THE DIALECTICS OF REPRESENTATION

SUSAN WELLS

THE DIALECTICS
OF REPRESENTATION

THE JOHNS HOPKINS UNIVERSITY PRESS
Baltimore and London

This book has been brought to publication
with the generous assistance of the
Andrew W. Mellon Foundation.

The Johns Hopkins University Press
701 West 40th Street
Baltimore, Maryland 21211
The Johns Hopkins Press Ltd, London

*The paper in this book is acid-free and meets
the guidelines for permanence and durability
of the Committee on Production Guidelines
for Book Longevity of the Council on
Library Resources.*

Library of Congress Cataloging in Publication Data
Wells, Susan.
  The dialectics of representation.
  Bibliography: p.
  Includes index.
  1. Literature and society.   I. Title.
PN51.W37 1985   809'.93355   85-7575
ISBN 0-8018-2506-7 (alk. paper)

FOR HUGH

CONTENTS

PREFACE AND ACKNOWLEDGMENTS

This book is about the relation between literature and social life. Specifically, I am looking at the ways that images of social life emerge in fiction and at the ways that readers interpret those images. The questions this book confronts have been emerging for the last ten years as central topics in literary theory.

This book approaches such questions by examining representation dialectically. Let me explain what these terms imply for this study. By invoking works of fiction under the rubric of representation, I mean to imply two things: that there is some relationship between social life and the work of art, and that this relationship is not simple. I am not working here with plays and novels as self-contained systems or as series of codes or as clusters of images, but with plays and novels produced and read by social beings, often in connection with some social project. That connection is never a simple matter of reflecting the world in a work of literature: social life is mediated and transformed by the writer; the work is interpreted and transformed by the reader. The work of literature, then, is not an object, but a process. Moreover, the work is a process in which contradictory elements coexist, in which parts and wholes are independent, in which negation and affirmation are closely joined—in a word, a dialectical process. I focus on two moments of that process: the moment of the typical, in which the work establishes its connection to social life and an intersubjective bond with its readers, and the moment of the indeterminate, in which the work resists interpretation. By *dialectics of representation,* then, I mean to imply both a connection between social life and literature and a way of understanding or reading that connection.

The method of this study is critical hermeneutics, especially the tradition of critical hermeneutics that has characterized both subjective, unorthodox Marxism, including such figures as the young Lukács, Mikhail Bakhtin, Lev Vygotsky, and Raymond Williams, and also the writers associated with the Frankfurt School, especially Herbert Marcuse, Walter Benjamin, and Jürgen Habermas. Obviously, this diverse list of writers, not all of whom were interested in literature, does not indicate a critical program, and still less a body of doctrine. These writers, however, do represent an interpretive tradition, characterized by a recognition of the historical situation of the text and the reader. To recognize the historical situation of the text is not to replicate either its initial production or its reception, but attentively to shape models of the historical subjectivity—what Raymond Williams calls "structures of feeling"—that form its context. It also implies that literary texts are relatively autonomous, that we cannot see them as so many instances of false consciousness or of ideological delusion. Thus, the work of the critic, rather than being privileged as "scientific," is constrained by the demands of critical subjectivity, including the demand that interpretive categories must not themselves be exempt from criticism.

An earlier version of chapter 3 appeared in *ELH* 48 (Spring 1981), under the title "Jacobean City Comedy and the Ideology of the City." An earlier version of chapter 4 appeared in *Minnesota Review* (Fall 1978), under the title "Self-Cultivation, Political Reaction, and the *Bildungsroman.*" I have quoted from Bertolt Brecht's poems "The Playwright's Song" and "Speech to Danish Working-Class Actors on the Art of Observation," using the edition by John Willett and Ralph Manheim (London: Eyre, Methuen, 1976).

I acknowledge a great debt to the readers of this manuscript, beginning with R. J. Kaufmann and Warwick Wadlington at Texas. I also thank James Schmidt, Doug Kellner, Wayne Rebhorn, Charles Rossman, Leonard Tennenhouse, Nancy Armstrong, and Michael Ryan. I have especially appreciated the readings and help of Michael Scrivener and of Hugh Grady and the editorial work of Eric Halpern. Deborah Currie and Rudy Barron typed the manuscript, and Cynthia Foote edited it painstakingly, saving me from many foolish errors: those that remain are all my own. Finally, the institutional support of the University of Louisville Faculty Fellowship, the Wayne State University Faculty Fellowship, and the Josephine Nevins Keal Fellowship allowed me to finish this book.

THE DIALECTICS OF REPRESENTATION

1

THE DIALECTICS OF REPRESENTATION

Representation in Paul de Man and Fredric Jameson

Contemporary literary theory focuses on two questions: the question of reference and the question of reading. Both are posed as investigations of representation, seen alternatively as the relationship between a literary work and the other structures of social life, and as the intellectual and social practice of reading.

It is almost inevitable that only one pole in such a relationship will be the focus of any single critical discussion. And indeed, if we categorize modern literary critics as proponents of one or the other theme, a coherent, if crude, schema emerges: on the side of reference, traditional literary history; on the side of reading, I. A. Richards; the development of referential criticism in psychoanalytic and Jungian theories, with their recodification of the represented object, and reader analysis and reader-response theories. Theories that try to think about representation simultaneously as reference and reading practice are both rare and diverse. I would give as examples the work of E. D. Hirsch, Jacques Derrida's reading of Rousseau, and the interpretive practice of Fredric Jameson. Not all of the studies that connect reading and reference elaborate that connection dialectically; for Hirsch and Derrida, such a method is deeply suspect.

The work of two major contemporary critics, Paul de Man and Fredric Jameson, is a good place to begin our own investigation of representation. Such a comparison helps to trace the relations between reference and reading, to understand what happens when one or the other of these concepts is submerged or excluded. In the course of this comparison, I also define some key terms and establish some methodological principles. So instrumental a discussion, of course, cannot hope to be comprehensive: this contrast of de Man to Jameson may throw certain edges of the problem of representation into high relief, but it certainly flattens the contours of each writer's work. With that apology, let me begin.

De Man and Jameson have set themselves quite different critical projects, and they proceed from entirely contradictory theoretical assumptions. For de Man, reading is central. Witness, for example, Wlad Godzich's introduction to de Man's reissued *Blindness and Insight*,[1] titled "Caution! Reader at Work!" The terms of this homage replicate precisely de Man's sense of reading as a labor, an interpretive act with its own creative force, its own formal exigencies. They also convey a carefully muted implication that reading is a subversive or risky activity, one in which the reader's preconceptions are at risk. But the warning sign makes no inflated claims: it reads, after all, "Caution!" and not "Danger!"

Jameson, on the other hand, emphasizes the importance of reference. His major theoretical work, *The Political Unconscious*,[2] begins with the slogan, "Always historicize!" For de Man, history is a system of tropes; for Jameson, tropes are the clever disguises of history. For Jameson, the rhetoric that guides a text's interpretation, its sedimented reading habits, are themselves historical artifacts, the accumulated detritus of representational norms that a patient critic archeologically sifts. But for de Man, the tropes *are* the text in its rhetorical functioning, and the task of the critic is tracing the "tropological displacement of logic."[3]

De Man's *Allegories of Reading*[4] is a prolonged investigation of allegory as a narrative practice that acknowledges the disjunction of signifier from signified. In fact, "any narrative" is primarily "the allegory of its own reading" (*AR,* 76), and for de Man, all denominative discourses are narrative. As enactments of the distance between signified and signifier, narratives are performances of error, of undecidability, dramatizations of the impossibility of either avoiding or being satisfied with multiple, contradictory readings. Allegory, to borrow the terms of de Man's earlier study, is the trope by which blindness and insight are indissolubly linked.

Allegories of Reading discusses these themes with mandarin subtlety. De Man's explication of allegory ascends the levels of discourse, beginning with acoustic patterns and moving through local figures, such as chiasmus, to the more global figures of metaphor and metonymy and to the theme of reading. The chapters on Nietzsche raise questions of narration, of aesthetic genres (theater vs. music), and of modes of discourse (philosophy vs. literature). In the final section on Rousseau, de Man takes up the relations among language, passion, and social order. With many detours and indirections, de Man has replicated the *cursus* of traditional rhetorical study, moving from grammar through history and literature to politics and ethics. And methodologically, the levels of de Man's readings are similarly graduated. He begins by deconstructing texts, then moves to deconstruct readings of texts, critical histories of texts, methods of discussing critical history, and eventually deconstruction itself. But in other ways, the book does not "develop" at all. The levels of discourse it ascends are unmarked. On its path, it meets, as if by accident, a series of themes, including time, selfhood, value, history, universality, consciousness, and guilt, which are consumed by rhetorical analysis. Their fragments mark the text's progress, and also memorialize the demolition of the central topics of phenomenological criticism. But this critique is seldom explicit; it is carried out monologically. Even the discussion of Althusser that underpins de Man's chapters on Nietzsche is largely a matter of allusion and oblique quotation. On the most elementary rhetorical level, the text circles back on itself. We read a subtle dismantling of chiasmus in the first chapter; the same figure appears triumphantly in the last, where a section of *The Confessions* is referred to as "a text of desire as well as desire for text" (*AR,* 289). It is almost as if *Allegories of Reading* were organized to subvert the peculiar narrative expectations that we bring to a work of criticism: that it develop, be comprehensive, proceed through its texts in chronological order, and reach a conclusion.

If we look at what *Allegories of Reading* has to say about reference and indeterminacy, we must first notice that neither term is wished away. Indeterminacy, of course, is central to de Man's work: it is derived from the arbitrary operation of denomination, which presents intrinsically metaphorical names for things, ideas, and sensations as if they were real, "substituting certitude for ignorance" (*AR,* 161). But, if we attempt to evade this dilemma by standing fast in the consciousness of our ignorance, de Man reminds us that reference is a process that no discourse escapes: "All discourse *has to be* referential but can never signify its referent" (*AR,* 160). There are no dignified spectators in the rush to the signified: all readers will join in that indecorous search, all will find something, and all will be deceived.

It will not do, then, to accuse de Man of reading as if nobody ever looked for meanings in the text.[5] De Man is aware that the search for meaning is obligatory, intrinsic to the rhetorical patterning of the text. But we might look more closely at the ways in which *reference* appears in de Man.

Reference is defined early in *Allegories of Reading* as "the nonverbal 'outside' to which language refers, by which it is conditioned and upon which it acts" (*AR,* 5). This quotation echoes Derrida's slogan that there is nothing outside the text, blandly invoking his rejection of the terrain of reference even as referentiality is being posed as a problem. As *Allegories of Reading* develops, de Man will deny not so much the existence of a realm "outside the text" as our ability to distinguish such a realm reliably from that of the text. Both reference and the rejection of reference stand "under the aegis of an inside/outside metaphor that is never being seriously questioned" (*AR*, 5). The nature of reference has been quite properly subsumed into the broader question of representation: reference can only be understood as a moment in the representational system of relationships between a text and its "outside." For de Man, that system enacts a series of reading conventions.

Something is lost in this translation of the question of representation into the act of reading. The notion of reading is compromised by its own narrative telos, so that reference is understood as a naive first step that the careful reader will quickly transcend, even while reference's power to entangle the reader in the delusive reconstruction of a text is acknowledged. Reference, then, plays a role in de Man's work oddly similar to that of ambiguity in classical New Criticism: it is the critic's worthy opponent, the crux that can be battled but never resolved, that must instead be harnessed, its power put at the service of critical discourse. Both the New Critical resolution of ambiguities into discrete, balanced patterns of meaning and de Man's dissolution of the referential moments of the text into problematic rhetorical patterns can be seen as alternate strategies for capture and containment. Both are powerful methods for transforming questions of representation into questions of reading.

But of course, New Criticism as a reading practice centered the subject, the reading subject and the written subject. It concerned itself with ethical problems, the very problems that de Man so strenuously brackets in the "inside/outside" metaphor he so consistently dismantles. De Man, then, transposes New Critical methods to a world without subjects. If Rilke's meditations on the "gentlest law" are, in some sense, acoustical figures, then so much the more is Nietzsche's critique of subjectivity and of the referential power of language a figure of reversal and substitution, and Rousseau's discussion of the relations among sovereigns, states, and individuals an "unreadable" realization of the polarities inside/outside and active/passive. Intersubjectivity, along with reference, has become an unavoidable error that makes language possible and knowledge impossible.

And indeed, de Man elaborates an explicit critique of intersubjectivity. This critique begins with an observance of the affective and intentional fallacies: neither the writer's intention nor the reader's response is a reliable gauge of the possibilities of the text. Speaking of Rilke's complicity with his audience, de Man observes:

"It is not difficult, for a reader alerted to the ambivalences of the relationship between the self and its language, to demystify this seduction. The intersubjective reading grounded in common sentiment, in the 'transparency of the heart,' does not allow one to reach the area of Rilke's poetry that is not affected by this demystification" (*AR*, 21). Here, intersubjectivity figures as a kind of barrier across discourse, a sanction against knowing the text in its fullness, an etiquette of discourse that forces us to be quiet while the text steps on our toes, until criticism liberates us. But what if we understand intersubjectivity, not as a limit to discourse, but as a condition of saying anything at all? It is only in intersubjective discourse that those categories subverted in *Allegories of Reading* can even be called into question. In the work of Jürgen Habermas, those categories, presented as truth, rightness, comprehensibility, and sincerity, are themselves systematically derived from the conditions of intersubjective discourse. If intersubjectivity is not read as an abstracted relation between an immaterial reader and a generalized writer, but rather, in Bakhtin's terms, as instancing that dialogical ground that is the only space where languages reveal themselves in their specificity, then de Man's rejection of intersubjectivity is not justified.[6] To exclude the communicative and properly intersubjective grounding of language renders arbitrary the search for reference, the desire to represent and to understand representation, even the desire to read. Since reason has been divorced from intersubjectivity, the reader's desire to interpret is left ungrounded; it is a disembodied appetite. Reading becomes an unmotivated by-product of language or of narrative power; the work of the reader is pursuit of error and delusion. We might do well to question a theory that, like de Man's, is so deeply at odds with itself, a theory that ends by mystifying its own central notions.

We can mark the first movement of this conflict, I think, in a casual stipulation de Man makes at the outset of *Allegories of Reading:* "Indeed, as the study of grammatical structures is defined in contemporary theories of generative, transformational, and distributive grammar, the study of tropes and of figures (which is how the term *rhetoric* is used here, and not in the derived sense of comment or of eloquence or persuasion) becomes a mere extension of grammatical models, a particular subset of syntactical relations" (*AR*, 6). But it is the excluded senses of *rhetoric*—commentary, eloquence, persuasion—that are intersubjective on their face, since there is no persuasion without a judging audience, no commentary without a scholarly audience, no eloquence without a responsive audience. De

Man criticizes these senses of *rhetoric* as "derived": Nietzsche will later be asked to authorize that criticism. But we must question this exclusion on a number of grounds.

There is good historical evidence that the persuasive elements of rhetorical theory were developed first.[7] Tropes and figures were only minor themes in the first rhetorical handbooks, those of Corax and Tisias, which concentrated on the structures of judicial oratory, materials for proof, and the handling of probability and authority, considering style only peripherally. In fact, the philosophical critique of rhetoric in Plato was elaborated almost simultaneously with the first codification of figures by Gorgias. The lists of tropes that we associate with rhetorical handbooks were developed much later by the Stoic rhetoricians, although Aristotle's discussion of metaphor was the authority for many later treatments of figural language. The Stoics valued the tropes, paradoxically, as strategies for avoiding ornament, since they eliminated the need for archaic or borrowed words.

Such a historical digression is perhaps more suggestive of the connections among naming, dialogic forms of language, and rhetoric than conclusive as a demonstration of which aspects of "rhetoric" are "derived" and which are fundamental. And we might question what such distinctions mean in a book that, like *Allegories of Reading,* devotes a whole chapter to the notion of genealogy. Let us look more closely at that discussion, which is deeply concerned with questions of rhetoric and intersubjectivity.

The argument of de Man's chapter on genealogy conforms to the basic schema of the book: we are led through two readings of the text. The first reading, which usually recapitulates current critical opinion in its most advanced, theoretically sophisticated form, often takes the content of the text at face value, using advanced tools to operate on that content rather than to determine it. This sense of the text's meaning is then placed within brackets, and a second, rhetorical and allegorizing reading of the text is performed, demonstrating that the conclusions triumphantly reached by critical analysis had, in fact, been both anticipated and enacted by the text. De Man distinguishes the two readings: the first is a substantial reading, "motivated by thematic statement considered as *meaning*"; the second is rhetorical, "motivated by thematic statement considered as *structure*" (*AR,* 87). In the case of *The Birth of Tragedy,* the first reading generates a critique of Nietzsche's opposition of Apollonian to Dionysiac in Derridean terms: this opposition assumes that origin and purpose are inextricably linked, and reenacts the valuations of presence, truth, voice, and music that Derrida criticizes as logocentrism. De Man then embarks on a "more rhetorical" reading of Nietzsche, pointing out that the oppositions between Dionysiac and Apollonian, between music and word, and even the connection between origin and purpose are framed in a rhetorical structure the reliability of which Nietzsche has already put in question.

That rhetorical structure, however, enacts precisely the sense of rhetoric that de Man had excluded in the first pages of *Allegories of Reading*. Speaking of Nietzsche's style in *The Birth of Tragedy,* de Man notes censoriously that his exploitation of the "complicity between the 'I' of the narrator and the collective 'we' of his acquiescing audience functions relentlessly, underscored by the repeated address of the audience as 'my friends.'" De Man gives several examples of this complicity, and ends by saying: "A longer enumeration of examples is superfluous, since they are as numerous as they are obvious in their strategy: this orator is in need of a very benevolent audience if it is to accept a shaky system of valorization" (*AR,* 94). For de Man, the more overtly the intersubjective, persuasive aspects of the text surface, the more doubt is cast upon its logical categories; dramatization, pathos, and subjectivity appear as strategems for making the worse case appear the better. Rhetoric has been divided into two forms: the rhetoric of tropes, which foregrounds the indeterminacy of language and is therefore good, and the rhetoric of persuasion and eloquence, which foregrounds the intersubjective force of language and is therefore bad. With this division, de Man affiliates himself with what he elsewhere calls a "recurrent philosophical topos" (*AR,* 173)—that of the philosophical distrust of rhetoric, specifically of rhetoric as a means of affecting an audience. His metaphor for the intersubjective aspects of the text, in fact, is that of seduction.[8] De Man's attempt to exclude the dangerous material of subjectivity, however, is not fully successful: these forms reemerge as the discredited pole in Nietzsche's binary opposition. Since de Man moves very quickly to a discussion of the fragile and arbitrary nature of valuations based on binary oppositions, one might be tempted to read his initial exclusion of intersubjectivity as a temporary gesture, laying down a theme only to catch it up again in the highly recursive structure of *Allegories of Reading*. But such a reading, to borrow de Man's sexual language, would be perverse, concentrating on what is unsaid in the text and neglecting what it does assert on its face.

Instead, let me consider the implications that de Man's rejection of intersubjectivity has for his understanding of reading and interpretation. We can approach this topic best by considering his treatment of the hermeneutic circle, a method understood by various authors as a critical device, a metaphor for the act of reading, or an ontological principle. [9] Stated in its most general form, the hermeneutic circle is a recognition that the meaning of a portion of a text can only be recovered from an understanding of the text as a whole. This understanding can be grounded on the universality of human nature, as in classical hermeneutics; in the shared prejudices of tradition, as in Gadamer; or in the norms of communicative action, as in Habermas. But in any case, it is grounded in understandings among subjects who approach each other through the text, despite distances of time or cultural disjunctions.

For de Man, however, hermeneutics is forcibly bracketed as a method of achieving understanding. At the end of the last chapter of *Allegories of Reading,* de Man closes his reading of Rousseau's *Confessions* by asserting: "The main point of the reading has been to show that the resulting predicament [of excess cognition] is linguistic rather than ontological or hermeneutic" (*AR,* 300). And in an earlier discussion, de Man had rejected hermeneutic metaphors for both Freud's project and the application of psychoanalytic methods to the text. Such a rejection of hermeneutics did not characterize de Man's earlier book, *Blindness and Insight.* [10] There, de Man simply took issue with the New Critical "romantic" error of seeing the unity of the work as an expression of its organic coherence, rather than as an implication of the hermeneutic method's predisposition to unify the text. But even in this early treatment, de Man excluded intersubjectivity from his understanding of hermeneutics. Explicating Heidegger's notion of *Forhabe,* the forestructuring of understanding, de Man said, "For the interpreter of the poetic text, this foreknowledge is the text itself" (*BI,* 30). The careful reader, then, is the one who approaches the labor of interpretation, not with some ideas about its significance, but with the "text itself" somehow luminously present, already suggesting the meanings that will generate interpretation. The problem of temporality, one of the central issues of hermeneutic theory, is truncated. The forestructuring of the text in Schleiermacher or Gadamer or Habermas involves historical distance, beginning with the distance between writer and reader, but including the histories of reading and interpretation that cue our responses, even to contemporary texts. For De Man, this distance shrinks to the interval between a reader's taking up "the text itself" and concluding its interpretation. The predicament of the reader who negotiates this narrow round is, of course, already "linguistic rather than ontological or hermeneutic."

In *Allegories of Reading,* a book that is much harsher in its critique of hermeneutics than *Blindness and Insight,* the themes that de Man associates with hermeneutic theory—temporality, circularity, the totalization of meaning—are dispersed through the text, each treated as a rhetorical figure. Without a grounding in intersubjectivity, hermeneutics becomes a bag of tricks, a source of themes rather than a method. The rhetorical reading that de Man counterposes to hermeneutics, whatever its strengths, excludes not only important senses of rhetoric but also the understanding of history that has been one of the strengths of hermeneutic theory.

Hermeneutic theory provides grounds for understanding the relationship between reading and reference, for thinking about both themes at once. It is therefore one of the most promising methods for reflecting about representation without divorcing the text's relation to social life from its relation to the reader. And, if hermeneutic theory has been flexible enough to serve as a method for Christian exegesis, liberal humanism, phenomenology, and the critical theory of the Frankfurt School, we might hope that it could be adapted to modern literary theory. One of the most creative attempts to modify hermeneutics in order to take into account new critical methods is the work of Fredric Jameson, especially *The Political Unconscious,* a book for which history is a central concept. The book begins by situating reading, writing, and criticism: "Our presupposition, in the analyses that follow, will be that only a genuine philosophy of history is capable of respecting the specificity and radical difference of the social and cultural past while disclosing the solidarity of its polemics and passions, its forms, structures, experiences, and struggles, with those of the present day" (*PU,* 18). And for Jameson, both history and interpretation are, in some sense, intersubjective, even if that subjectivity is transformed, politically situated, and virtually transindividual. After all, it is only metonymically that the "polemics and passions" of the past can express solidarity with those of the present. Jameson, therefore, is quite right to describe this project as the formulation of a "new and more adequate, immanent or antitranscendent hermeneutic mode" (*PU,* 23). He shares fundamental assumptions with hermeneutic theory: his revision of that theory to take into account new interpretive methods preserves both its power to account for historical specificity and its intersubjective force.

Jameson's interpretive theory is focused on the question of representation—of the relations among texts, their represented worlds, and the internally represented worlds of the readers. Interpretation is a matter of unfolding the text's formal qualities and its ideological structure; it is also a matter of establishing a relation between a given text and the multitude of other narratives through which we "know" both history and our own society, by means of which we reflect on our past and hope for our future.

We might begin a comparison of Jameson's and de Man's work with some remarks about what is gained and what is lost in such a radical shift in focus; in moving to Jameson, we have moved from a criticism of tropes to a criticism of historical relations, from the interpretation of the rhetoric of the text to a hermeneutic of the text as an expression of the political unconcious. The literary critical world controlled by these new problematics is a world rich in objects—on two representative pages of *The Political Unconscious* we meet Bloch, Frye, folk dances, minuets, Oedipal narratives, fairy tales, the Grail, and Eichendorff's *Aus dem Leben eines Taugenichts*. If de Man is the Flaubert of contemporary criticism, ruthlessly abolishing its narrative structures, Jameson is its Balzac, the constructor of an ample critical object world. And in this world, texts are, like Balzacian characters, quite heterogeneous: they relate to their social context on different levels, and in different ways; these relationships differ for different audiences, and realize themselves on different levels of meaning. For de Man, on the other hand, critical reading is a radically centripetal process: texts may be very different from one another, but they all contain meanings that contradict what they might seem to be saying, and they all hold these contradictions in suspension. Further, de Man's contradictory discourse takes place outside time and space, in a reading practice that is tacitly limited to the text, ancillary statements by the author, and the authoritative commentaries.

But Jameson's critical practice also has its contradictions and equivocations. In particular, three central concepts in *The Political Unconcious* have doubled interpretations. Jameson controls this doubling by excluding indeterminacy from interpretive practice, radically reducing the role of reading in his theory.

The unique strength of *The Political Unconscious* is its attempt to bring together Hegelian and Althusserian methods and problems; this effort expresses, among other things, a political project of reconciling the traditional cultural practice of Marxism with the theoretical legacy of the New Left. The interpretive practice of the central chapters of *The Political Unconcious* effects such conjuncture, but the theoretical explanations that bracket Jameson's readings interpret the notions of history and totality in a contradictory way. The theme of subjectivity, which is less overtly realized in the text, is also deeply contradictory.

Jameson introduces the theme of totality by radically retranslating it. In Kojève's Marxist version of Hegel, once widely accepted, totality was the concept that promised the unification of being and discourse, the possibility of complete and unproblematic knowledge:

Totality is revealed Being or self-conscious Being (which Hegel calls "absolute Concept," "Idea," or "Spirit"): it is split by Negativity into given static Being (*Sein*) and its discursive "ideal" opposite; but it is, or again becomes, one and homogenous in and by this doubling . . . when the Totality of being is correctly revealed by the "total" or circular Discourse of the Wise Man. . . .

As the *Result* of Negation, Totality is as much an Affirmation as is the Identity which was negated in order to become Totality.[11]

For Jameson, however, totality is a strategic rather than a transcendent concept. It is a mark of a systematic attempt to objectify the world, and to establish the boundaries of a system's coherence, simultaneously marking them as boundaries and warning the reader to test the truth of the relations that hold within them. The notion of totality, then, is not seen either as a simple reflection of an already-connected world or as the speculative achievement of a thinker who unifies the world in wise discourse. Rather, it is a "negative and methodological" concept (*PU,* 53), one that functions most forcibly as a caution or guard against thoughtless reliance on the ready-made generalizations of "common sense." We might even say that it is a rhetorical rather than an ontological concept.

At other times, however, Jameson's deployment of the notion of totality is affirmative and substantial rather than negative and methodological. Such an affirmative use of totality is suggested in his imperative that the main contradiction in the ideological structure of a work be identified. It surfaces explicitly in the impulse to form a hierarchy of interpretations: "As a matter of practical criticism, it must be clear to anyone who has experimented with different approaches to a given text that the mind is not content until it puts some order in these findings and invents a hierarchical relationship among its various interpretations" (*PU,* 31). And this affirmative notion of totality motivates the assertion of the political as the ultimate horizon of interpretation, the ground on which all other readings are, like Kojève's Negative, revealed as provisional realizations of a truth that is, at last, unitary.

Very often, the figure for that unitary truth is History. Here again, one of the basic concepts in the text is deeply equivocal. At some points in *The Political Unconcious,* history is given the ontological and epistemological status of a totalizing, affirmative, concept: "History itself becomes the ultimate ground as well as the untranscendable limit of our understanding in general and our textual interpretation in particular" (*PU*, 100). Here, history is not a set of relations, not a series or ensemble of narratives, but a strategy for exclusion—what cannot be subsumed under its sign cannot be understood. We cannot know anything but history, both in the relations of social life and in our reading practice; insofar as anything is understood, that understanding realizes history.

But elsewhere in *The Political Unconcious,* we find a much more limited notion of how history can be known. In the initial statement that although history is not a narrative, it can only be known as a text (*PU*, 35), we can read a recognition that multiple interpretations of history are inevitable; we might even conclude that the boundary between real and fictional narratives would be difficult to fix. Other statements about the relation between history and narrative are more positive, but retain a hermeneutic openness. We are told, for example, that the materials of history "recover their original urgency for us only if they are retold within the unity of a single great collective story" (*PU*, 10): here, history is unitary as a matter of rhetorical strategy, to strengthen a persuasive narrative in aid of insurgent common sense. Whatever the problems in this understanding of history, it is not an affirmative totality.

Jameson's rhetorical understanding of history, however, is sometimes abandoned in favor of speculative certainty. When history is a knowable totality, subjectivity can only be untrustworthy and unreliable; only when history is rhetorical can the writing of history have intersubjective force. We might even read a recognition of the relation between rhetoric and intersubjectivity in Jameson's invocation of the mind to validate the impulse toward hierarchized interpretations. Such a mind, "which is not content until it puts some order in these findings," would be understood in historical terms as a place where the ensemble of ideological codes, reflected social experiences, and "scientific" practices meet, producing some combination of prejudice and authentic reflection, however compromised and provisional. But more often, subjectivity appears as a breach of decorum, almost a moral error. For example, Jameson claims that "only the dialectic provides a way for 'decentering' the subject concretely, and for transcending the 'ethical' in the direction of the political and the collective" (*PU*, 60). We can hear in such a statement an echo of the diverse but connected critiques of the subject that have emerged in new French critical theories; it might be helpful to mention some of the bases of these critiques, reviewing, as it were, Jameson's footnotes.

Psychoanalytically, the work of Deleuze and Guattari elaborates a critique of the centered subject under the name of Oedipus, counterposing to the unitary ego of Freud's family romance an alternate understanding of desire that takes territorializations, flows, and blockings as its primary figures. In Foucault, the subject is a historical, heuristic form, a form that has been worked through and used up, so that the real object of investigation, discourse, becomes visible: "From within language experienced and traversed as language, in the play of its possibilities extended to its furthest point, what emerges is that man has 'come to an end,' and that, by reaching the summit of all possible speech, he arrives not at the very heart of himself but at the brink of that which limits him." Finally, for Louis Althusser, subjectivity is an artifact of humanist and historicist misunderstandings. In following Marx's concept of the relations of production, says Althusser, we do wrong to admit human agents as "subjects"; the true subjects here are the definers and distributors of places and functions within the system of production. And, lest we misread this exclusion as a temporary and tactical one, we can find its extension and formalization by Balibar. Speaking of Marxist theory, he states, "Men do not appear in the theory except in the form of supports for the connexions implied by the structure, and the forms of their individuality as determinate effects of the structure."[12]

All of these rejections of subjectivity have several themes in common. First, the individual subject is not to be displaced through a moral project, however ethical the rhetoric of the writer might become—which, in the case of Deleuze and Guattari, is quite ethical indeed. Rather, the subject is seen as *already* displaced, or *about to be* displaced, either in actuality or in theory. Second, this displacement is always in favor of some other concept—the schizo, language, desire—that will absorb the explanatory function of the centered subject. Finally, what is objected to in the subject is a lack of relation— a lack of relation to the multiple possibilities of desire, or to the constituting power of discourse, or to the constraints of social relations. Subjectivity is seen as the concept that forbids and blocks the establishment of crucial relationships.

With the first of these three gestures, there can be no real difficulty: it is essentially a historicizing move. The subject did not always exist as it does now; neither will it remain unchanged. But we should note immediately that, for Althusser at least, such a statement is nothing more than a liberal accommodation; in criticizing similar theories, Althusser compares them archly to the Aggiornamento of Vatican II: everything is supposed to change, but it ends up remaining quite the same after all.[13]

Having said so much, we should consider what difference it might make to the critique of subjectivity if such a critique itself were historicized. And it is here, I think, that the work of Theodor Adorno becomes important. It was Adorno, after all, who charted the radical reduction and decomposition of subjectivity in the context of advanced capitalism,[14] a decomposition that he labeled as the reduction of being to species being or the predominance of the universal. And it was also Adorno who forecast the force of this analysis: "A candid look at the predominance of the universal does all but unbearable psychological harm to the narcissism of all individuals and to that of a democratically organized society. To see through selfhood as nonexistent, as an illusion, would easily turn all men's objective despair into a subjective one." Adorno proposes, as counters to this despair, the objectification of systematic thought, self-consciousness, and self-reflection.[15] We could do much worse. But we might do better, perhaps, by counterposing a more rhetorical understanding of intersubjectivity to the contemporary theory that opposes a monadic individual subjectivity over against global, totalizing notions such as structure and discourse. Such a relation would begin with the reflexivity of relations among subjects, rather than constituting the subject in isolation and then convicting it of failure to relate to some other concept. Such an understanding, it is convenient to note, was already implicit in Hegel, and was analyzed by Lukács.[16] It is at work in Adorno's refusal to grant primacy either to individuals or to universals. In our present context, a rhetorical understanding of intersubjectivity would amount to the assertion that language does not operate without the intervention of human subjects, that relations of power imply reciprocal constraints, and that acts of discourse are relationships as much as they are structures. Intersubjectivity, then, is a rhetorical concept that locates relations of power and discourse within communities of speakers and hearers. It asserts, finally, the power of speakers and hearers to transform the discourse that they enact.

For Jameson, such a notion of intersubjectivity is alien; although his criticism is most certainly rhetorical, it is a rhetoric that seeks to evade the limits of reading and writing subjects. This evasion, to return to the main line of my inquiry, requires Jameson to exclude indeterminacy from his reading practice.

The Political Unconscious is full of discussions of reading. What it presents, however, is more properly a theory of critical discourse, a theory for the unfolding of reference. It is a theory that arrives at the text *post festum,* operating on its content in order to restore the text to a concept of totality that is too often affirmative and a concept of history that is too often transcendent. And such a restoration can only be effected by the exclusion of intersubjectivity and indeterminacy.

Jameson begins by identifying three levels for a historical hermeneutic: relation to political history, including references to quite topical events; relation to broad social forces, realized as ideology with its gaps and contradictions; and "history in its vastest sense," the level on which the form of the work is related to the broad succession of modes of production, the slow transformations of social relations. In the work of actual interpretation, on the other hand, Jameson more often focuses on the relations between two levels: a psychological level, in which the family is related to systems of desire, and a historical level, in which elements of the text are related to its social and political situation. In either case, for either the threefold hermeneutic that Jameson asserts initially or for the twofold hermeneutic of his explications, the same question emerges: how do these levels relate? In *The Political Unconscious,* all the levels, in the final analysis, harmonize. Each work speaks differently, but all of its various messages come together. Either they are transformations of the same ideologeme, or they relate to a unified situation in symmetrical ways. Even when they are not so neatly contradictory, nothing in the text is really undecidable; there is nothing that cannot be clarified by the taking of thought. Thus, the interpretation forms a unitary whole, a "word" on the text at hand. And quite often, History stands as enforcer of that word, as a positive totality that guarantees it.

We might take as an example Jameson's reading of Balzac's *La Rabouilleuse,* where familial conflict is seen as a realization, with some strategic changes, of certain psychopolitical conflicts that are also instanced in Balzac's life. These conflicts, translated into narrative, are signs of a "fundamental family situation which is at one and the same time a fantasy master narrative," which is itself to be read as the "mediation of class relationships in society at large" (*PU,* 180). This use of *mediation* seems perilously close to the mechanical assertion of homologies among levels of a totality that Jameson had rejected earlier (*PU,* 39). Both the historical class relationships and the fantasized family relationships are seen as instances of Desire, as fantasies of wish fulfillment that also include images of all the obstacles to their realization. Thus, desire merges with history; to fantasize a desire is also to fantasize that which resists desire. History has become a demonic, active force, the final sign under which the reading is to be subsumed, reducing all the figures of the text to indexes of accommodation and impossibility.

Such a reduction is certainly effective in reducing indeterminacy. But it is not very satisfying as a way of carrying out Jameson's more properly hermeneutic project, the elaboration of an intersubjectively satisfying sense of literature in its relation to history, a chapter within the "single great collective story." It is in aid of this political project that Jameson formulates, in the last chapter of *The Political Unconcious,* his Marxist version of Paul Ricoeur's "double hermeneutic" (*PU,* 185): a hermeneutic of unmasking, of ideological analysis, and also a Utopian hermeneutic that searches for the prefigurative truth in all ideological expressions. Jameson's dual hermeneutic, then, is in many ways a satisfying summation of all the provisional hermeneutic formulations of *The Political Unconscious.* It maintains a historical focus, since both its positive and negative moments are grounded in class relations. But the need to establish a positive totality is evaded, since the two moments of ideology and utopia are not to be reconciled. Neither, in fact, is given priority; they are "simultaneous" and interdependent interpretations of the text. The dual hermeneutic suggests possibilities for developing a criticism that does justice to both the specificities of texts and the exigencies of political commitment. What the dual hermeneutic does not do, however, is to admit of any real indeterminacy.

This might seem to be an odd criticism to make of a theory that asserts dual, nonidentical readings, readings no interpretation can ever hope to decide between. But that is exactly the point. Without the attempt to decide, to determine, there can be no indeterminacy, but only alternation of perspectives. Such an alternation preserves Jameson's suspicions of the intersubjective: it is in the form of the competing interpretations of diverse readers, or those marking divergences between readers and authors, that indeterminacy presses on us most concretely. Without some acknowledgment of the uncertainty and contingency of reading, the reference of literature to social life appears as a fact about literature rather than as a rhetorical relation among reader, writer, and text. The work of the reader, then, becomes invisible, is subsumed in the finished artifact of the interpretation. And the axioms on which that interpretation is based pass outside the arena of critical discussion. The reader of critical discourse cannot be expected to decide among them on any grounds other than their efficacy in interpretation. Marxism, then, is a preferred critical method, not because of any political or philosophical judgments that a reader might make, but because it alone is capable of subsuming other interpretations. The abstraction of this position, of course, is quite at odds with the commitment that informs Jameson's text, but it may explain the frustration, almost the bad temper, with which Marxist critics like Eagleton or Said have responded to the political, rather than the literary, dimensions of *The Political Unconscious.* [17]

I began this introductory investigation by counterposing the problem of representation to the problem of reading. De Man's study focuses on the problem of reading and ends by reducing reading to an arbitrary, unmotivated act. Jameson's study focuses on the representation of history, understood from a Marxist perspective, and ends by excluding Marxist understanding of history from critical reflection. In both cases, the attempt to exclude what is dangerous and subjective—the persuasive elements of rhetoric, intersubjectivity, or indeterminacy—has short-circuited critical reflection on the basic notions of the study. What is needed, I think, is an understanding of these relations that is dialectical in two senses: in seeing the deep relationship of interdependence between reading and reference, and in opening its own presuppositions to critical reflection. I propose to investigate the dialectical relation between those aspects of the text that connect it with the lived world and those that resist such connection. In analyzing these relations, I will refer to the aspects of the text that suggest a connection with the world as *typical,* and to those that resist interpretation as *indeterminate.* A dialectical analysis of representation will attend to the interplay between these two aspects of the text, so that the representation neither vanishes into the world nor dissolves into an individual reader's experiences. Such an analysis will be alert for the interpenetration of opposites, so that we might understand opposing moments of the text as preconditions for one another: there can be no reference without distance, no resistance to interpretation without an interpretive project. But perhaps, as we extend our analysis, we will come to see them as alternate ways of organizing the relations among text, world, and reader, alternates always threatening to merge, so that the deepest indeterminacy marks the most referential moment of the text, and the most compelling reference beckons out of the deepest indeterminacy.

Both the relation between the text and the world and the relation between the reader and the text are specific mediations. That is, something is being done here, material is being *worked on,* things change. The text labors over the world and transforms it by representing it; the reader transforms the text by interpreting it. We might recall Marx's exposition of the great mediating systems of industrial capitalism: religion, money, the state. In all of these analyses, the mediation is neither a simple deception nor an expression of truth to be taken at its own word. Rather, the mediation is seen as a kind of transformation, responding to its own necessities, of basic social relations. Similarly, as we take up the relations established by literary representations among images of the world, realized texts, and their readers, we will be analyzing these relations as ways of transforming and mediating lived experience, transformations shaped by their own necessities, including the necessities of form and genre.

If, in their typical moment, representations recall Aristotle's dictum that poetry is more philosophical than history, it is because the typical aspects of the text present themselves as being faithful to the underlying nature of events, to the essential significance of characters and personalities. The indeterminate aspects of the work challenge the reader by asserting that the work is not real, that it has been abstracted from the lived world. The indeterminate calls attention to the artificial nature of the text; through its indeterminate aspects, the forms of thought that produce representations are opened to investigation. In both instances, a dialectical analysis becomes implicated with questions "outside" the text—the nature of historical events, the forms of thought—by virtue of its very immersion in the text.

We have been speaking of the typical and the indeterminate as "aspects" of the text, as if they were separable parts, available in pure form for analysis. Such a conception violates the demands both of hermeneutic logic, in which whole and parts are seen as interdependent, and of even the simplest forms of dialectics, which discourages the disconnected consideration of parts and whole. Perhaps, then, we might borrow a term from sociolinguistics (which borrowed it from music), and speak of two *registers* of the text, a register being a collection of syntactic and semantic traits distinguishing a special mode of a language. Sociolinguists speak, for example, of "intimate" or "formal" or "professional" registers. Registers include clusters of features on all levels of language: an intimate register, for example, implies a special vocabulary, some syntactic features (questions, suspended statements), rhetorical tropes (private jokes, plays on words), genres (reminiscence, fantasy), and rhetorical strategies, or conceptions of the speaker and listener. Analogously, in the "language" of representation the typical and indeterminate registers include features at all the significant levels of the text: verbal tropes, narrative strategies, formal devices, and manipulations of genre. Like sociolinguistic registers, typicality and indeterminacy are interdependent and mutually defining: each has its own structure, and together they also constitute the general structure of the language that governs them. And, as the linguistic analogy suggests, the typical and indeterminate registers can each dominate a text; one register can be so heavily marked that the text seems to be simply referential, or impossible to interpret.

In the remainder of this chapter, I will discuss the typical and indeterminate registers and use them to analyze Shakespeare's *Richard II* and *A Midsummer Night's Dream*. In the second chapter of the book, I will examine two works, one in which the typical register dominates and one in which the indeterminate is dominant. In John Webster's Jacobean tragedy *The Duchess of Malfi,* the basic social relation between public and private is represented typically, enacted through the Duchess's clandestine marriage to her steward. But this celebration of understanding cannot be dramatized—it would not exist for us at all—without the indeterminate subjectivity of the Duchess's two evil brothers, who see ghosts, prefer the darkness to the light, and present mad spectacles. I will then examine Henry James's *The Turn of the Screw* as a work in which the indeterminate register is dominant. The text presents us with a series of unresolvable questions: Are there ghosts? What do they mean? Is the governess crazy? These questions are all silently supported by the typical level of the story, in which the social relation of possession is explored in the multiple senses of sexual possession, possession of goods, and self-possession.

In the third chapter, I will move to generic questions, examining the Jacobean city comedy as an attempt to contain ideological and historical pressures that had rendered the self-understanding of the city of London problematic. And in the final chapter, I will examine a more complex genre, the bildungsroman, a genre for which typicality is a controlling assumption, since in these novels one life is seen as an image of many. But even so conventional a bildungsroman as *David Copperfield* uses indeterminacy as a structural principle, while for a modern author like Doris Lessing, the representational power of an individual life becomes problematic, and the novel itself becomes more indeterminate.

The basic plan of this book, then, is to move from a theoretical discussion of basic concepts through concrete studies of individual works, arriving at some broad generic questions. Let me begin this movement by analyzing the typical register.

The Typical Register

The typical register of the text establishes its referential power. For a text to be read as referential, two contradictory relations between the text and lived experience must be established: the text must resemble the world of the reader, and it must be intelligible. A text that simply records everyday events, for example, seems arbitrary and uncertain in its reference, unless it also suggests that some structure informs those events, that some significance shapes them, even if that significance is subtle, atmospheric, a matter of mood. But of course, everyday life notoriously resists attempts to invest it with meaning. From the beginning, then, it is clear that the typical register of the text must be more than a simple record of events.

We can, perhaps, deepen our understanding of these contradictions by examining the surprisingly long and complex history of the term *typical.* Even the etymology of *typical* is contradictory: it denotes the mark of a blow, and thus the direct pressure of the real. It also suggests a sign, a mark left as a signal, and from this sense is derived its meaning for biblical hermeneutics, in which typology is the search for the "marks" of events in a biblical text. The contradiction between the type as a blow and the type as a mark is a simple form of the contradiction between the typical as a resemblance to everyday life and the typical as a structure of signification. The more recent history of the term preserves these contradictions, which I hold can be resolved by seeing typicality as a structure of intersubjectivity.

Let me summarize this history briefly, and then embark on a rather lengthy discussion of it. *Typical* enters the vocabulary of literary study from three early modern sources: the criticism of the Russian realists Belinsky and Chernishevsky, the literary historical work of Hippolyte Taine, and the logic of Hegel.[18] The first two of these sources characterize the objectivist and scientizing sense of *typical:* for them, the typical is simply that which resembles lived experience. Hegel's use characterizes a more dialectical and intersubjective sense, in which the demands of intelligibility are also recognized. Along with many other concepts rooted in Hegel's logic, typicality entered Marx's writing, and thus—with frequent, if silent, refreshment from the moralizing springs of Russian realism—became part of the apparatus of Marxist literary criticism. But some of the Hegelian sense of the term survived in two other contexts. Wilhelm Dilthey's romantic hermeneutic theory emphasized the text's intelligibility rather than its resemblance to experience, and the classical German sociology of Georg Simmel recovered much of the dialectical flexibility of the term. And heir to all of these traditions, a romantic in his youth, a student of Simmel, and a creative—if erratic—Marxist theorist, George Lukács, placed typicality at the center of his theory of representation.

We can deal rather summarily with the Russian realists and with Taine, since their significance is mainly historical. Chernishevsky saw the typical character as an artificial replication of the general qualities held in common by a group.[19] His "typical character," then, is close to the "type character" or stock character of literary handbooks and Roman comedy: the braggart soldier, the religious hypocrite, the lusty widow. Such types present themselves as unmediated images of unreflected social experience. In them, "what everyone knows" about widows or soldiers or fundamentalists takes shape and walks the stage. The type character might stand, then, as an example of the typical's direct resemblance to lived experience. But of course, things are not so simple. When we want to dismiss a character as unrealistic, wooden, or purely literary, we describe him or her as "just a type." We acknowledge, in this description, that unreflected social experience is not, after all, very good experience, and that we demand some kind of mediation, some transformation of what everyone knows, before we are willing to accept an image as true.

Taine's understanding of the type can perhaps stand as an example of minimal mediation. Hippolyte Taine held that the artist does not exactly imitate objects themselves, but their "relations, and above all, their proportions." For Taine, as later for Zola, the artist was a social physician or a naturalist of humanity, studying society scientifically. For Taine, the type was a kind of species, to be determined by repeated and detailed observations rather than directly subsumed from conventional wisdom. Taine's artist, then, was not limited to passively recording commonplaces; like the scientist, he was expected to make heroic discoveries. As Taine said of Balzac: "His doctors have no greater pleasure than the discovery of a strange and forgotten malady: he is a doctor and does as they do. He has many times described passions against nature of a kind that cannot even be indicated here."[20] The mediation that produces typicality, for Taine, is the simple tenacity of the artist, his lack of squeamishness in handling the repulsive instance. The artist no longer reworks what everyone knows; he finds exotic examples and presents them in scientific categories. The representation, then, is still essentially a record of lived experience, but social life is reconceived to admit romantic aberrations.

Both the Russian realists and Taine, however, see the typical as a relation between the author's general ideas and his or her method of instancing particulars. For Chernishevsky, both the individual and the general are simple reflections of existent social reality. For Taine, the general, or universal, is a mental category, and the particular is empirical, but the connection between them is passed over in silence. It is to Hegel we must turn, then, for a theory that sees the typical as a mediation, confronting the tension between the individual instance and the general notion, the contradiction between the demands of resemblance to experience and those of intelligibility.

Hegel did not use the term *typical* in any sustained way, although it might be possible to find equivalents to this term in cognates like *Particular* or *Individual*.[21] Nor was he much concerned with the problem of representation. However, Hegel's understanding of the dialectical relation of parts and wholes and his application of this dialectic to the problem of subjectivity in *The Phenomenology of Mind* have provided a framework within which other theorists, notably Marx, have reflected on the basic relations of representation. And his investigation of the relations between parts and wholes is a convincing resolution of the problem of relating individual instances to intelligible general constructs.

Let us examine Hegel's analysis of the part-whole relation in *The Encyclopedia of the Philosophical Sciences:*

> The Notion as Notion contains the three following "moments" or functional parts. (1) The first is *Universality*—meaning that it is in free equality with itself in its specific character. (2) The second is *Particularity*—that is, the specific character, in which the universal continues serenely equal to itself. (3) The third is *Individuality*—meaning the reflection-into-self of the specific characters of universality and particularity; which negative self-unity has complete and original determinateness, without any loss to its self-identity or universality.[22]

Hegel goes on to say that he is not speaking here of "immediate or natural" individuals, but of Individuals seen as expressing a totality— the full range of variations, experiences, and transformations possible for a coherent or self-specifying notion. At the same time, he distinguishes the notion from an ordinary abstraction or generalization, which is formed by "forgetting" the specific qualities of beings in the world and identifying them only through what they have in common. Such abstractions, which would include concepts like "assets," or "farm animals," do not really exist, and the specific instances from which they are formed exist independently of any abstraction that might be formed about them. No cow changes because it is categorized as a herbivore. The series of relations that Hegel describes here, however, is one of complete interdependence and interpenetration. This series of self-transformations is possible, however, only if we conceive of the universal, the particular, and the individual in a dialectical way, a way somewhat at odds with common-sense ideas about these categories.

The Universal, Hegel says, with "undimmed clearness finds itself at home in its antithesis." It is a Universal, then, which is not asserted blindly as truth, but which has already been formed in discourse, has already been subject to mediation and negation. It is not a general idea; it is very specific, and that specificity is not the result of an external determination, but of its own development of its implications and latent possibilities. Hegel gives as examples of such Universals "God and man in their true universality,"[23] commenting that they "cost thousands of years to enter into the consciousness of men." The universal notion of humanity, then, cannot be seen as a simple generalization, or collocation of facts about a biological species. It is a highly specified notion, implying a series of ideas about what human beings are, have been, and ought to be.

The specifications evolved by the Universal comprise Hegel's Particularity; it is because these specifications are self-originating rather than externally imposed that the Universal can be said to "continue serenely" in them.[24] And individuality implies the full development of both the Universal, in its signifying power, and the Particular, in it determinate specificity. While Universality, Particularity, and Individuality each imply the whole development of the notion, only at the moment of Individuality does that implication—and therefore the historical situation of the Notion—become explicit.

An application of these logical categories to art is not far to seek—we can find them used for Hegel's analysis of classical art in his lectures on aesthetics. Discussing the classical form of sculpture, which "has attained the pinnacle of what illustration by art could achieve," Hegel adopts a framework identical to that of the *Logic:* he will consider, first, Universality, then Particularity, and finally Individuality. It is worth noting that while these logical relations are by no means entirely immune from the idiosyncratic myth of art history that informs the *Aesthetics,* they are analytic rather than historical categories, describing a work's internal structure as much as its referential force. What is universal about classical art is not the relation between the work and its social setting, not the work's capacity to provoke an aesthetic response from many viewers, but its ability to deploy the category "human" in both its content and its form so that they "come into the most complete correspondence with each other." It is in its internal relations, not in its ability to reflect historical events, that Hegel locates the universality of classical art. Similarly, particularity is virtually a generic concept, invoking the classical "presentation of a range of particular gods and powers over human existence."[25] And, just as the particular of Hegel's *Logic* is a specification that loses none of the self-originating power of the universal, so in the *Aesthetics* the particular is a totality of qualities, harmoniously presented as an individual.

There are some links between this series of transformations and our investigation of the typical. First of all, we can see the universal, particular, and individual as a series of mutual representations, each term mediating and transforming the others, each referring to the others and threatening to dissolve into the others. (Hegel, we should note, would not have been impressed with such an image.) This series of mutual representations, further, suggests the possibility of overcoming the contradiction between everyday experience and intelligibility that has marked our investigation of the typical register of representation. Hegel's logic suggests that such a contradiction stems from a faulty understanding, both of actual experience and of meaning and intelligibility. If significance is not understood as an abstract, general "message" over against the text, and resemblance to the lived world is not understood as a random array of sensations, the gap between these two moments of the typical register becomes more negotiable. And in fact, everyday experience never presents itself to us innocently, without mediation; it is through general categories that we organize our experience as it happens. And these general categories, in the best of cases, will not be empty abstractions or stereotypes, but notions that have been formed in social discourse—notions, therefore, formed by a consciousness that recognized the possibilities of their transformation and development. We might consider, by way of illustration, the interplay of everyday experience and general categories in a genre like science fiction, where a category like "the alien" simultaneously reveals the hidden structures of everyday experience and discloses unforeseen implications of the notion of humanity.

Intelligibility and the power of evoking experience emerge in Hegel's *Aesthetics* as the transcended contradiction between diverse qualities and their presentation in individual images, the triumphant resolution of the conflict between natural objects and universal meanings. But neither intelligibility nor the power of invoking everyday experience is a simple attribute of language. Both of them imply mediation and reflection, and we can read Hegel's *Phenomenology of Mind* as an extended description of such mediations. In the movement of *The Phenomenology,* we can find a tacit recognition that it is only intersubjectively that we can speak either of resemblance to lived experience or of intelligibility. Neither of them is inherent in a text; neither is the free creation of an individual mind. This recognition becomes explicit, I think, in Hegel's discussion of the relation of Master and Slave, in which experience of the world, the texture of consciousness, and the transformation of the natural world itself are all determined by social relations. And in a later passage of *The Phenomenology,* Hegel describes the development of the idea of the Universal in terms that explicitly recall his treatment of part-whole relations in the *Logic*. Describing a consciousness caught up in the desire for pleasure, for the enjoyment of another independent consciousness, Hegel states that such an enjoyment is self-contradictory.[26] It assumes a self-understanding of consciousness as independent, but the independent consciousness searches for realization in an other. When this contradiction becomes apparent, the pleasure-seeking consciousness confronts in the other a manifestation of the Universal: it is only because they both express a Universal that two individuals can be a source of such pleasure to each other. The categories of the *Logic*— here invoked as unity, difference, and relation, in all their interdependence—have become categories of consciousness, rather than simple logical markers. While such an experience is not a happy one, we are concerned less with the fate of the pleasure-seeking consciousness than with the way this moment in the phenomenology illustrates the intersubjective grounding of the links among the individual, the particular, and the universal. That relation is not perceived by thinking about logic, although it is a logical relation; instead, it grows from the experience of an other consciousness, and from what that experience reveals to someone who had considered himself an "individual self-existent being." Hegel says that to search for pleasure is to seek to take possession of life; but that the consciousness that sought to take life "rather thereby laid hold on death," because it was profoundly changed, and can no longer see itself as independent. The interrelation of Universals, Particulars, and Individuals has become a pressure against the being of the pleasure-seeking consciousness.

Let us consider what this line of thought might mean for our understanding of the typical moment of representation before we resume the thread of our narrative, the history of typicality. First, Hegel has provided us with a model of the relation of parts and wholes, of experience and meaning, that is entirely dialectical. We find here no trace of Chernishevsky's exemplification, or of Taine's empty idealism. And Hegel suggests that the dialectic that shapes typical representation is connected with the experience of intersubjectivity. However, although this analysis acknowledges the claims of history, we have lost any concrete sense of historical situation, especially since the historical analysis of Hegel's *Aesthetics* is clearly unacceptable.

Hegel's model of the relations of particulars and universals cohered with Goethe's discussion of the representational power of the type, and so penetrated the literary discourse of romanticism. But the typical was always in danger of being absorbed into the allegorical, the strongest traditional model for linking literary image and significance. Victor Hugo, for instance, presents a definition of the type that is a virtual paraphrase of Hegel's *Logic:* "A type does not reproduce any man in particular; it cannot be exactly superimposed upon any individual; it sums up and concentrates under one human form a whole family of characters and minds."[27] But, in giving examples of the type, Hugo resorts to simple allegory. Achilles is the type of the slayer; Hamlet, of the dreamer. And indeed, in literary discourse, *type* has become a byword for ahistorical representation and criticism.

The next major philosophical writer after Hegel to concern himself with the question of the typical, however, was Marx, whose writing was nothing if not historically situated. And, oddly enough, the work in which Marx takes up the question of individuation is also his only extended work of literary criticism, *The Holy Family.*[28] In this early work, Marx comments on a popular novel by Eugene Sue, *Les Mystères de Paris,* which had been favorably reviewed by the Young Hegelian Szeliga. Szeliga and the other Young Hegelians simplified Hegel's infernal machine of representations and replications to a set of reductions and reflections. Individuals were treated under the rubric of "the Mass," and universals became mere abstractions, such as "truth" or "virtue." The relation between individual and universal was simple: individual characters exemplified universal traits. *Les Mystères de Paris,* then, with a little juggling, could be read as the story of the penetration of Mass by Spirit. Such a reading has more in common with traditional allegory, in which a figure invokes a univocal significance, than with the dialectical typicality we have been projecting.

Marx insists that the idealism of the Young Hegelians, ahistorical and unmediated, is simply a complicated form of empiricism. For example, the Young Hegelians constituted the object of their reflections by conflating concrete things and social relations, so that for them a house was a "*concrete* speculative unity, a *Subject-Object* which is the house and the houseowner in one" (*HF,* 167). Marx held that this method is doubly confused. It includes in the "speculative unity" accidental features of houses—dormer windows and sliding doors become part of the speculative understanding of houses. And the Young Hegelian method cannot account for the contradictory ways that owner, builder, and renter experience the house; intersubjectivity vanishes as a category. That conflict is dissolved: the house as "speculative object" is capable of reducing all relations to a specious self-identity. This method is one in which badly chosen examples are crudely linked to badly constituted universals.

In insisting on the historicity of the objects of knowledge, Marx also demonstrates the politically repressive quality of the Young

Hegelian method. On an immediate level, Marx found Szeliga de-humanizing: since characters were ignominiously reduced in his article to examples of virtues and vices, they became victims of his moralizing puritanism. Marx objected that Szeliga's method made the plot of a novel a series of interactions among fictional labels rather than a careful working out of the concrete social web of motivations. On a conceptual level, Marx found Szeliga unable to formulate a vision that deeply challenged the order of things as they are. His theory of justice, Marx said, was: "confined to stating that everything determinate is an opposite of the boundless generality of self-consciousness and is, therefore, of no significance; for example, the state, private property, etc. It must be shown, on the contrary, how the state, private property, etc., turn human beings into abstractions, or are products of *abstract* man, instead of being the reality of individual, concrete human beings (*HF*, 193)." The concept of abstract man, the putatively equal "citizen" of juridical theory, may be an impoverished concept, but it is not therefore without power. The state does indeed have the power to treat individuals as abstractions, and private property is capable of reducing even the most skilled and inspired labor, as Marx later pointed out, to a ratio of abstract labor power. The critique made by the Young Hegelians, confined to objections against the conceptual poverty of such abstractions, lacked any purchase on the social institutions that actualized the impoverished notions of "citizen" or "labor" as impoverished social relations. The Young Hegelians refused to engage these conceptions on the terrain of social life.

Marx's treatment of these themes reworks, in polemic tones, the central points in Hegel's discussion of the relations of Universals and Particulars, and applies them to the problem of representation. By criticizing Szeliga's celebration of unmediated objects and commonplace characters as reflections of the Universal, Marx reasserts the centrality of mediation in rendering everyday experience intelligible. By turning a house into a "concrete speculative unity," a direct representation of a Universal, the Young Hegelians failed to do justice to the conceptual complexity of our experience of houses. At the same time, Marx sees Szeliga's inability to trace out the mediations that connect self-consciousness to the determined social world as an emptying of the power of the universal; if everything, equally, pales before it, then the universal is simply an abstraction, independent of any individuation, deprived of any historical location or transformative power. Finally, both Marx's critique of the Young Hegelian stance as the personification of "spirit" over against the inert "mass" and his scorn of Sue's moralizing imply a perspective in which the interpreter claims no privileged access to the transcendent, but rather works to make the text intersubjectively accessible, so that its ability to "turn human beings into abstractions" is subverted.

Marx's posthumous *Grundrisse,* a more discursive work, integrates these historical and critical concerns into an overtly Hegelian logical structure. Marx writes: "The concrete is concrete because it is the concentration of many determinations, hence unity of the diverse. It appears in the process of thinking, therefore . . . not as a point of departure, even though it is a point of departure . . . for observation [*Anschauung*] and conception."[29] The concrete, here, has functions analogous to Hegel's Particular. The concrete is determined; it is not a static example, but a moment in a process. The concrete is not simply a piece of the world appropriated as an investigative tool: it is a mental reality, what Marx will call elsewhere in the *Grundrisse* a "product of the thinking mind," a product consciously elaborated to help the mind observe the lived world on a clearer, more adequate, conceptual level than simple empirical observation could provide. The concrete, then, is a particular kind of representation, which functions both as a heuristic device (a "point of departure for observation") and as a logical paradigm ("concentration of many determinations"). It mediates, therefore, experience and intelligibility. To illustrate this dual quality, Marx uses the example of the concept "population," which without considerable labor of the "thinking mind," can only be apprehended abstractly, as a heap of individuals characterized by bare common residence. The labor of the thinking mind would not involve enumerating all the individuals in the class: such an empirical procedure would simply replace the empty abstraction with a dimly understood heap of instances. Rather, certain mediating concepts such as "class" are required. But these concepts, Marx says, resolve themselves into even more determinate ideas, such as "exchange" and "means of production"—until, Marx says, we arrive at the simplest determinations, such as labor power: "From these the journey would have to be retraced until I had finally arrived at population again, but this time not as a chaotic conception of a whole, but as a rich totality of many determinations and relations."[30] If Hegel's treatment of part-whole relations provided us with a dialectical tool for understanding the basic tensions of typicality, and Marx's critique provides us with a way of situating these structures historically, we can turn to the next major figure to concern himself with the typical, Wilhelm Dilthey, for an illustration of how a dialectical method located in history could be compromised by the claims of scientific certainty.

Dilthey used typicality to describe the basic structures of perception, to analyze the representational power of art, and to project a method for the "human sciences." In all of these contexts, the typical was both a record of experience and a specific device for reflection on experience. As Dilthey put it in his essay on Hegel: "Artistic creation produces types which raise and intensify the manifold of experiences to an image and thus represent it. Thus, the opaque and mixed experiences of life are made comprehensible in their meaning through the powerful and clear structure of the typical."[31]

In his aesthetic theory, Dilthey's understanding of typicality does justice to the dialectical fluidity of Hegel and Marx. The typical mediates experience and intelligibility. It is not a simple empirical record—the representation "raises and intensifies" everyday experience. Dilthey's use of the type in historical investigations, however, may well merit the stock criticism of typical systems, that of being crudely abstract. Dilthey defined, for example, three typical world views—naturalism, subjective idealism, and objective idealism—and in spite of his repeated claims that these types are only heuristic, that concrete individuals are likely to be "mixtures" of all three, we must concede that no attempt to explain all intellectual history in three forms can do justice to the specificity of real social situations. In his aesthetics, however, Dilthey sees typicality as a deeply historical concept, since artists do not construct their types as elements in an abstract system. Rather, the type represents an individual vision, rooted in history, responsive to the conditions of space and time. Dilthey's aesthetic types, then, are both historical and intersubjective.

If we examine Dilthey's discussion of the logic of the type, however, we find indications both of his dialectical skill and of his tendency to misunderstand historical forms as ahistorical laws.[32] Dilthey advances two logical descriptions of the typical. The first is illustrated by the performance of a dancer or skater, in which the particular motions of the performer suggest other possibilities of movement, so that a single gesture somehow includes a whole range of alternates. To judge a performance as typical in this sense is to conjoin a factual description and an evaluation; the typical, Dilthey says, is a "norm lying between deviations." This description of the typical implies that typicality is an intersubjective relation: a performance can be typical only if it suggests alternate forms to an understanding audience. But in Dilthey's second analysis of typicality, the typical is an objective relation, and the artist who creates the typical images is, not a performer, but a scientist: "Art attempts to express what life is. The entire process of individuation of the human historical world comes to an understanding in poetry long before science strives to know it. And the means for the presentation of uniformities, the recurrence of differences, gradations, and affinities is typical vision."[33]

Here, the typical is a simple commonality, as it was for Chernishevsky or Taine. That commonality, further, has been dignified because it anticipates science: artistic understanding is more prescient than scientific explanation. But if artistic understanding produces certain knowledge, it cannot itself be known: it is a matter of an inaccessible "typical vision" rather than a shared relation between writer and reader.

Dilthey, unfortunately, was not the last writer for whom a scientistic notion of representation would coexist with a numinous theory of artistic inspiration: Lukács was entirely capable of such critical sleight of hand. And indeed, the diverse senses of *typical* codified in Dilthey became very influential, often for writers who did not have his dialectical skill.

Among the writers Dilthey influenced were the sociologist Georg Simmel and his students Max Weber and Karl Mannheim. Simmel used *typical* to describe our mental schemas of personality structures, and claimed that these schemas are the sole vehicles whereby we know other people, since we have no access to their interior lives. Mannheim and Weber were later to speak of an "ideal type," which Weber defines as a "conceptual pattern which brings together certain relationships and events of historical life into a complex, which is conceived as an internally consistent system."[34] The ideal type is a quasi-scientific tool for sociological investigation; as it was deployed by American empirical sociologists, the concept became simply a schema for organizing empirical remarks. In Weber's initial deployment of the concept, however, there is some recognition of the interdependence between the investigator and the object of his investigation, and some recognition of the ways in which the logic of social investigations differs from that of scientific experiment.

All of these strains in the odd history of typicality emerge in the writing of George Lukács. Lukács was a student of Simmel's, briefly frequented the same Prague study circle as Mannheim, acknowledged an early link with Dilthey, and had some affinity with Max Weber. As a major theoretician, Lukács expressed deeply contradictory impulses within Marxism. By background, conviction, and association, Lukács's interests were dialectical and subjective. But always, even when he was not a member of a party, Lukács was at heart a party theorist, and for many years he was the theorist of a party dominated by philosophical materialism and aesthetic reflectionism. Lukács managed to serve these two masters by asserting, alternately, the primacy of mimesis in art and the relative autonomy of aesthetics from social life. Lukács's definition of *the type* bears the mark of both assertions: "The central category and criterion of realist literature is the type, a peculiar synthesis which organically binds together the general and the particular both in characters and in situations. What makes a type a type is not its average quality, not its mere individual being, however profoundly conceived; what makes it a type is that in it all the humanly and socially essential determinants are present on their extremes, rendering concrete the peaks and limits of men and epochs."[35]

A peculiar synthesis indeed. Lukács's definition, like Dilthey's, yokes uneasily together a mystical conception of the power of art and a naive admiration for the predictive power of science. Rather than investigating the complex dialectic of everyday experience and intelligibility, Lukács simply invokes "organic bonds" that will hold those two categories together. The transcendent language of earlier theorists—terms such as "universal," "absolute," and "totality"—here gives way to a modest assertion of the relationship between the "general and the particular." Lukács reserves his totalizing language—"highest level," "ultimate unfolding"—for the invocation of history. But it is here, in the injunction that artists portray the "essential determinants" of a period, that Lukács makes crucial concessions to scientism. The "essential determinants" are logically prior to the typical image, and they give entry to a scientized version of Marxism, as a static external system. We are reminded that a page or so before formulating this definition of typicality, Lukács has urged the artist to emulate the early Marxists in keeping to the "true highroad of history, the true direction of the historical curve, the formula of which they knew" (*SER*, 5). History, here, has ceased to be an intersubjective ground of knowledge; it has become objectified, even reified.

If Lukács's understanding of typicality is part of an aesthetic appended to a rather dogmatic Marxism, this adjunct status paradoxically allows him to preserve some of the dialectical force that the concept had for Hegel and for the early Marx. Here among the epicycles of the theoretical machine, we must be prepared for some fancy stepping. Thus, the typical is not for Lukács what it would be for later Soviet writers, an inspiring hagiographic image. Nor is the typical image empirically determined; in recognizing the need for "extreme presentation of extremes," Lukács suggests that form has something to do with the nature of typical representations. Latent in Lukács's definition, then, is an aesthetic that need not have rejected the "excesses" of Joyce and Kafka.

I began by contrasting literary critical approaches focused on reading and representation; I can end this lengthy history of the concept of typicality by looking at these themes in a modern literary critical treatment of the typical, W. K. Wimsatt's "The Concrete Universal," and in an editorial on the typical from the Soviet journal *Kommunist*.

Wimsatt assumes that the work of art combines the general and the particular in a unique way—by forming concrete universals— and asks what connects the universal in a work to particulars.[36] Wimsatt holds that this connection is formed by the logical relation of the various parts of the work. For literary characters, thus, the logical relation among various traits produces the self-consciousness that distinguishes round from flat characters; for metaphors, the tacit relation of the elements to each other produces the central abstraction of the poem. The concrete universal is therefore both an ethical and a rhetorical ideal, subduing the complexity of poetic materials to maturity and unity.

Only in the most ghostly form does Wimsatt's essay preserve the dialectical integrity of the question it confronts. Although the essay begins with a sense that the referential power of poems is something that needs explanation, Wimsatt soon locates that explanation in the favorite New Critical category of the harmonious relation of elements of the work to each other. The question of reference is left behind; the work relates to itself through its unified form, rather than to the world of social life. The question of reference, however, is not so easily exiled. It returns in the abstractions concrete universals are said to invoke—sterile topics, like "communion, telepathy in solitude," for Wordsworth's "The Reaper," for example. And the question of reference returns with a vengeance in Wimsatt's anomalous claim to scientific certainty: "a criticism of structure and of value is an objective criticism. It rests on facts of human psychology. Such a criticism, again, is objective and absolute, as distinguished from the relative criticism of idiom and period."[37]

We would not expect such scientism from a literary critic writing in the fifties. We might expect to find it in a 1966 central committee resolution of the Communist Party of the USSR. We would not be disappointed. In the resolution "On the Question of the Literary and Art Treatment of the Typical,"[38] the search for universals becomes a mandate for the composition of monumental works, a demand for political and stylistic orthodoxy. The "science of Marxism-Leninism" assures that any realistic work will automatically convey the proper political moral. The work of art requires no mediation; it simply records and projects privileged abstractions. The term *typical* has been totally debased, and it is not surprising that it lost currency. Except for scattered instances, it has been ignored in Western Marxist literary criticism.

Thus, its dialectical wildness tamed, the concept of typicality was displaced from its central location at the intersection of metaphysics and the rhetoric of representation. It found a safe, if boring and provincial, home at the margins of orthodox Marxist criticism, and after learning formal good manners, we adopted under the rubric "concrete universal" as a flywheel in the machinery of New Criticism.[39]

Since it is our aim to renovate the concept of typicality, to restore it to usefulness, what can we say after reviewing this tangled history?

First of all, to understand the typical is to revise our basic notions of the relations of parts to wholes, by abandoning the common-sense idea that only the concrete is real, and that the group name is nothing but a pale abstraction. Instead, we need to see that concrete instances and abstractions are mutually determining, are both products of the "thinking mind," and are not related to each other through the logic of categories, but are formed along the axes of fundamental social relations. Consider how impossible it would be to discuss women's images in literature if only statements about women's experience that could be demonstrated as empirically true about a majority of women were admitted to the discussion. Consider further the possibility of a discussion that made operational all abstractions about women (women's nature, feminine intuition, feminine psychology, women's roles), rather than reflecting on them as ways of formulating experience, expressing aspirations, or intervening in history. As this example suggests, our "normal" reading procedures, whether we are professional or lay readers, demand an understanding of part-whole relations that is more dialectical than normal category logic: we attempt, however crudely, to see an interconnection between the particular and the universal, and we attempt to locate that relation in history.

And indeed, we cannot avoid the question of history once we have begun to talk about the representation of social relations—relations of material production, political subordination, sexual division of labor, and cultural hegemony. Because such relations are quite subject to change, and tend to vary among cultures and periods, they cannot be discussed fruitfully outside of historical contexts. Since norms of reading are also part of the apparatus of cultural hegemony, these relations will also be at issue in various interpretations of the text; therefore, social relations can be contested in various renderings of the typical. The concept of typicality, then, returns us to the traditional notion of hermeneutic accountability: the interpreter is responsible for the reading, and therefore, in a sense, for the text. But such accountability is not seen as a moral relationship in which the interpreter is soiled or ennobled by the text. Rather, the interpreter and the text call one another to the question, interrogating what is missing, lost, or suppressed in text or interpretation. Hermeneutic accountability, in this framework, can be seen as an implication of the text's subjectivity. As the critical theorist Jürgan Habermas put it in *Knowledge and Human Interests:*

> Hermeneutics must assimilate the dialectic of the general and the individual that determines the relation of objectification and experience and comes to expression *as such* in the medium of the "common." If this is so, then understanding itself is bound to a situation in which at least two subjects communicate in a language that allows them to share—that is, to make communicable through intersubjectively valid symbols—what is absolutely unshareable and individual. Hermeneutic understanding ties the interpreter to the role of a partner in dialogue. *Only this model of participation in communication can explain the specific achievements of hermeneutics.* [40]

It is intersubjectivity that enables typical images to mediate particular and general, to be presented in concrete fullness and also to invoke universals. Such mediations establish the text as a dialogue between author and readers, a dialogue in which the constraints of language and ideology can be subverted. The centrality of mediation further implies that the text cannot be reduced to an object; the reader who has had a part in forming the categories under which typical images are subsumed cannot turn against those categories and images as if they were alien. A reader can, of course, reexamine his or her interpretation of a text, but such an act is self-reflective; it is not an inquiry about structures outside the relationship between text and interpreter.

Since the typical is at once a means of relating parts and wholes and a means of establishing a text's intersubjectivity, it joins the logic of the text with its rhetoric. To read a text typically, then, is to see its basic codification of social reality as a moment in the relation we are able to establish with it and to see our relation to the text as the realization of a moment of its codification of social reality. The text, then, is neither a record of instances, or a series of ornaments. The relations between the text, the world, and ourselves interpenetrate.

The mediations of intersubjectivity, the location of a text in history, the juncture of logic and rhetoric, a dialectic between instances and universals—all these formulas tell us something about the typical, to be sure. They do not tell us, however, how the typical actually emerges in the text or in the interpretation. Perhaps we should end this discussion, then, with an inventory of some ways in which the typical register of the text is particularly accessible or strongly marked. Then, we will turn to the analysis of the typical register of Shakespeare's *Richard II.*

To begin at the most comprehensive level, realism as a self-conscious literary movement can be seen as an attempt to exploit the typical register of the text. Lukács, as we have seen, understood the typical as the central category of realist literature; it is probably more appropriate to see realism as a subspecies of typical representation. In self-consciously realistic literature, we commonly find a chain of affirmations, internal and external to the text, linking its particular instances to some more global system of affirmations. A story by Balzac, for example, might be bracketed by the sociological explanation of Balzac's framing narrative; we might also place it according to the generic rubrics of *La comédie humaine,* or the project, modeled on natural history, outlined in Balzac's foreword to the series. Later readers have framed Balzac's stories in other systems of signification: Marx's assertion that he learned a great deal of political economy from Balzac elevated him to the orthodox Marxist canon as a "social realist"; Barthes's virtuoso reading, *S/Z,* showed how linguistic systems can be projected as the frame of the story. In all of these instances, the story is seen as a formulation of an intelligible statement about the world, a statement that can be brought into coherence with other sets of intelligible statements. Realism presents each work as a moment in a lucid, coherent discourse. Any of the framing devices seems to bring the events of the story, improbable and romantic as they might be, into focus; each frame assumes and comments upon the others, until they form a web of interpretations.

We might also consider such a critical history, a history of affirmations, as a manifestation of the typical register. Texts that have provoked debates for generations of critics foreground their own indeterminacy, and we shall later focus on one such text, *The Turn of the Screw.* But what is perhaps more puzzling is the text that always seems transparent, the text for which one interpretation succeeds another in a stately procession—even though the interpretations are contradictory—the text like *David Copperfield* or *The Doll's House,* about which there seems to be nothing to say. Such an interpretive history is a record of collaborations between the text and the interpreter to confirm the transparency of the text, to see it as simply a record of experience, already redolent with significance, for which the interpreter's labor is superfluous.

In the same key, a narrator who appears to be reliable, or at least well disposed toward the reader, often figures in the typical register. As J. Hillis Miller showed in *The Forms of Victorian Fiction*,[41] such a narrator can be asserted as a model of integrated consciousness, a fully formed subjectivity trusted to judge fairly each of the fragmentary minor characters. Such a narrator images out the intersubjectivity of the typical register, personifying it in the text so it is not only a logical and rhetorical feature of the representation, but also appears in a human guise.

On the lexical and syntactic level, the typical register is marked by such tropes as metonymy, in which a concrete object is used to indicate the world that formed it. Such figures are not empty; they remind us of Marx's early maxim that "for the eye to become a human eye it must have a human object."[42] Metonymy, then, is an economical figure for social commentary, as in Joyce's catalogs of the flotsam of Dublin life. Other tropes that mark the typical register include some of those that Freud identified as means of representing repressed ideas in dreams: indicating logical connection by simultaneity, or causality by collocation, showing a dangerous resemblance by means of a less dangerous one; creating composites, or encoding the subject of the work in its form. Unlike other forms of dreamwork, displacement and condensation, these tropes do not produce images that demand explanation, but instead images that insist on their normalcy. In all of these typical forms, outward appearance is presented as the truth of the world: relation in space implies logical relation; formal categories are communicative rather than arbitrary; the connections among images are finite and manageable. In all of these tropes, the typical register appears as a vehicle for connecting specific and universal, for connecting the text to lived experience, and for connecting the logic of the work to its rhetoric. In all of these tropes, the typical appears as a friend to the interpreter, an intersubjective ground on which the text can be approached and interrogated.

The Typical Register in Shakespeare's *Richard II*

Let us use this theoretical framework to interpret Shakespeare's *Richard II*. My reading will not generate a startling reversal of critical opinion about the play; what is of interest in this initial foray is method.

Let us begin by situating the text historically, orienting ourselves to the terrain of the play's typical relations. We can safely assert, relying on modern historians, that Shakespeare's period saw the development of something like a modern state in England. The English state changed from the household establishment of the king to an autonomous structure, capable in theory of fully governing the realm and organized according to relatively bureaucratic and rational, rather than personal and customary, norms. For Shakespeare, writing in such a period, the dynastic wars were a politically charged subject, recalling the crucible in which this state had been formed. And for us, a modern audience, the construction of the state form that even now governs us is of more than antiquarian interest. Let us take, then, that state as a common location, a piece of shared ground from which we can begin to survey the horizon of the play, onto which we can summon the images it invokes. Such a procedure allows us to integrate our understanding of the ideological apparatus available to Shakespeare with our immediate experience of the play. In the forty years of historical commentary on Shakespeare's history cycle, quite a few features of this apparatus have been identified, from the orthodox chain of being posited by Tillyard through the investigations of Machiavellian statecraft or the redaction of the Elizabethan political consensus proposed by various revisionist theorists.[43] If this information aids us in recreating the world of the play, it does not also make the play's world our own. As Robert Weimann puts it, the task of interpretation must take into account the contexts of both writer and reader: "For the literary historian and critic the question, then, is not whether to accept both worlds as points of reference, but rather *how* to relate them so as to obtain their maximum dimension . . . to have as much of the historical significance and as much of the contemporary meaning merged into a new unity."[44]

How then does the state shape the relations of representation in *Richard II*? The state, first, is a "new thing" within the universe of the play. Instead of being assimilated and naturalized by political ideology, the state is a scandal, a stumbling block in the way of routine observation, a thing to be explained. Consider, by way of contrast, Steinbeck's *Grapes of Wrath*, where the activity of the state is transparent and unproblematic. The Elizabethan writer faced the problem of reshaping the conventions of chronicle history, heroic drama, and moral interlude to the new form of the state. Shakespeare's solution to this problem provokes us, as readers, to rethink the state, since the normal tropes in which realist literature recuperates the state as a natural structure are absent from *Richard II*. In its representation of the state, then, *Richard II* can challenge us, say something new to us.

The state is also a virtually unique place in modern discourse for examining questions about community, about the nature of public life and its relation to private life. It is thus a vehicle for discussing the proper relations of individuals and groups. Marx pointed out long ago that a certain alienation and distortion are implicit in this process, whereby "every common interest" is "straightway severed from society, counterposed to it as a higher, general interest snatched from the activity of society's members themselves."[45] But this very alienation establishes a certain congruence between the state and the typical register of representation: the state is a concrete structure representing a range of individual experiences. Our horizon, then, conjoins with that of the play's original audience, who saw the sovereign-subject relation as both pattern and source of every relation between a superior and an inferior—and thus, for all important social relations. For the Elizabethan, the sovereign-subject relation mobilized all the terms in the lexicon of power, from the totalized language of awe in prescribed homilies: "so doth God himself in the same Scriptures sometime vouchsafe to communicate his name with earthly princes, terming them Gods," to the more intimate terms of Stafford's speech to the Council of the North: "Princes are to be the indulgent nursing fathers to their people. . . . Verily these are those mutual intelligences of love and protection descending and loyalty ascending which should pass . . . between the king and his people."[46]

If the Elizabethans saw social institutions in terms of personal relationships, we see communal relationships among persons in terms of social institutions. Thus, by a strange spiraling of ideology, the relations between Renaissance sovereign and subject provide us with ideological forms complementary to our own: the gaps and vacancies in our ideology are indicated by what has been made explicit in theirs. The state, which is both an institution and the personal tool of the sovereign, thus provides, in Henry James's famous phrase, a circle within which social relations appear to end, a circle we share with the play's original audiences, and that circumscribes the play's typical register.

The relations between subject and sovereign, or more specifically, among Richard II, Bolingbroke, and other characters in the play, thus become representations, both of the shifting relations of public and private life and of the scope, power, and impersonality of the new monarchy. Shakespeare organizes this representation in a number of formal patterns, from the archaic allegory of the garden scene to the Senecan deposition scene. The traditional forms of chronicle play, moral interlude, and royal tragedy describe a monarchy that could no longer be traditional.

However, *Richard II* is not a simple conflict between archaic and modern state structures, with Richard personifying an attractive but doomed traditional monarchy and Bolingbroke the rising but humanly inhospitable modern state. Such a representational structure

would be simply allegorical, and *Richard II*—unlike, say, *Richard III*—
has a typical register demanding enough to subordinate the allegorical
strains of the play. Rather, both characters display complex relations
to the problems posed by the modern state, so that those problems
are mediated by intersubjectivity. Richard tries to solve the problems
of a modern state with the tools of traditional rule; he ends by re-
treating to the private, to a sphere of significance "outside" the state,
a location for intimacy and interiority. Bolingbroke, on the other
hand, challenges the state on the basis of his private "right"; his subjectivity becomes an instrument of rule.

This representation is not a mirror for princes, or for magis-
trates; it is rather a translation of political problems into terms
accessible to the intersubjective imagination. The varying accommo-
dations of Richard and Bolingbroke demonstrate different possibilities of the situation. Richard is unable to master the forms of the
new state: he continues to rely on familial and customary forms of
rule, forms that always fail him as he undertakes modern projects.
The institutions of customary society, arrayed before us in the first
scene—the ducal council, ceremonial trial by combat, the oath—rest
on relations of consent and of mutual obligation. They do not cohere
with the impersonal, almost bureaucratic, relations of authority that
characterize an omnicompetent state on its way to becoming an absolute monarchy—in Elizabethan terms, an *imperium*. Such dissonance
would be only a stylistic problem were not Richard also engaged in
acts that required all the powers of the developed state. His farming
of the realm for taxes would have reminded the Elizabethan audience
of Henry VIII's misnamed "Amicable Grant," another blank-charter
tax that had excited so much resistance it had to be repealed. He is
engaged in the perennial task of subduing the stateless Irish to the
nascent empire, and he keeps the style of an absolute monarch; he is
blamed for "too great a court and liberal largess".[47] He attempts to
impose upon his most powerful vassals the forms of equality before
law observed in a modern state: "He [Bolingbroke] is our subject,
Mowbray, so art thou" (1.1.32), thus endangering the familial forms
that shore up his slender support. Richard, then, is trying to be two
different kinds of king, a customary feudal king and the ruler of an
imperium. The contradictions of this enterprise force him doubly into the sphere of the private—he treats the realm as his private property
("landlord of England art thou, not king," 2.1.113), and in his
monologues, Richard expresses the only private subjectivity available
in the play. We will return to this theme.

In the character of Richard, four heterogeneous elements are conjoined: the modern state, customary society, private property, and private subjectivity. Richard, of course, cannot reconcile the contradictions among these elements. But in his passage from public life to private life, Richard presents the contradictions to us as a series of subjective experiences. By mediating these problems through the character of Richard, the play simultaneously invites us to investigate these themes and assures us that they will bear investigation. If Richard can live out the troubled relation between the state and customary society, then surely we can think out that relation. Rather than being subordinated to a series of allegorical categories, the characters of *Richard II* mediate the contradictory categories in which the play organizes lived experience, so that political and cultural processes are presented in their intersubjective forms.

Bolingbroke also mediates these contradictory elements, but in quite a different way. He is a magnate; his private grievance—Gloucester's death—thereby derives public force. But in the context of the omnicompetent state, Bolingbroke is only another subject. He appears initially as an embodiment of archaic forms, a champion going into combat "lusty, young, and cheerly drawing breath" (1.3.66). Later, as bare abstract subject, he will defend primogeniture as a universal law. Paradoxically, it is this double quality of Bolingbroke—carrier of customary privilege and isolated individual struggling for his due—that allows him to justify himself in respect both to the rights of customary society and to the duties of a modern subject. His struggle for his own becomes a common cause. Thus, when Bolingbroke asserts, "I am a subject, / and I challenge law" (2.3.134-35), his location within two systems of subordination gives his modest claim sovereign force. Bolingbroke's skillful exploitation of his dangerous position contrasts with Richard's bumbling, since Richard cannot manage even so public an obligation as the Irish wars without seeming greedy for private profit. And, while Richard's personal subjectivity threatens to absorb his ceremonial decorum, Bolingbroke invests himself with that glamour of power that was to the Elizabethans an attribute of royalty. Richard, at a crucial moment, is reduced to a body:

> throw away respect,
> Tradition, form, and ceremonious duty;
> For you have but mistook me all this while.
> I live with bread like you, feel want, taste grief,
> Need friends. Subjected thus,
> How can you say to me I am a king?

(3.2.172-77)

But Bolingbroke is able to use his body as weapon and advertisement; Richard observes his "courtship to the common people," as he goes "wooing poor craftsmen with the craft of smiles" (1.4.28).

In the final act of the play, both kings are isolated: Richard at Promfret Castle and Bolingbroke at court. These twin images of isolated individuality invite us to reflect on the relations of royal dominance and subordination that constitute the play's public and private worlds. And since we, who do not live in a world ruled by kings, do live in a world where even the most intimate relations are determined by public norms of power, these reflections open the play to us, open our lives for us, allow us to interpret the play as a typical representation of the relations that shape our own world.

It is not surprising, then, that critical responses to this play, and to the history plays in general, have reflected quite faithfully twentieth-century understandings about the state. Traditional critics like Tillyard, writing at mid-century, preoccupied with notions of order, saw insurgent readings of the history plays as anachronistic and unhistorical. In Tillyard's memorable formula, the "delusion" that Hal was wrong to cast off Falstaff "will probably be accounted for, in later years, through the facts of history. The sense of security created in nineteenth century England by the predominance of the British navy induced men to rate that very security too cheaply and to exalt the instinct of rebellion above its legitimate station." Like Tillyard, New Critics were preoccupied with the question of how individual integrity could be protected from the distortions of politics.[48] Both of these concerns respond to the problems raised by fascism and world war: anxiety for the future of parliamentary democracies and a profound distrust of mass movements and mass enthusiasms. Critics of the sixties, on the other hand, turned from the celebration of authority to a critique of artifice and an investigation of personal politics,[49] echoing the central topics of contemporaneous political discourse. And a critic writing in the eighties, Gordon Ross Smith,[50] reads the history plays as a complaint against violence, corruption, and waste—a post-Watergate Henriad, by way of *Sixty Minutes*. There is nothing magical in his play that makes it relevant to so many historical situations. Rather, it is because *Richard II* phrases its investigation of the basic relations of political domination as a conflict between two discrete individuals that these relations are mobilized, unfolded, mediated in different ways. And since such mediating devices are presented intersubjectively, responses to the characters in this play can simultaneously reflect deeply subjective concerns and lend themselves to "objective" formulation. The most common way to take up a new hermeneutic stance toward *Richard*

II, then, has been to call for a reexamination of the historical record, to announce a new, more faithful, recreation of the "background" of the play.

Let us consider again how the play itself treats the theme of subjectivity. Specifically, let us examine Bolingbroke and Richard as we encounter them in the last act. Representative of familial and customary claims, Bolingbroke is nonetheless seldom shown with his own family. No queen appears by his side, his heir is present in this play only as a nasty rumor, and his other sons will only appear in the second part of *Henry IV*. The family, the classic arena of private life, has been compromised, for Bolingbroke, by his instrumental use of it; he is skillful at deploying other people's families for domination, as in the comic crisis of Aumerle's treason. Lack of familial ties, however, does not exhaust the theme of Bolingbroke's isolation: unlike Richard, who favors the royal "we," Bolingbroke always announces himself as a solitary "I." But like his family relations, Bolingbroke's individuality has lost its subjective force in being used as a political tool. His personality is instrumentalized, as in his equivocal, almost opaque, reaction to Richard's murder: "Though I did wish him dead,/I hate the murtherer, love him murther'd" (5.6. 39–40). Throughout the rest of the history cycle, Bolingbroke's most distinctive voice will be heard only in his mourning for his own isolation from his son.

The case of the obsessively subjective Richard is more complex. In his soliloquy at Pomfret Castle, Richard recasts the lament of the deposition scene—"I must nothing be" (4.1.201)—into private terms. Loss of office is for Richard, as it was to be for Othello, loss of public being, but lacking Othello's capacity for desperation, Richard endeavors to create instead an entirely mental world, populated by the creatures of his imagination. That world, to be sure, is compromised by the treason and penury that determine Richard's status as a deposed monarch: his subjectivity cannot substitute social relations for itself. And his invented people fall into the easy categories of public life: they are ambitious or scoundrels, royal or impoverished. Thus his enterprise, to "people this little world," simply repeats the relations of power that he failed to understand in public life. Finally, the whole project founders upon Richard's corporeality, upon the scandal of the royal body wasted by time.

We can see *Richard II*, then, as an investigation of a number of linked, contradictory pairs:

modern state / communal society

private subjectivity / private property

public life / private life

In all of these pairs, relations between parts and wholes, generalities and specific instances, are at issue: we consider various ways of understanding the relations between individuals and social groups. But the text, as I have said, does not present these pairs to us allegorically. The two main characters cut across these axes, so that the character whose political beliefs are most alien to us today, Richard, presents the most fully developed subjectivity, while Bolingbroke, who is more familiar ideologically, seems subjectively distant and opaque. The typical register of the play, then, links its logic and its rhetoric: we are invited to keep alive the dialectical play of its categories by preserving a mobile imagination; the typical register of the play refuses to allow our sympathies to lie down peacefully next to our prejudices.

For Shakespeare's audience, however, somewhat different problems would have emerged. The royal characters of *Richard II* allowed Shakespeare's audience to reappraise their concept of royal rule. Neither king would have been easily assimilable to Renaissance ideology: neither is a tyrant; neither is fully legitimate. Shakespeare's audience would also have met in the play a representation of the modern state, a state they had encountered but had not yet given a name. The pair, Richard and Bolingbroke, present between them all the claims of customary rule and all the necessities of modern sovereignty. For an age so preoccupied with the themes of obedience and rebellion, such a spectacle must have been vertiginous, since the play endorses neither Richard's retreat to privacy nor Bolingbroke's instrumental subjectivity. Thus the play would have suggested questions its audience had not begun to ask in its more narrowly political discourse. It functioned, then, as a representation: an indication of a world other than the one it depicts; a solemn setting forth of what had been presented to the audience in social life but not recognized.

For us, this representation also prompts reflection on the fundamental relations of public and private. Since the nineteenth century, the play has been accessible less as a meditation on usurpation and legitimacy than as an investigation of the ways that Richard's sensibility is at odds with his royal role. We can see the play as a critique of this kind of subjectivity, of Richard's isolated and interiorized self-interrogation. The play invites us to see his self-conciousness as a displaced sovereignty, as the reflex of an exile from power. Indeed, there is no privacy in this play that is not shaped by relations of domination. We can read the garden scene, in which the queen eavesdrops on gardeners and learns of her husband's deposition, as an overt statement of this theme—there, a character who is a "little better thing than earth" (3.4.78) discusses events of state. But further reflection on this scene would require us to consider the paradoxical status of the Renaissance pastoral, which combined a dream of privacy and seclusion with a tradition of political commentary. Such generic considerations would lead us to connect the Renaissance theme of domination with the modern theme of the public and private, a promising line of thought and one we will take up in the next chapter.

To read *Richard II* as representation, then, is to trace out the relations between individuals and groups that the play calls into question, understanding that those questions phrase themselves differently for different historical audiences. A hermeneutic approach to the play's typical register will not resolve the questions that arise in the course of these reflections: it will surely not answer the questions of traditional criticism by assigning the proper ratios of blame to Richard and Bolingbroke, or evaluating Bolingbroke's coalition tactics. Nor would a hermeneutic approach stop, as we have, at the play's typical register; it would also confront the more puzzling, alien, and resistant aspects of the play. But a hermeneutic approach to the play's typical register does illuminate its intersubjective power. We can use this approach both to analyze the differences between the texts we read and those that Shakespeare's audience encountered and also to show the links, translations, and shared horizons of consciousness that bring these texts together. The play, then, speaks to us, but its location in history has been respected.

The Indeterminate Register

The typical register takes as its domain the relations between individuals and groups, the location of a text in history, and intersubjectivity as an interpretive ground. But everything accidental and contingent, everything that rubs against the historical grain or runs on a bias to the main axes of social relations, everything that resists interpretation and refuses intersubjectivity—in short, a great deal of social life and of literature—cannot be subsumed in the typical register of representation, and constitutes instead the indeterminate register. The indeterminate register gives the text a quality of contingency: it is the aspect of representation that suggests a rational kernel to students' complaints that close readings are just "reading into" a text—the work is sufficiently opaque to make all interpretations seem labored and implausible. While the typical register of the text affirms an intersubjective relation between writer and audience, the indeterminate register presents a text that lives its own life, autonomous from both writer and reader. Let us look more closely at this concept.

It is possible, with some application and a bit of good luck, to write a history of the word *typical.* Although the term seems transparent, without a history, it has managed, in its obscure wanderings through the unfashionable quarters of literary and philosophic discourse, to quietly accumulate a store of contradictory meanings, and these meanings indicate fairly precisely what the problems of typical representation might be. The history of indeterminacy as a term in literary studies is shorter, more focused, but scarcely less complex. *Indeterminacy* surfaced as a major term in literary criticism as a translation of Roman Ingarden's *Umbestimmtheitsstellen,* which is sometimes also rendered as "places of indeterminacy." For Ingarden, the words of the text provided a schema from which the reader projects certain fictional states of affairs.[51] Since no text can directly replicate the multiple determinations and specifications of even the simplest "state of affairs" in the world, the text's schematic structure is necessary to its verbal economy. The sketchy places in such a schema are called places of indeterminacy. They are undefined aspects of the narrative the reader must make concrete. Readers may concretize the schema well or poorly; ideally, for Ingarden, one's concretization of the text is adapted to its basic structure.[52] Ingarden recognizes the problem of circularity in this formulation, but claims that the "essentially necessary structural elements" should correspond in the acts of reading and writing.

This reticence of Ingarden's, it seems to me, raises some problems. In attempting to circumvent the intersubjective demands of the hermeneutic circle, Ingarden quickly becomes mortgaged to the objectified "essential structure" of the work, which is neither schema nor concretion, neither authorial, textual, nor readerly, neither virtual nor actual, but which somehow controls all these locations and mediations of the work. Ingarden has reinvented Dilthey's positivist illusion, that the text somehow "contains" a real subjectivity that a correct interpretation can recover. A ghostly second structure is erected over the concrete experience of the work, intervening at crucial moments in the process of interpretation to tip the scales in favor of objectivism; this second structure will later arise as the "spirit of the work," which, according to Ingarden, judges whether a particular concretion is adequate.[53]

Ingarden's conception of indeterminate places in the text is useful, however, because he demonstrates that indeterminacy is not simply a local aberration, a tremor in the smooth unrolling of meaning, but rather a necessary and pervasive quality of the text. This perception is amplified in Wolfgang Iser's *The Act of Reading: A Theory of Aesthetic Response.* He objects that Ingarden's concept of indeterminacy is only useful for describing indeterminacy in "illusionistic," or conventionally realistic texts. Instead, Iser proposes that indeterminacies—blanks or negations—are those breaks in the syntax of the text that permit the reader to articulate his strategy for approaching the text. Thus, indeterminacy is a sort of "propellant" conditioning the reader's formulation of the text. The text's blanks and negations "make it possible for the fundamental asymmetry between text and reader to be balanced out, for they initiate an interaction in which the hollow form of the text is filled by the mental images of the reader."[54]

Clearly, this vision of indeterminacy is a way of reconceiving the text; the work has become intersubjective in its very constituting structure, in its very resistance to interpretation.

If indeterminacy is linked to intersubjectivity for Ingarden and Iser, for Paul de Man it is an expression of the impossibility of grounding the text in intersubjective relations. Indeterminacy, for de Man, is located neither in the text nor in the reading nor outside the text, but in the impossibility of disentangling reference from referent, of holding on to the metaphorical status of concepts like "man," "passion," and "perfectibility"; "Language can only be about something such as man (i.e., conceptual), but in being about man, it can never know whether it is about anything at all including itself, since it is precisely the *aboutness,* the referentiality, that is in question" (*AR,* 161).

We should question de Man's attribution of knowledge to language—a hypostasization that is already implied in de Man's rejection of intersubjectivity—but there is much to be gained from his radical formulation of indeterminacy, since readers certainly do not "know" in any positive sense whether texts are about their overt topics, their representational strategies, or themselves. Further, de Man's formulation of the depth of indeterminacy illustrates the dialectical connection between indeterminacy and typicality: a text is indeterminate because it is impossible to state, a priori, what it is typical *of,* even if we assume a counterfactual reader who has full knowledge of the text's social situation. The moment of reference and the moment of reading converge.

Such a challenge to objectivist norms has not gone unanswered; Geoffrey Hartman, for example, has attempted a normalization of the concept of indeterminacy, conflating it with the more familiar New Critical and existential term *irony.*[55] Hartman defines irony as a temper of mind that resists the closure of reflection; such openness and play are seen as essential constituents of literature. Irony, then, and by implication indeterminacy, is no longer confined to the reader's struggle to interpret a text; it has been generalized, connected with basic notions of truth and of ethical behavior. But in relocating the domain of indeterminacy from the cramped, intimate quarters of the ignoble act of reading to the higher ground where questions of meaning and truth are considered, Hartman has blunted and neutralized the concept. Indeterminacy becomes an adjunct to the specific content of the text: the text says something determinate, and then we decide—indeterminately, ironically—whether or not to believe what the text says. But in Iser's or de Man's treatment, indeterminacy is a precondition to anything being said at all; it is not merely a commendable attitude for readers, but an inescapable implication of the act of reading. In Hartman's treatment, indeterminacy is recuperated to the traditional problem of ideas and belief in poetry; but if the concept of indeterminacy is taken seriously, as an aspect of representation, the problem of ideas and belief is itself bracketed, becoming a subsidiary question in the analysis of the situation of the interpreter.

Although Iser's treatment of indeterminacy is useful, it does have some shortcomings. The notion of indeterminacy as a blank or negation avoids objectivism, but Iser's description of the positive content of the work does not. Iser assumes that content under the rubric of "schema," and generally conceives of it as a series of recombinations of preexisting cultural themes. Such an analysis reduces the labor of abstraction, of forming and interpreting the typical image, to a series of formulaic choices, and it oddly anticipates poststructuralist notions by excluding subjectivity from the text. Although Iser's explicit aim is developing a subjective theory of reading, he has allowed subjectivity to enter the text only in its gaps and absences: insofar as the text *is,* it is objective. The problems inherent in this project emerge when Iser quotes Piaget approvingly: "In a word, the subject is there and alive, because the basic quality of each structure is the structuring process itself."[56] Whatever the significance of this sentence in its original context, for Iser it invokes subjectivity under a rubric that echoes traditional notions of divine presence: God is not a palpable being in the world, but the shaping force behind the act of creation. Subjectivity, then, is not accessible to reason or analysis: it is an unseen, validating presence behind the objective structure of the work. This mysterious subject, like Ingarden's "spirit of the work," furiously turns the wheels of literary structure, but is not encumbered by any location in time, space, social class, or history. Iser allows an objectivist conception of the text to coexist with an unreflective notion of isolated subjectivity. The limits of this conception, I think, can be overcome by reconceiving the given text in less schematic, more dialectical terms, taking indeterminacy as an aspect of what is given in the text, as well as what is absent from it. If intersubjectivity is placed at the center of the text, its typical and its indeterminate registers are linked.

Indeterminacy is the register in which the work represents itself as a text, in which the illusion that the text gives onto a different world is dissolved, and in Heidegger's term, the "ready-to-handness" of its intersubjective structure is called into question and made visible. It is in its indeterminacy that the specifically textual character of the work is represented. In the indeterminacy of its representation, all trompe d'oeil is abandoned: the speaking picture asserts itself as a series of marks on paper. By insisting on its fictionality, the text becomes paraodoxically realistic—it is only what it says it is, a text. Thus, the indeterminate aspect of the text functions as a representation of the process of representation, as a self-representation. Reflexivity emerges as an intrinsic quality of all literary texts, even the most stodgy Edwardian novel: it is the unavoidable obverse of typicality. Indeed, the concept of indeterminacy suggests that the reflection theory of representation might prove adequate if it abandoned its central metaphor of a mirror and adopted that of the moon, the inconstant moon, marked by craters and chasms and subject to eclipse.

Having said all this, however, we find ourselves entangled in a contradiction. We have said that indeterminacy is marked by gaps and negations, and that it is also an aspect of the positive content of the text: it is not simply "something missing," but also "something there" in the text. In order to understand how this can be, let us look closely at some of the rhetorical structures that characterize the indeterminate register. By analyzing what these structures have in common, we can move to a fuller conceptual understanding of indeterminacy.

While the typical register is concerned with questions of parts and wholes, the indeterminate is concerned with questions of appearance and reality, surface and substance. On the verbal level, then, indeterminate representation will make use of ironic, enigmatic, or gnomic constructions, of all those tricks of language that declare that the real meaning is elsewhere. Indeterminate representation, further, has recourse to foregroundings of language that both the conventional and the avant-garde novel employ; the evocative and complex style of Joyce's *Portrait of the Artist as a Young Man* exemplifies the first strategy; the fireworks of *Finnegans Wake,* the second. Both novels, by calling attention to the verbal adroitness of the author, refuse to masquerade as transparent accounts. Characters can be deployed to emphasize their indeterminacy: an author may duplicate or double them, calling attention to their fictional quality. The narrative may include a dream sequence or be structured according to the logic of dreams or be otherwise dislocated or segmented. The text may be presented from a patently shifting or unreliable point of view; such a text will not surrender its indeterminacy, no matter how much we badger it to settle down into its typical significance. Parody, placing the text "alongside" other texts, may be a tool of indeterminacy, while certain enigmas or puzzles in the text, which entice us into collusion with its typical register (Who *was* the man in the mackintosh?) also insist on its indeterminacy (Why is this man in the mackintosh always turning up?). Logically, equivocations and ambiguities in the text make explicit the reader's labor in tying together the narrative; thematically, incursions of the supernatural frustrate the secular reader by forcing the text to remain unresolved. Generically, that whole strain of literature that invokes an "elsewhere," the group of texts that have on their face no real referent—utopian literature in all its moods—is a domain of indeterminacy.

All these tropes have two qualities in common: they are abstract, and they are negative. We have already mentioned the need for a more dialectical understanding of abstraction; we now need to consider this question again, and to search for an emancipatory understanding of negativity as well. Again, we must untangle the confusion fostered by school English, for which an abstraction is a general statement, and to "be negative" is a rude habit.

Let us first consider *abstraction*. What does it mean to say the indeterminate register is marked by abstraction? The typical register, as we have seen, also requires the formation of abstract categories as vehicles for interpretation. But abstraction functions differently in the indeterminate register. First, because indeterminacy invites reflection on the text as text, it moves the hermeneutic task to a relatively abstract level. In working with the indeterminate register, the interpreter considers, not the relations of social life portrayed in the text, but how the text portrays them. The indeterminate is a representation of representation; this reflexivity implies one level of abstraction.

Second, indeterminacy isolates and foregrounds the work of abstraction that constructs the typical register of the text; in the most concrete images of the text, indeterminacy uncovers the labor of the thinking head. And it is here that the distinction between abstraction and generality becomes crucial, as Hegel said, "for the sake both of cognition and of our practical conduct."[57] Generality can be seen, making certain allowances, as a quality inhering in objects: since experience with rocks and with copper tells us that blue rocks may well contain traces of copper, we can, crudely, locate the link between the descriptive generalization "blue" and the predictive generalization "containing copper" in the rocks rather than in our investigation. (This connection, of course, leaves unexamined the basis of such an investigation, and the question of how its generalizations constitute themselves as part of the determined social discourse of natural history.) But dialectical universals do not permit even such a crude and temporary linkage. Our judgment that the modern state divides public and private life could not rest on any experience "of" the state, since the notion of a divided life implies some prior or projected unity, some ground of connection inaccessible to experience but formed by reflection on its basic categories and the possibility of their transformation. In the typical register, such reflections take concrete form, *as if* they had been embodied in social experience. The indeterminate does not permit us to glide over that *as if*. By insisting that the image is not an unmediated description of social life, it foregrounds the mental labor of reflection that produced it.

None of this should be taken to mean the indeterminate register is inhabited by shadowy entities, things that are and are not. Universals, and the processes of abstraction that produce them, exist quite concretely as objects of thought; the typical register exists quite concretely as one moment in the dialectic of representing such objects, and the indeterminate, as another. Indeterminacy emphasizes the paradox inherent in all representations; representations are not objects in the same sense as tables and chairs, but enter into their full existence when their material being as marks on a page has been swallowed up and forgotten, and they have become thoughts in the mind of the reader. If this paradox is obscured by the concrete appearance of the typical representation, the indeterminate register of the text does not permit us to forget it; it is an ambassador of the act of reading within the text.

Indeterminacy, then, is abstract in two senses: it is a representation of the abstraction that forms the text, and it is therefore an abstract, reflexive structure. Both of these abstractions are at the heart of every text; indeterminacy cannot be confined to postmodernist or baroque works, still less dismissed as decorative or as a distraction from the serious business of representing the world as it is. (That world, in any case, includes our thinking minds, which can also be represented.) Rather, indeterminacy is produced in the text by the very process of typification, by the reader in his or her first moment imagining out the text.

Neither the typical nor the indeterminate register can be considered the primary moment of representation, although an individual work can be dominated by either register. Neither register is the truth of the work: neither subsists independently, and each implies the other. The indeterminate image makes sense only within the context of a literature that also includes determinate, typical images, while those determinate images could not be produced without the mental activity that is represented in indeterminate images. Such mental activity cries out to be admitted into the world of the work, the world it has produced, and the text, voracious in its appetite, in its desire to make a meal of everything in the world of experience, turns its representational power upon itself and constructs from the very processes that generated it the indeterminate image. And having been produced in such an acrobatic feat, the indeterminate becomes available for the representation of all sorts of other difficult materials, all the hidden, contingent, and private forms of experience, all those aspects of social life that cannot be realized typically, since they resist any normalization. The indeterminate image fulfills Benjamin's injunction that "truth is not a process of exposure which destroys the secret, but a revelation which does justice to it."[58]

The indeterminate, to use Iser's word, "propels" not only the primary act of reading but also the whole process of interpreting the text, seducing the interpreter into the belief that the text can be fully unfolded, that its ambiguities can be resolved, that the whole indeterminate register, in fact, can be collapsed into the typical register. Were it not for this delusion, interpretation would become a simple philological rendering of the linguistic structures of the text, and any difficulties in the text would be allowed to stand patent and unresolved. It is only when the text appears, however momentarily, not as a representation, but as a state of affairs in the world that it can cry out for interpretation and resolution. This is true whether *state of affairs* is understood to refer to social life, authorial intention, ideological forms, or the structures of language.

A critical hermeneutic of representation, of course, cannot exempt itself from this delusion: if we try to interpret the work sympathetically, we will sooner or later become implicated in its structures, however we distance ourselves from them later, when our interpretation becomes critical. We can, however, try to maintain a consciousness of the intersubjective performance in which we are participating, to use the trail of the disappearing consciousness of representation as a guide to interpretation.

The dialectic of typicality and indeterminacy calls into question critical theories that privilege either the typical or the indeterminate register, traditionally under the rubrics of realism and imagination. Among such theories I would include Lukàcs's notion of objective reality as the ultimate ground of literature and Northrop

Frye's analogous grounding of literary discourse in the universal activity of the imagination. Each instance of such theorizing calls its opposite into being: consider the relation between naive Marxism and the early New Criticism, or the displacement of antiquarian historical studies by abstract structural explications. Such aesthetics are, as these examples imply, subject to the crudest ideological manipulations; they are also unable to follow the complex movements of the dialectic of representation. A critical hermeneutic will refuse to privilege either moment in that dialectic.

I have also said that the indeterminate register is the domain of negation. Let me return to that theme. Once again, negation can be derived from the basic structure of the part-whole relations that characterize the typical register, if those relations are understood dialectically. For common sense, the relation between generalizations and concrete instances is positive: to say that this apple is a fruit is to affirm the apple, the fruit, and their connection. But if we move from a logic of categories to a logic of dialectical relations, the connection between individuals and universals becomes deeply negative: the particularity, the resistance of the concrete instance, "speaks against" the universal; the signifying power of the universal demonstrates the poverty of the particular. For Hegel, negativity simply fueled the exhaustive dialectical progression, a progression eventually leading reflection back to its origin, and constructing a totality. Thus, negativity was placed, ultimately, at the service of affirmation, although Hegel did characterize the Particular as a "negative self-unity." But, as Adorno put it, "the contradiction weighs more heavily now than it did on Hegel, the first man to envision it."[59] If we have renounced any desire to find closure for interpretation in the stasis of totality, our hermeneutic must make a place for negativity, must understand that the negative, like the abstract, is not an external obstacle to the smooth progress of interpretation, but a precondition to the reader's production of the text, and his or her constant companion in the labor of interpreting it.

Negation operates in the indeterminate register both logically and rhetorically. Logically, the negative is derived from the mutual contradiction of particular and universal. Returning to Adorno: "The judgment that a man is free refers to the concept of freedom; but this concept in turn is more than is predicated of the man, and by other definitions the man is more than the concept of his freedom."[60] Such contradictions, inherent in the very structure of representation, have generated endless critical debates, as scholars have struggled to form categories that can explain characters like Falstaff (Vice, Lord of Misrule, natural man, spirit of play), and then criticized those categories to liberate the individual character from them. But of course, even to summarize a critical dispute in this way is to collude with the disappearance of representation—to assume a being, Falstaff, about whom categories can be predicated and negated. To look more closely at the logic of negation, we must examine the very language of representation, which presents us with images, but not their full realization; with actions, but not all of their interior quality; with explanations, but not a warrant for their authority. Insofar as the text presents us with something other than a fully elaborated experience, then, it is negative.

And this negation is also rhetorical, since everything that is absent from the text can be supplied by an understanding reader. In fact, to import a favorite trope of existentialism, unless it were experienced as an absence, nothing in the text would be elaborated by a reader. Whole, unblemished, and positive, the text could be simply consumed. The indeterminate, then, refuses to give us what we want from the text in the way we want it; it forces us to collude with the representation in telling us something new. The text refuses to be reduced to its positive content, refuses to become referential, negating its own referential power and also negating the reader's desire for reference. The indeterminate, then, is the sign under which the text appears as an opponent to the reader—as tricky, elusive, even fiendish. In all these affectionate reproaches, the reader salutes the text as an active negativity, a zone where meaning and reference are not allowed to rest and where the readers themselves are put at risk.

Thus, the hermeneutic of the indeterminate enjoins us, readers infected with the negativity of the text, to search it for things that could have been written otherwise. If the classic watchword of typical representation is Hamlet's advice to the players, with its injunction to hold the mirror up to nature and bracket the artifice of their representation so skillfully that it is invisible to the audience, we might find an analogous watchword for indeterminate representation in Brecht's request to the actors of our time:

> a time of overthrow and of boundless mastery
> Of all nature, even men's own—at last
> To change yourselves and show us mankind's world
> As it really is: made by men and open to alteration.[61]

What is valued here is not the radiant image of the mirror, but mobility, transformation, and openness. The work of literature is seen, not as an image, but as a performance—a performance that, in its constant and overt refashioning of the tools of art, claims as its own and renders present the "at last" of utopian time.

Thus, we arrive at the final quality of indeterminacy: its critical and utopian edge, a quality already suggested by Adorno's discussion of freedom. By insisting upon the status of the work of art as a product of labor, writers' and readers' labor, the hermeneutics of the indeterminate reveals the whole world of meanings as a world made by labor. All concepts and ideas, all products of the thinking mind, lose their reified status as direct copies of experience; all are revealed as human creation rather than innocent restatements of the world.[62] Such a hermeneutic, in opening literary representations to inquiry and reflection, cannot be confined to the world of the work; the world that is represented is also put at risk. The fundamental canon, then, of the hermeneutics of indeterminacy is that of all utopian literature: "It could well be otherwise."

The indeterminate aspects of the work prevent us from ever totalizing our interpretation of it, no matter how seductive its typical register. The text, so long as it contains any indeterminate elements at all, can never be closed, can never aspire to the deadly stasis of a representation that simply repeats in conceptual form the essential determinants of social life.[63] To quote Adorno once again, here from his critique of Lukács's *The Meaning of Contemporary Realism:* "Art does not provide knowledge of reality by reflecting it photographically or 'from a particular perspective' but by revealing whatever is veiled by the empirical form assumed by reality, and this is possible only by virtue of art's own autonomous status."[64]

Let us turn, then, to a concrete instance of "revealing what is veiled" and analyze the indeterminate register of Shakespeare's *Midsummer Night's Dream.*

Indeterminacy and *A Midsummer Night's Dream*

A full analysis of *Midsummer Night's Dream* would begin by unfolding its typical register, which is concerned with the contradiction between social power and the contingent, unmanageable force of passion. To state matters schematically, this contradiction is initially posed as an opposition between the social forms of patriarchy and passion, a force that is seen as a source of individuation against the collective norms enforced by the father and the prince. The lovers, on the other hand, express their individuality in choosing a beloved, just as the fairy queen preserves her page as a memento of a personal history rather than surrendering him to Oberon's company. An analysis of this register of the play might meditate on the opposing images of boundaries (cloisters, city walls, the "mazes indistinguishable" of the disordered earth) and of the moon, tutelary planet of passion and transformation. Such an analysis would subject to hermeneutic scrutiny the opening lines of the play:

> *Theseus:* Hippolyta, I woo'd thee with my sword,
> And won thy love by doing thee injuries;
> But I will wed thee in another key,
> With pomp, with triumph, and with revelling.[65]

In these lines, relations of force and relations of passion are brought up against each other: we are confronted with a deviant instance, in which the bonds of marriage—which for us are free, subjective choices, and even for the Elizabethans required for their validity an irreducible minimum of freedom from constraint—appear as simple expressions of unmediated violent force. The dilemma posed by these lines is expanded in the play's opening scene: How can sanctioned force be reconciled to passion and interiority?[66] For Theseus, social force can simply be transmuted into legitimated passion. But for us, the problem posed by the typical register is to find relationships capable of doing justice to both poles of this dilemma. And this is a representational problem; indeed, it is a problem of relating parts and wholes. For *A Midsummer Night's Dream,* as for so many other Renaissance comedies, marriage will be affirmed as the transcendent union of individuals with both their own deepest needs and the most basic structures of social order; the problem of the play is to find an adequate representation of this most conventional of solutions, one that takes into account the ways in which marriage is no solution at all to these contradictions.

The indeterminate register of the play is the agency through which this representational problem is solved. Indeterminacy breaks up the simple dichotomies of act 1, where power tries to determine the course of love. As the play's action moves to the wood, the place of indeterminacy, identities shift and nothing is certain. Considerable scholarly labor has been expended in discovering the sources of the fairy creatures who populate the wood, and the list of possibilities is impressive: rural folk legend, joke books like Tarleton's *News out of Purgatory,* romances like *Huon of Bordeaux,* the native dramatic tradition with its prankster devils, and the high allegory of the *Faerie Queene.*[67] Equally disparate are the verdicts of Elizabethan common sense about the fairies: they don't exist; they do exist. They are the satyrs and fauns of antiquity. They are the dead—ghosts or dead pagans or unbaptized children. They are devils disguised, or devils pure and simple. They are elemental spirits, part of nature, representatives of its sexual and nurturing power. They are—most ingeniously—

"spiritual animals" of a "middle Nature, between Man and Angel."[68]
All of these theories and conjectures find their voice somewhere in
the play. This polyphony, I think, is not simple eclecticism on Shakespeare's part; rather, by mobilizing all possible understandings of the
fairies, he establishes them as enemies of all fixed and static forms.
They are reorderers of identity, and they require the reader to continuously reinterpret the play. Thus, the fairies appear by turns as
amoral and beneficent, purely fanciful and decorative ("some war
with rere-mice for their leathern wings," 2.2.4), and seriously symbolic ("And then I will her charmed eye release / From monster's
view, and all things shall be peace," 3.2.376-78). They attract and
resist all the culturally current categorizations that might have been
applied to them: they foreground the arbitrary and contingent
quality of all conventional characterizations. As long as the fairies are
on stage, the typical register of the play is called into question, and
all its promise of intersubjective transparency is deferred. For example, let us consider a passage whose language is—for this play—rather
tame, but whose syntax is quite revealing:

> Puck: I took him sleeping (that is finish'd too)
> And the Athenian woman by his side:
> That when he wak'd, of force she must be eye'd.
>
> Enter Demetrius and Hermia
>
> Oberon: Stand close; this is the same Athenian.
> Puck: This is the woman; but not this the man.
>   (3.2.38-42)

Puck's mission had been to enforce an intersubjective harmony between man and woman: the warrant of that harmony was the intersubjective understanding between Puck and Oberon. Oberon gave
Puck unmistakable signs, category signs, leading him to Lysander
and Hermia: a man and a woman, sleeping separately on the ground,
wearing Athenian garments. And in all good faith, Puck followed
those signs, with results that are erratic, unreliable, resistant to interpretation: we see the right woman, but not the right man.

    Such strangely shifting categories have other, subjective impli-
cations. For the lovers, force and violence have, until now, been
external threats; they might face angry fathers or stern princes, wild
beasts or serpents, but among themselves love, amity, and courteous
rivalry prevail, guaranteed by a secure set of categories. Each of the
young people enters the wood knowing whom they love and who
loves them; all their relationships are based on the assumption that

those categories will be stable. Now, through the indeterminate agency of the fairies, those categories are violated, and the language of force erupts:

> *Hermia:* If thou hast slain Lysander in his sleep,
> Being o'er shoes in blood, plunge in deep,
> And kill me too.
> . . . .
>
> *Lysander:*   Vile thing, let loose,
> Or I will shake thee from me like a serpent!
>   (3.2.47-49, 260-61)

In two very serious ways, then, the agency of the fairies has disturbed the initial equilibrium of the play. First, while the play opens with the assertion that passion individuates, we find in the wood that passion has reduced the young people to abstractions, to the bare categories "Athenian," "man," and "woman." While the lovers may insist that there is only one unique beloved, the play insists that anyone can love anyone else. So, in their manipulation of the Athenian lovers, the fairies have operated as agents of this indeterminacy. It has been pointed out that the play begins with a mismatched triangle: Lysander and Demetrius both love Hermia; Helena's love for Demetrius is unrequited.[69] The fairies work all possible permutations of this mismatching, including a totally disordered state in which all relations of love are met with hate: Hermia loves Lysander, who hates her and loves Helena; while Helena loves Demetrius, who hates her and loves Hermia. This confusion is jockeyed into a second, even more competitive and disordered set of triangles; both Lysander and Demetrius love Helena and hate Hermia. Hermia and Helena hate each other, as do Demetrius and Lysander. The point of these transmutations, as well as of the more serious and comic passion of Titania and Bottom, is to mobilize the senses in which passion is not a force for individuation or self-definition, but a way of losing oneself. The lovers make their way, amazedly, through a disordered community in which any one of them can substitute for another. They become for each other what they have already been for us—abstract young men and young women. The lovers have become infected with the fairies' indeterminacy: they experience themselves as interchangeable. In the forest outside Athens, indeterminacy is not a condition of knowledge, something on the edge of the mind's peripheral vision, but a direct experience.

The second disturbance to the play's initial equilibrium concerns the relations between power and passion. The play begins, as I have said, by presenting love as a relatively unproblematic relation thwarted by the external violence of state and patriarchy. In this world, where brides are won in battle, Lysander ruefully and banally admits, "the course of true love never did run smooth" (1.1.134). But the lovers soon face difficulties more intimate than differences of blood or years, family opposition, or the chances of war, death, and sickness. Their wanderings in the wood demonstrate that violence is not simply an external threat: it was always a possibility in their relations with each other. If, in the wood, all love each other in turn, nearly all threaten or strike each other too. Hermia will claw out Helena's eyes; Lysander rudely shakes off Hermia; Lysander and Demetrius will duel for Helena. If their changing loves demonstrate the abstract quality of passion, their violence is an image of its negation, and the fairies' evocation of this violence reverses the equation that constituted the play's initial typical register. Rather than forming individuals in spite of the social force of patriarchy, passion is seen as abstracting individuals and unleashing a random order of force and violence:

> *Titania:* Out of this wood do not desire to go;
>   Thou shalt remain here, whether thou wilt or no.
>   I am a spirit of no common rate;
>   The summer still doth tend upon my state;
>   And I do love thee; therefore go with me.
>
> (3.1.152–56)

Titania has reversed the order, but retained the logic, of Theseus's wooing of Hippolyta.

This experience, paradoxically, permits the lovers to find, at the end of their wandering, a way of understanding each other as irreducibly free and separate, so that Helena, waking, says in amazement:

> I have found Demetrius like a jewel,
> Mine own, and not mine own.
>
> (4.1.191–92)

Her assertion, I think, closes the play's investigation of the relation between eroticism and social power. The lovers have confronted their own limits and the limits of their passion; unreasonable fathers and strict princes will quickly see the light of day. Since force and order are no longer external constraints, the young people are quickly reconciled to their elders: both generations have reinterpreted family, marriage, and passion.

The next business of the play is interpreting the experience of the forest, an experience retold in a series of negatives: "The eye of man hath not heard, nor the ear of man hath not seen, man's hand is not able to taste, his tongue to conceive, nor his heart to report what my dream was. I will get Peter Quince to write a ballet of this dream. It shall be call'd 'Bottom's Dream,' because it hath no bottom" (4.1. 211-16). The affairs of the forest are defined by their indeterminacy, their resistance to definition. All that can be done with such an experience is to re-present it, to make a "ballet" of it.

Later, Theseus and Hippolyta try to agree on the sense of the lovers' improbable account, a story that displays certain qualities of abstraction and negativity: it cannot be reduced to empirical plausibility; it defies all normal conventions of causality and emotional verisimiltude. Theseus and Hippolyta, then, are like bemused readers of a new novel, puzzled by its indeterminacy. Theseus wants to reduce the lovers' story to its empirical base, to find the bush behind the bear, but Hippolyta realizes the intersubjective truth of this experience, truth evidenced by "all their minds transfigur'd so together" (5.1.24).

The indeterminate register becomes dominant a third time as we watch the court characters witnessing the mechanicals' performance. Here, we are presented with an image of ourselves as spectators. We are invited to find in the play that Philostrate calls "nothing, nothing in the word" (5.1.78) an image of the intersubjective collaboration that is the precondition for all literary representation. And this representation of its own image to the audience must have been especially striking if, as is often supposed, the play was originally performed at an aristocratic wedding.[70] The courtly spectators in *Midsummer Night's Dream* are not uncritical, but they are also ready to collaborate in creation, and their example instructs us as interpreters. We are not to reduce these images; neither are we to reject them as fancy and moonshine. And even Hippolyta's detached respect is not, finally, enough. Rather, we are to step inside the dramatic circle and, with our own imaginations, amend the images that have been presented to us.

But of course, this injunction to see the play like a good audience, what Shakespeare's contemporary John Webster called an "understanding auditory," is too simple. It tames the indeterminacy of the play, subsuming it under familiar romantic terms, allowing us to forget those uncomfortable moments when the play was our opponent, and we could not easily collaborate with it. And so the last moment of this dream reinvokes that mood; Puck enters, perhaps from the new dimension of the stage "hell,"[71] speaking of owls, shrouds, graves, Hecate, and darkness. The indeterminate is reasserted as Oberon and Titania ban this very darkness and deformity in their guard and blessing on the newly married couples:

> And the blots of Nature's hand
> Shall not in their issue stand;
> Never mole, hare-lip, nor scar,
> Nor marks prodigious, such as are
> Despised in nativity,
> Shall upon their children be.

> (5.1.409–14)

Marriage, of course, is the traditional solution to the contradictions between order and eroticism, and this play, as I have said, affirms that solution. But the play seeks to include as representations quite resistant materials, including the blindly creative power of a Nature whose hand is anything but steady.

It is in this context that, in Puck's epilogue, the illusionistic and fictive nature of the drama is asserted one final time. The dramatic spell is dissolved only by invoking the power of the audience. The hermeneutic circle that interprets the play's indeterminacy as an image of all creative and transformative powers dissolves into the circle of spectators and actors, the circle that is the source and boundary of all representation.

2

DOMINANCE OF THE TYPICAL, DOMINANCE OF THE INDETERMINATE

The Two Registers and Representational Strategies

In the first chapter, I referred to a "dominant" register. *Dominant* means that one register sets the problems that occupy the text, or that it generates reading strategies under which a full interpretation can be subsumed. Dominance of one register does not imply, however, that it contains the key to the text, or that any text can be understood without coming to terms with its full working as a representation. Nor does dominance of a single register mean that interpretive work must begin with that register. Since a dialectical method tries to see in each part the operation of the whole, our interpretation can begin anywhere in the text.

The relations between the two registers, however, are not exhausted by two bare possibilities—dominance of the typical and dominance of the indeterminate. Within a text, the registers may be at odds, may contest for domination. Within a genre, a strategy may evolve that balances the two registers to set or resolve some representational problem. Such a strategy, internalized by readers, creates a frame of expectations that later writers may satisfy or violate.

In analyzing representational strategies, I will use a method like the one Marx proposed in *The Grundrisse*—working from an abstraction through mediating concepts to more determinate ideas. I will move from the initial abstract discussion of representation, through the mediating concept of the dominant register in this chapter, to the determinate instances of historically situated genres in subsequent chapters. By following this path, we will, perhaps, be able finally to arrive at representation again, "as a rich totality of many determinations and relations."[1]

To discuss the dominant registers, I will use a traditional form, explication of texts, looking at John Webster's *The Duchess of Malfi* (1613), in which the typical register dominates, and Henry James's *The Turn of the Screw* (1898), a text dominated by the indeterminate. In both these texts, the protagonist is an isolated woman, and both of them recount stories of unequal love, supernatural visitations, secrets and mysterious deaths. And in both texts, the dialectic of representation is quite complex.

Dominance of the Typical and *The Duchess of Malfi*

The Duchess of Malfi is marked by the uneasy dominance of its typical register. The problems this play takes up resemble those posed in Shakespeare's history plays—relations of sovereigns and subjects, of public life and private intimacy. Like Shakespeare's histories, *The Duchess of Malfi* investigates these problems as questions of representation, questions of the relations of parts to wholes, of individuals to groups, of the hidden to the manifest. And, like *Richard II, The Duchess of Malfi* phrases this investigation in the language of the typical register. But while the indeterminate elements in *Richard II* are consistently subordinated, in *The Duchess of Malfi* they make a bid for autonomy, if not domination. Interpreting this play, then, will broaden our understanding of the representational possibilities of the typical register and will sharpen our analysis of the dialectic between the typical and the indeterminate registers.

Since *The Duchess of Malfi* is not so familiar as *Richard II* or *A Midsummer Night's Dream,* perhaps a summary of the play's action would be useful. The widowed Duchess of Malfi, against the wishes of her brothers, secretly marries her steward, Antonio. Bosola, who has been paid to spy on her household by the brothers, discovers and betrays the marriage. The Duchess's brother Ferdinand imprisons, torments, and finally murders her. In the last act, Bosola helps Antonio to revenge the Duchess, while the brothers deteriorate rapidly—Ferdinand hallucinates that he is a wolf, and the Cardinal sees ghosts. Antonio and Bosola are both killed in the final carnage.

This grisly, but by no means unusually tangled plot weaves together two strands of discourse that Jacobean drama normally separated. The matter of domestic tragedy—questions of fidelity, family ties, and the good order of the household—is joined with the matter of historical tragedy—questions of honor, legitimacy, and the good order in the state. The typical register of the play phrases both the public state questions and the private family questions in terms of part-whole relations and concentrates them through the character of the Duchess and the indexing image of her body. *The Duchess of Malfi* is thus a quite different play from *Richard II,* in which the public sphere is a sphere of isolation, developed as a reflex to the contradictions of public life. Here, public and private are both contradictory. and together they form a system of problematic part-whole relations.

The play's typical register is organized by the contradictory relations of its private sphere.

The Duchess of Malfi begins by invoking a conventional view of the relations between sovereign and subject, between public and private life. Antonio says that the French court is admirable because, "in seeking to reduce both state and people to a fixed order," their king has begun "at home" (1.1.6-7, 8). Home, for the king, is the court, the fountain of honor, the source of all public and private virtue. To reform the king's home, then, is to replace politic flatterers with good counselors. The opening of the play provides us with a series of ideological equations: the king, as an individual, represents the kingdom; the king's public life represents the private lives of his subjects; the king's private life is represented by his public activity. These equations prescribe a double replacement: the king substitutes for his subjects, and the king's public life substitutes for his private life—a twofold substitution that favors both public life and sovereignty. *The Duchess of Malfi* does not, however, take this ideological figure at face value, but challenges its representational logic by disturbing the play's initial equations. In *Richard II,* as we have seen, the private sphere was ordered by either the claims of private "right" or the interior world of private subjectivity. In *A Misummer Night's Dream,* the family mediates public and private, satisfying both the claims of individual passion and the sanctions of social norms. In *The Duchess of Malfi,* however, the family becomes identified with privacy and interiority, a domain of peculiarly intersubjective meaning. The state and public life, on the other hand, are emptied of representational power, and become the arena for a combat of wills and appetites. We can read the play as an experiment in moving the typical register from the sphere of the public to the sphere of the private, radically altering the structure of each sphere and their relation to each other. In the play, the Duchess performs this transformation for us.

> *Cariola:*   Whether the spirit of greatnes, or of woman
>   Raigne most in her, I know not, but it shewes
>   A fearefull madnes.
>
>   (1.3.576-78)[2]

As the Duchess's maid perceives, there is a contradiction for her between the "spirit of greatness," that magnanimity held to be the crowning virtue of princes, and a "spirit of woman," a spirit that chooses out Antonio, woos him with "only half a blush," and marries him in a private, unconventional ceremony. These two "spirits" both try to "reign" over her. The figure of the Duchess is a scandal because she cannot be assimilated to the normal system of public-private relations or of part-whole relations. She has established a virtuous court, but that court has not exhausted her subjectivity. She has established a family, but within that family she does not maintain her proper subordinate role. She has enforced a split between private life and public life, establishing Antonio as ruler of the night and lord of misrule, while she rules the public world of day. Finally, in setting herself against her brothers and establishing a secret family, she has also divided herself, making herself incapable of the public display of an untouched self, of the instrumental deployment of subjectivity, that the exercise of Renaissance sovereignty required. To reject the state and public relations of representation in favor of domesticity and the family may seem unproblematic. What could be less controversial, for conventional ideology, than for a woman to renounce public life for the sake of domestic intimacy? This reaction, however, assumes a nineteenth-century valuation of family life rather than an understanding of the relationship of public and private that was contemporary with the play. As Adorno said: "To antiquity this intimacy was wholly alien; according to Plato's *Phaido,* Socrates, who generally speaks just in favor of inwardness, sends his closest relatives away just before his death, in order to be able to converse undisturbed with his friends. Only in modern times did the family transpose the demands of society to the interior of those entrusted to the family, make them into the family's own affair, and thereby 'internalize' the human beings."[3] Such a change in the valuation of domestic life, which probably did not reflect a radical shift in family size or structure,[4] reached its most intense expression in Reformation spirituality, that crucial vehicle for the creation of an autonomous sphere of the private. It was within the family that the inward spirituality and Christian liberty that characterized Reformation doctrine were to be expressed.[5] For English reformers, this implied spontaneous family prayer, searching counsel and admonition, and mutual corroboration of religious experience—a whole machinery, in fact, for generating a private life, a vocabulary for discussing it, and a set of norms controlling it. When the Duchess laments, "in the eternall Church, Sir, I doe hope we shall not part thus" (3.5.84–85), she echoes the Reformation commonplace that every household should be a "little church."

To interpret this text, then, requires us to bracket some of our normal assumptions, to see family relations in an unfamiliar light. We cannot construct a reading of the play that mirrors its reception by Webster's contemporary audience. In fact, to attempt such a re-creation would be the last refuge of reflectionism: if the play does not contain a mirror image of the world, we might try to find in it a blue-print for a vanished consciousness, the consciousness of its original audience. But if we cannot resurrect that audience's consciousness, we can do justice to the intersubjective force of the play's typical representation. By confronting us with an image of domesticity as it was being invented, *The Duchess of Malfi* invokes everything that is for us still difficult, promising, and subjectively dangerous about the family. The Duchess says, as she prepares to woo Antonio:

> I am going into a wildernesse,
> Where I shall find nor path, nor friendly clewe
> To be my guide.
>
> (1.1.404-68)

And the text places us in a wilderness, too—not the same wilderness as the Duchess's, but one that has a common border with it.

Thus, when we speak of the typical register locating *The Duchess of Malfi* in history, we face a certain paradox. History simul-taneously links us to the play and separates us from it. We live in a world for which the equation between domesticity and intimacy has been taken for granted, sentimentalized, and exposed as a means of domination. But our world is also fundamentally the same as Web-ster's, in that both are structured by a division between public and private life. The private emerges in this play as a new sphere, uncom-prised and radiant with possibilities—a vision of domesticity it is not easy for us to share. But the structure of this private world, the rela-tion between it and public life, and the utopian hopes that formed it: these are not alien categories, but arcs in a horizon of consciousness that encloses both us and the original audience of the play, although we scan that horizon from different positions.

As a sort of index or "friendly clewe" to these structures and relations, the play provides us with the image of the Duchess's body. In our analysis of *Richard II*, we have already referred to the conven-tion of the king's two bodies, an interpretive topic traditionally as-sociated with that play. In *The Duchess of Malfi*, we encounter a different sort of royal body, invoked most memorably by the Duchess in her courtship of Antonio:

> This is flesh, and blood (Sir,),
> 'Tis not the figure cut in Allablaster
> Kneeles at my husbands tombe.
>
> (1.1.519-21)

While for received ideology the king's royal body is an image of the whole nation and is invested with typical force, in this play the Duchess's royal body, the alabaster figure, is static, remote, dedicated to mourning. Typical force resides in her eroticized, individual body. We encounter that body whenever we enter the Duchess's domestic world. She is the "sprawling'st bedfellow" (3.2.16); she vomits; she eats apricots greedily; she calls out in childbirth; her hair turns grey. We are continually placed by this image in a world of fragile and fertile bodies: the symbolic distinctions that normally shape our experiences of the body—experiences of division, status, and class—are subverted. The body emerges as an expression of common experience, to provide an index for the play's pattern of typicality. We are continually reminded that we share some common bonds with the Duchess, bonds the Renaissance would have characterized as those of "kinde," and that Marx analyzed as those of "species being."[6]

These relations of representation are grounded, for the Duchess and Antonio, in intersubjectivity, specifically in intersubjective dialogue. As Habermas puts it:

> The intersubjectivity of the world . . . is not a generality under which individuals are subsumed in the same way as elements under a class. It is, rather, the case that relations between I, You (other I) and We (I and other I's) are established through an analytically paradoxical achievement. The speakers identify themselves with two mutually incompatible dialogic roles and thereby secure the identity of the I as well as that of the group. The one (I) affirms his absolute non-identity *vis-à-vis* the other (You); but at the same time both recognize their own identity by accepting one another as irreplaceable individuals.[7]

This formulation suggests a homology between intersubjective dialogue and typical representation: both are relations of inclusion that do not require the subordination of individual moments or speakers. In *The Duchess of Malfi*, the dialogue between the Duchess and Antonio simultaneously transfers value and significance from the public world to the world of the family, creating the play's typical register, and establishes an intersubjective relation between the Duchess and Antonio as nonidentical speakers:

> *Antonio:* These words would be mine,
> And all the parts you have spoke, if some part of it
> Would not have savour'd flattery.
>
> .   .   .   .

> *Duchess:* (You speake in me this, for now we are one.)
> (1.1.541-43, 569)

Each finds in the other's speech an expression of subjective intimacy, but each one's speech remains the discourse of an other.

Since it must be created by discourse, intersubjectivity is not simply given to us as a virtual image in this play; something must happen before we can see it. The first act of the play permits us to do that work, establishing the play's typical register as we move from the received ideology to a new sphere of the private, a sphere of domestic intimacy. In the course of this act, the ideological equation of the sovereign's public life with the subject's private virtue becomes associated with the Duchess's two wicked brothers, and is therefore dramatically compromised. The brothers, to anticipate our analysis of the play's indeterminate register, see the public significance of the sovereign's private life as a vehicle for self-aggrandizement, thus abstracting and negating received ideology. When the brothers warn the Duchess that her private life will inevitably have public consequences, for example, they enforce this warning by hiring Bosola to spy on her. And Ferdinand blatantly imposes his subjectivity on his subordinates: he forbids them to laugh before he does. In the brothers, the representational power of the sovereign has become a vehicle for domination and deceit.

The Duchess, on the other hand, opens a new terrain for the private by creating a language of domestic intimacy, a language that she teaches to both Antonio and the audience. She renounces all equivocating public language—"a tyrant doubles with his words"—and insists that degree and domination will not affect the world of her marriage. And the guarantee of that world is her own body, "flesh, and blood (Sir,)," the body that embraces, desires, and ultimately joins Antonio.

The Duchess invokes a world of domestic intersubjectivity, but we see that world only intermittently in this play: the marriage is hidden, emerging only when it is in danger, its secrecy enacting its intimate and interior quality. What we see when the marriage is dramatized, however, is not a realm exempt from the relations of domination, but one in which they have become objects of play, pretexts for joking. In the play's domestic world, normal systems of subordination have not been abolished; the Duchess's utopian invocation of the "birds, that live i' th' field / on the wilde benefit of Nature," who "may choose their Mates / and carroll their sweet pleasures to the Spring" (3.5.25-26, 27-28), is not realized in her own life. In the play's domestic world two systems of subordination are at odds:

Antonio is the Duchess's inferior in political rank, but her superior in gender. This dissonance, rather than generating tragic discord, allows Antonio and the Duchess to establish themselves simultaneously as identical and nonidentical, to use Habermas's cumbersome term. They are not equals—the notion of equality, in fact, was profoundly alien to the Jacobeans—but they are able to play the relations of subordination off against each other, so that neither character is subsumed by the other. And, since neither character is exhausted by conventional systems of representation, both characters appear at once as individuals, exempt from stereotyped constraints, and also as representations of the basic relations of domestic life rather than its conjunctural details.

The intersubjective world of the Duchess and Antonio, then, joins the rhetoric of the play to its logic. Our assent to these two characters reenacts the intersubjective dialogue they have initiated. We find, first, in the image of the Duchess's body, an answering voice, a response to our interrogation of the play. That body, the dramatization of which must have been a scandalous breach of decorum to the Jacobeans, is for us a reassuring sign of commonality. The Duchess's individual physical being is a recognition of our own. Our interpretive dialogue with the play, then, can begin with a recognition of the "identity" of the play as speaker. We begin to interpret its typical register by seeing the Duchess and Antonio as people like ourselves, by affiliating with the group (family members, lovers) for which they are such compelling representations.

But this affiliation is too simple. That which, in this play, seems most exempt from history is also that which is most deeply determined by history: family sentiment, tenderness of the body, desire for homely intimacy. All of these categories, which seem natural and obvious to us, the play struggles to establish as bases of significance. We are led, then, to recognize the play as a "nonidentical" speaker, since its assertion of domestic life as a sphere of meaning is distorted by the terms of our initial assent to it. This assertion, for Webster's audience, was not a truism to be consumed, but a difficult mediation to be performed. We can trace the path of their performance, even though we cannot re-create its subjective quality: to see the private in this way meant to put at risk the normal relations of subordination, setting them at odds with one another. It also meant leaving the public sphere without adequate representation: if the prince's power to invoke a commonality is transferred to private life, then how can the public be invested with significance? How can it even become intelligible?

Paradoxically, when we approach the play as a mediated, historically determined representation, as an expression of a subjectivity quite different from our own, we open a final horizon of consciousness that includes both us and the play's original audience, and find a link between its representational strategy and our interpretive strategy. Both for the Jacobeans and for us, private matters were entering the domain of history, pressing, by different routes, into the world of public discourse. For the Jacobeans, the family was entering history, coming to have a history, establishing itself as a reflex to the newly defined sphere of the public, differentiating itself from the other corporate entities associated with church and state. For us, the family is entering history on a conceptual level; new feminist scholarship and social history have enabled us to understand the family as a historical, rather than a "natural" or "given," form, and we see domesticity as an institution situated in time rather than as an eternal refuge from the cares of public life. In both cases, the sphere of the subjective, of privacy, requires re-presentation. We share with the Jacobeans the need to rethink the relation of the public and the private, although our reflections are cast in different terms.

To fully understand the play's typical register, however, we must move beyond those aspects of the play that invite our identification, that announce their resemblance to social life. We must also confront what is resistant to interpretation if we are to see the play as a representation, a performance linked to social life but also alienated from the norms of received experience. Let us turn, then, from the play's typical register to its indeterminate register.

Indeterminacy and Contested Representation in *The Duchess of Malfi*

If the typical register of the play subverts received ideology and establishes a realm of domestic intimacy, the indeterminate register receives that subverted ideology and presents its own distorted version of the Duchess's domestic world. This indeterminate world is structured by a reduced, abstracted, negated version of intersubjectivity.

Let us examine first the indeterminate negation of received ideology. Traditional ideology provided the brothers with a rationale for domination and the naked exercise of power; their own private lives are so distorted by this use of power that they recognize no nonidentical subjects, to use Habermas's term. For example, when the brothers first confront the Duchess, warning her against remarriage, they rehearse bits of conventional wisdom, drawing from the truisms of sexual lore:

> So most Widowes say:
> But commonly that motion lasts no longer
> Than the turning of an houreglasse.
>
> (1.1.335–37)

of politics:

> You live in a ranke pasture here, i'th Court.
>
> (1.1.340)

of morality:

> Those lustfull pleasures, are like heavy sleepes
> Which doe fore-run mans mischiefe.
>
> (1.1.363–65)

It is, as the Duchess says, "terrible good councell" from characters who have already been established as amoral villains. Indeed, this series of platitudes is followed by the Duke's joke about the "part without a bone" and his gift of his father's dagger to the Duchess. Thus, the catalog of received ideas, a catalog that devalues the private and the bodily, is followed by a threat, an invocation of the penis, a reminder of patriarchal power.

The indeterminate register of the play discredits received ideology by associating it with the disturbed and disordered subjectivity of the brothers: it joins skewed common sense with psychosis. The Duchess enters a wilderness so that she can create a world of domestic intimacy: the brothers wander in a wilderness of their own, a wilderness in which ideological forms and subjective experience are both self-referential. Received ideology rationalizes their self will; subjective experience is for them self-enclosed and resistant to interpretation.

If the Duchess lives in a world of other subjects, however compromised that world may be, the brothers negate intersubjectivity. For them, all social forms are reflections of themselves; all other individuals present simple commensurable variables, to be taken into account instrumentally, but ruthlessly suppressed if they become inconvenient. For the brothers, other subjectivities are so abstract that they can be represented by the bare figure of exchange: any subordinate can be bought. Neither the Cardinal nor the Duke recognizes any independent private sphere; neither of them hesitates to use his office for private purposes. The Cardinal banishes his sister by ecclesiastical authority; the Duke uses the law for his own ends. In place of a private intersubjective world, the Duke and the Cardinal have constructed a world of secrecy and concealment, a world built on sub-

ordinates whose services are purchased for cash—a network of in-
formers, a mistress kept by gold and fear—a world controlled by the
habit of plotting and bribing.

In this world, the ties of family are not dialogic. As a private
relation, the family does not rise to the brothers' consciousness;
only as a dangerous extension of the boundaries of the self does the
family become a problem for them both. For Ferdinand especially,
family is incomprehensible and incommunicable, a material and
irrational tie of blood:

> Damne her, that body of hers,
> While that my blood ran pure in't, was more worth
> Than that which thou wouldst comfort, (call'd a soule).
>
> (4.1.146–48)

If the public body is more valuable than the private body, it is infinitely more valuable than private subjectivity, "call'd a soule." If
the Duchess's body was for us a clue to the typical register of the play,
it is to Ferdinand a galling reminder of his own body. Ferdinand is
trapped by the equation he had himself constructed: if his private
will is the sole legitimate source of public power, then all other wills
are simple reflections of his own. They have been absorbed into his
subjectivity, and he then becomes vulnerable to their aberrations.
Ferdinand's desire for domination, like the search for pleasure that
Hegel described, confronts him with the recalcitrant, irreducible
other he had sought to evade, and confirms the power of others over
him. When the Duchess marries in secret, she reverses the relations of
power and representation. Ferdinand rightly feels that the very integrity of his body has been lost. He is suddenly vulnerable; his
individuality has been dissolved into a public sphere that is now un-
accountably out of control. He longs to apply "desperate physike"—
to the Duchess, to himself, to the realm. The boundaries between the
world of others, the members of his family, and himself, never very
securely conceptualized, collapse:

> I could kill her now,
>   In you, or in my selfe.
>
> (2.5.82–83)

This mad vision is an abstraction and a negation of the Duchess's project. In place of her concealed world of domestic intersubjectivity, the Duke creates a concealed world in which his subjectivity
absorbs all others, in which the family is a self-referential web of

appetite, eroticism, and the desire to dominate. If the Duchess's is a world of domestic intimacy, we can describe the world of the brothers as its negation, or borrowing Freud's term, as an uncanny world.[8] And in fact, Freud's word for uncanny, *unheimliche,* is derived from *heimliche,* which means, among other things, homelike, cozy, domestic. The uncanny shapes the indeterminate register of this play; this is a theme to which I will return.

I have said that the indeterminate register is an abstraction and negation of the Duchess's domestic world. For the brothers, subjectivity is an abstraction. While the Duchess raises and enriches her servant Antonio, the brothers degrade and waste their dependents. They are surrounded by interchangeable monads, any one of whom—they think—can substitute for any other. All offices—except the naked, original use of force—can be deputized; there is no other who cannot be manipulated, suborned, or eliminated. For the brothers, reason and discourse, like the hoariest ideological cliches, are simple pretexts, embodiments of desire with no density of their own. Thus, Ferdinand expresses his hatred of his sister in whatever grammar of desire comes to mind at the moment—sexual appetite, pride, greed for "an infinite mass of treasure," zeal for the family honor—all are, abstractly, interconvertible, since there is never anyone, least of all the Duchess, to whom they must be communicated.

The dialogue between the Duchess and Antonio has created an intersubjective world; they find themselves performing the "analytically paradoxical achievement" of recognizing the nonidentity of one another. But neither brother attempts such discourse. They cannot use speech for any other reason than to convey orders and threats or to elicit information. It is not surprising, then, that the brothers cannot speak to each other or to the Duchess. For them, speech is an act of will, a way of imposing on subordinates, so that in their scenes with each other, the Duke and the Cardinal often carry on simultaneous monologues. And neither of them can speak to the Duchess, especially after her remarriage. The Cardinal confronts her only in the ceremony of banishment, a transformation of the "noble ceremony" of pilgrimage. The sacramental vows, sacrifices, and gifts of rings that should structure that ceremony are placed at the service of a purely private passion. And so transformed, they require commentary and interpretation. They become indeterminate.

> *1st Pilgrim:*   What was it, with such violence he took
>   Off from her finger?
> *2nd Pilgrim:*   'Twas her wedding ring,

> Which he vow'd shortly he would sacrifice
> To his revenge.
>
> (3.4.39–42)

The Duke also communicates with his sister by means of shows: the presentation of a dagger, an appearance by night, the unveiling of corpses, a masque of madmen. Like the Cardinal's, Ferdinand's spectacles are essentially demonstrations of force. He is all too ready to supply an interpretation for them, and that interpretation almost always is an assertion of his power over his sister's subjectivity:

> (*SD:*) *Here is discover'd (behind a Travers;) the artificiall*
> *figures of Antonio and his children: appearing as*
> *if they were dead.*

> *Bosola:* He doth present you this sad spectacle,
> That now you know directly they are dead,
> Hereafter you may (wisely) cease to grieve
> For that which cannot be recovered.
>
> (4.1.64–66, 68–71)

These spectacles summarize and concentrate the indeterminate register of the play: they abstract and negate the relations presented concretely and positively in the typical register. The Duchess hides her family; the Duke reveals them to her, no longer hidden, no longer her family. The Duchess creates an intersubjective sphere based on her participation in the commonality of domestic life: the Duke tries to control that domestic life without being subjected to it. The Duchess establishes relationships based on dialogue: the Duke creates a sphere of meanings divorced from public discourse, but inaccessible to intersubjectivity. Both brothers' spectacles are displays of power, attempts to reduce both the audience and the performers to abstract counters that the brothers can deploy at will. The Duchess's maid, Cariola, describes the effect of these shows; she says that the Duchess has become:

> Like to your picture in the gallery,
> A deal of life in shew, but none in practise:
> Or rather like some reverend monument
> Whose ruines are even pittied.
>
> (4.2.33–36)

The Duke's spectacles undo what the Duchess and Antonio had done, by reducing her to a public, monumental image and making her an abstracted representation of herself.

And these spectacles are deeply indeterminate. They announce their obscurity by being performed in the dark; the Duke always provides an explanation for them, but his explanation is not always convincing. Just as the Duke will use any language that comes to hand to explain his hatred of the Duchess, he multiplies reasons for his torment of her. But all these reasons negate the Duchess's privacy, assert that he is in control of her subjectivity:

> *Bosola:* Why doe you doe this?
>
> *Ferdinand:* To bring her to despaire.
>
> (4.1.139–40)
>
> . . . .
>
> *Servant:* I am come to tell you,
> Your brother hath entended you some sport:
> A great Physitian, when the Pope was sicke
> Of a deepe mellancholly, presented him
> With severall sorts of mad-men, which wilde object
> (Being full of change, and sport,) forc'd him to laugh,
> And so th' impost-hume broke: the selfe same cure,
> The Duke intends on you.
>
> (4.2.40–47)
>
> . . . .
>
> *Duchess:* Even now thou said'st,
> Thou wast a tombe-maker?
>
> *Bosola:* 'Twas to bring you
> By degrees to mortification.
>
> (4.2.175–79)

Further, the density of the Duke's last spectacles—the masque of madmen and Bosola's series of disguises as tomb-maker, bellman, and executioner—seems to transcend the limits of the Duke's self-referential vision. They achieve this density of terror because their indeterminacy allows them to become independent of the characters who present them. What the Duchess faces in those final spectacles is no personal opposition; rather she confronts the dangerous, unknowable aspect of the world she has constructed. Domestic intimacy, here, presents its indeterminate face; it becomes *unheimliche*.

Freud defines the *unheimliche* as "that class of the terrifying which leads back to something long known to us, once very familiar."[9] And he gives a catalog of uncanny objects and events, a virtual prop list and precis of the *The Duchess of Malfi:* wax figures, reflections in mirrors, doubles and twins, a severed head ("Send Antonio to me; I want his head in a busines," 3.5.35), a hand cut off at the wrist, spirits and ghosts. Freud sees all the items on this gory list as expressions of an anxiety about the self, death, and castration. Fearing a loss of self, an uncanny consciousness creates a world of protective doubles, a world made of material more friendly than the alienated world outside. But these doubles become invested with the anxiety that created them; they are reminders of vulnerability and mortality, an anxiety expressed as castration fear.

In the fourth act, when the brothers have full control of the Duchess, the indeterminate and typical registers contest for domination of the play. The act presents us, first, with an indeterminate world, one in which identities shift, in which Bosola will appear four times in four different roles. It is a world in which the boundaries between public and private vanish: the madmen are consumed by their old occupations; the Duchess's noble rank is used to mock her. It is a world in which the body is not an intersubjective bond, but a source of vulnerability, "a little cruded milke, phantasticall puffepaste" (4.2.24-25). There, familiar things become threatening. The site of the Duchess's torment is her own palace. All this terror threatens some loss of self: Bosola presents death to the Duchess as the erasure of her noble status, the annihilation of her public self:

> Much you had of Land and rent
> Your length in clay's now competent.
>
> (4.2.185-86)

her reduction to an inert body:

> *Duchess:* Thou art not mad sure, do'st know me?
> *Bosola:* Yes.   *Duchess:* Who am I?
> *Bosola:* Thou art a box of worme-seede, at beste, but a
> salvatory of greene mummey.
>
> (4.2.121-24)

It is a world in which the abstract state of subordination exhaustively defines social being, in which Cariola and the children are killed for the mere fact of their relation to the Duchess. And it is a world in which Ferdinand feels anxiety only when he faces, in the Duchess, an alienated image of himself:

> She, and I were Twinnes:
> And should I die this instant, I had liv'd
> Her Time to a Mynute.
>
> (4.2.285–87)

This uncanny world is a self-referential and unhappy version of the intersubjective, intimate domesticity of the Duchess; the two worlds are in contradiction. In this contradiction is the source of the play's representational power. Webster will reassert the dominance of the typical register, but had he not contested that dominance by allowing the indeterminate register to take over certain portions of the play, *The Duchess of Malfi* could not have become a full representation. It is the brothers' opposition that enforces the secrecy of the Duchess's marriage; their indeterminate bond with her requires her to construct an overt representation of the inwardness and retirement that mark her domesticity. The secret marriage, then, grounds the Duchess's project in the deepest relations of public and private. Without the brothers, the Duchess would face no experience of negativity, absence, or abstraction. The family would have been a vehicle for easy transcendence. Because of the brothers, she must confront those aspects of domesticity not easily expressed in intersubjective discourse: unconscious eroticism, the desire for domination. Without the brothers, the sphere of private intimacy would be only a refuge from public life; because of their opposition, it must be constructed in the face of a public attempt to dominate the private. Without the brothers and the indeterminate world they so vividly constitute, the Duchess's story would be a simple exemplary tale, the presentation of a polished image, an alabaster body to be consumed without being understood. We should therefore take very seriously the Duchess's assertion that:

> Even in this hate (as men in some great battailes
> By apprehending danger, have atchiev'd
> Almost impossible actions: I have heard Souldiers say so),
> So I, through frights, and threatnings, will assay
> This dangerous venture.
>
> (1.1.385–89)

Given the crucial role of indeterminacy in *The Duchess of Malfi*, why have I said that the typical register dominates this play? There are a number of reasons. First, while the play's representation is contested between its typical and its indeterminate register, the typical register absorbs and transforms the indeterminate at the climax of the play, the long scene of the Duchess's murder. Second, Bosola, who acts as an agent of exchange between the two spheres, is at the end of the play absorbed within the typical register, and establishes its dominance.

Let us see how these dynamics work in the final actions of the play. The Duchess, as I said earlier, is not immune to the Duke's oppression. At one point, she is reduced to a mere image of herself. She loses even her sense of her own body:

> I am full of daggers:
> Puffe: let me blow these vipers from me.
>
> (4.1.107-8)

And faced with a deranged attempt to reorder her private life, she feels herself completely absorbed by a debased form of the public:

> I account this world a tedious Theater,
> For I doe play a part in't 'gainst my will.
>
> (4.1.98-99)

But faced with Bosola's final disguises, the Duchess recovers herself and her vision of intersubjective commonality. She locates the sphere of domestic intimacy in the "other world," borrowing the religious trope of a heavenly union, but her dramatic presence establishes that sphere, those norms of representation, in the subjective present. She regains her sense of the body as an index of commonality:

> What would it pleasure me, to have my throate cut
> With diamonds? or to be smothered
> With Cassia?
>
> (4.2.221-23)

During the Duchess's long dialogue with Bosola, the play's indeterminate register is subordinated to typical intersubjectivity.

Let me unfold that statement a little. Bosola, of course, has been the brothers' creature throughout the play, but he has done their errands with an increasingly uneasy conscience, has been more and more ready to question Ferdinand. Ferdinand delegated Bosola as his final emissary to the Duchess, but Bosola chooses, finally, to appear only in disguise. He takes his place as a kind of second—or third—

author of the final spectacles of the play, speaking always under the brothers' authority, inhabiting their uncanny world quite comfortably, but busy about his own affairs.

We cannot know, of course, what those affairs are: as a "melancholy," Bosola is a deliberately enigmatic character. We know that he is drawn to the Duchess and that he is deeply nihilistic. His shaping presence in act 4 deepens its indeterminacy, since the final spectacles cannot be read as expressions of any one subjectivity, and the subjective intention of Bosola, one of the chief performers, is simply irretrievable.

But Bosola's actions are shaped by some subjective intention. Even though this intention is not accessible to us, it is clear that in him the Duchess meets someone who recognizes her as a speaker, a partner in intersubjective dialogue. Bosola shifts and equivocates, but he also questions and answers, pacing the shifts in his performance to match the Duchess's mood and tone. Bosola is not the Duchess's equal; there is no affection or friendship or recognized dependency between them, and so in this last dialogue the Duchess has left the terrain of normal relationships entirely. But still, between them there is a dialogic bond, and that, for the Duchess, is enough. She recreates with Bosola a grisly version of the world of domestic intimacy she had constructed in wooing Antonio. Both scenes are marked by images of concealment, rings, cords, circles, oaths, and kneeling. In both of them, received ideas are subverted: with Antonio, the valuation of the public; with Bosola, the terror of death. In the last scene, the Duchess is able to assert with equal seriousness the claims of domesticity, privacy, and daily life, to reconcile her subjective identity with her noble status in the public sphere:

> I pray-thee, looke thou giv'st my little boy
> Some sirrop, for his cold, and let the girle
> Say her prayers, ere she sleepe.
>
> (4.2.207–9)
>
> I am the Duchess of *Malfy* still.
>
> (4.2.141)

The Duchess reinterprets each of the indeterminate spectacles she confronts, recasting it into typical terms: each becomes a way of asserting her subjectivity, an occasion for establishing her membership in the "excellent company" to be met in the other world. There the Duchess hopes for a full realization of her intersubjective project; the barriers of rank and public occupation dissolve as she welcomes death on her knees. Her final request reasserts in the simplest terms her concern for that body that we have seen, in so many guises, as the indexing image of the play's typical register;

> Dispose my breath, how please you, but my body
> Bestow upon my women, will you?
>
> (4.2.235–36)

With the Duchess gone, the burden of the typical register is carried by the unlikely figure of Bosola. He has demonstrated the infinitely malleable quality of his subjectivity, appearing in one role after another, casting off each costume without regret or rationalization. Bosola now finds himself implicated in the Duchess's subjective project: he worries about her state of mind and guards her corpse from dishonor. That body, index of the typical sphere, reveals to him his subjection to the abstract norms of exchange. Bosola describes his awakening in terms that shift from his familiar language of exchange to the language of subjective vision: he begins by speaking of a register, here meaning a ledger, and then refers to a perspective, a painting that formed a coherent image only when the viewer looked at it from the correct angle: [10]

> a guilty conscience
> Is a blacke Register, wherein is writ
> All our good deedes, and bad, a Perspective
> That shows us hell.
>
> (4.2.384–87)

Bosola's vision is temporary and fragmented; it cannot save him, but it does condemn the brothers. He dedicates himself to the discovery of secrets, to the resolution of indeterminacy—the protocols of revenge in this play.

And so the play ends with Bosola's spectacle, a reversal of the self-referential and uncanny shows of the brothers. If he blunders into killing Antonio, he murders the brothers according to his own script: he designs their deaths. The brothers have refused any dialogic relations. Their retainers are primed to ignore their final cries for help. Ferdinand has made public forms into a vehicle for private desires; he is deluded into seeing his final scuffle in an obscure room as a glorious battle. The brothers have used their subordinates as direct extensions of themselves; they will be held accountable for all their intended and unintended crimes:

Roderigo: How comes this?
  Bosola: Revenge, for the Duchesse of *Malfy,* murdered
        By th'*Aragonian* brethren: for *Antonio,*
        Slaine by this hand: for lustfull *Julia,*
        Poyson'd by this man: and lastly, for my selfe.
        (5.5.102–5)

If these lines of Bosola's are a final assertion of the problems of subordination and exchange, the final lines of the play summarize its treatment of subjectivity:

Integrity of life, is fames best friend,
Which noblely (beyond Death) shall crowne the end.
        (5.5.146–47)

Spoken by Delio, the reliable confidant, these sententious lines pose the problem of forming a complete subjectivity, one that has overcome divisions to become *integer*—whole, untouched. Such wholeness, we are told, can be reconciled with that extended public being that the Jacobeans valued as "good fame," although such a reconciliation is ruefully projected to the impossible territory beyond death. The play's last words affirm, however tentatively, the relevance of the Duchess's vision and the dominance of the play's typical register. Neither register of the play, however, can be understood or expressed except through the agency of the other. Without the brothers, there is no concealment of the Duchess's marriage, no representation of the essential inwardness of her subjective life. Without the Duchess's marriage, the brothers' attempts to abolish the boundaries between public and private would have remained the conventional activity of tyrants and villains, rather than becoming an uncanny doubling of selves.

In analyzing a representation dominated by the typical register, then, we find that we cannot evade the indeterminate. The indeterminate register enables us to read this text seriously; it is a precondition of our hermeneutic interrogation of the play.

But what happens when the indeterminate register does not, finally, place itself at the service of the typical? What happens when it dominates a text?

The Turn of the Screw, Indeterminacy, and the Dialectics of Possession

We find such a work in *The Turn of the Screw.* More familiar to us than *The Duchess of Malfi,* separated from us by three generations rather than ten, a staple schoolroom text, *The Turn of the Screw* has still eluded interpretation. It has been a bone of critical contention for forty years.

In analyzing a work such as *The Turn of the Screw,* the process of reading is overtly problematized, and the text's negation and abstraction are foregrounded. The typical level of such a work, however, is not just a rhythmic accompaniment to the improvisatory wanderings of indeterminacy—it assures us that the text has intersubjective meaning; it incites us to interpretation by presenting us with the text as an intelligible document.

Before we begin our explication, let us consider generally some forms that a dominant indeterminate register might take. The reader might be presented with certain finite questions, gaps in the text that invite his or her collaboration, as Iser might say. Melville's *Billy Budd* can stand as an example of such indeterminacy. The reader is prompted to ask why Claggart hated Billy Budd and is not prohibited from answering that question. Another, quite different indeterminate form presents the reader with a break or vacancy in the narrative, but then prohibits the reader from filling that break, perhaps by providing contradictory directions for reading, or by posing a situation so estranged that the reader is defeated in his or her effort to sketch out its missing contours. Jorge Luis Borges's "Tlön, Uqbar, Orbis Tertius"[11] might stand as an example of this use of indeterminacy. The reader is asked, first, to imagine Uqbar, a fictitious country in the Near East—a very modest and conventional premise. But then the reader must assent to Uqbar's imaginary counterpart, Tlön, with its idealist metaphysics, its improbable language, and its scandalous sciences. Finally, this more demanding, but still conventional direction to the reader—imagine an improbable alternate world—breaks out of its narrative bracketing. Artifacts of Tlön start to appear in "our" world, and the study of Tlön begins to absorb the imagination and energy of this world—a narrative predication that resists translation into the normal tenses and moods of summary. Our capacity for assent has been overloaded; our performance of the narrative has been short-circuited in order to provoke reflection on theses linked to the text's indeterminacy: the contingency of lived reality, the seductions of fiction, and the power of the reader over the text.

The story we are about to examine shares something with both forms of indeterminacy. *The Turn of the Screw* is exceptional both for its narrative power and for its ability to prompt speculation.[12] Readers respond to the story on both the levels that James claimed for it: as a compelling tale, an *"amusette,"* in which the unanswered questions that haunt the narrative simply provoke some extra shivers, and as a provocative trap "to catch those not easily caught" (*TS* 120), a goad to reflection. In this doubled use of indeterminacy, *The Turn of the Screw* is not exceptional; such a loading of the indeterminate register is a canonical variation of classical realism. Consider Dickens, stitching and tucking his tissue of narrative rationalizations, and then throwing the whole improbable structure into relief with a case of spontaneous combustion, a gratuitous drowning, or one coincidence too many. These devices seal us among the assenting readers, and also provoke us to reflect upon the process of reading, on the relation of the London of the story to the London of history. Or we might recall Balzac's story "La jeune fille aux yeux d'or," where the machinery of abduction and concealment indicates the hidden inarticulate eroticism of the narrative, simultaneously bracketing the events of the story and foregrounding their dreamlike quality.

But let us turn to the text at hand, a durable example of this doubled indeterminacy. My interest in analyzing *The Turn of the Screw* will be threefold. I will examine the relations of indeterminacy and typicality in the text, tracing its invitations to readers' assent and reflection. This analysis will lead to further reflections on the links among indeterminacy, abstraction, and negation. And in passing, I will investigate the rhetoric of indeterminacy, using the traditional method of close textual analysis.

The text as a whole is a representation of various forms of possession: possession, seen typically, of a house or a child or a lover; possession, seen indeterminately, by spirits or the idea of spirits. On the typical level of the text, the unnamed Harley Street uncle has engrossed all the lands, moveable goods, and chattels of the story; there is no sanctioned or secure ownership save his. His accidental inheritance of the children from his brother and of Mrs. Grose from his mother and his "carrying off" of the governess are cases in point. These relations are the preconditions, the pretexts, of the story, although they do not figure in it directly. Ironically, the story requires that the uncle abstain from active exercise of his rights of possession. Like Flaubert's novelist as god, he is everywhere present, but nowhere visible. And like a medieval god, if not Flaubert's, the uncle arranges his world in a calibrated series of ranks. At Bly, there are no equals. The children are differentiated by age and sex. The governess, because of her status as a lady, is nominally superior to everyone else, but the children are "little grandees" who will one day outstrip her. Mrs. Grose has certain rights of seniority and has known the children longer than any other living person, but as a servant she cannot aspire to exercise this knowledge independently. And then there is the orderly stairstep of underservants: "a cook, a housemaid, a dairywoman, an old pony, an old groom, an old gardener, all likewise thoroughly respectable" (*TS*, 5). In this story, relations of possession also imply inequality and domination. Each character's relation to all of the others is determined by the quality of his or her subordination to the uncle. The relations between superiors and subordinates, so problematic in *The Duchess of Malfi*, are here rationalized and made transparent—but not simple. As a member of the story's fictional audience remarks, it is possible to die of so much respectability.

I must stress that all the relations I have been naming, although they may involve the exchange of wages and labor, are represented as relations of possession rather than relations of hire. The uncle has all the characters at his disposition indefinitely—nobody is in any hurry to go anywhere until Miles becomes anxious about school. Within the bounds of the narrative, the uncle can dispose of characters more or less as he pleases. Thus, the relations of subordination on which the story is based come to have a somewhat archaic flavor: the uncle is surrounded, not by employees, but by retainers.

The chief of those retainers, the governess, does not have an easy time establishing her own authority over the others. She can only secure possession by feverish activity. As Cranfill and Clark note,[13] she grasps after people—holding Mrs. Grose in the hallways, roughly seizing Miles, clasping Flora's hand through half the night. Her language is also marked by metaphors of possession and exchange. She describes her ability to understand the haunting of Bly as something "given" to her from an unnamed source. She asks Mrs. Grose to "give" her the truth, or sees the housekeeper "taking" information. In one of her least sympathetic reflections, the governess imagines that the housekeeper had "offered her mind to my disclosures as, had I wished to mix a witch's broth and proposed it with assurance, she would have held out a large clean saucepan" (*TS*, 46). This perception gives the governess an "odd recognition" of her superiority; she won the right to use Mrs. Grose instrumentally, as her own subordinate. If, in *The Duchess of Malfi*, only Bosola and Ferdinand were capable of a relation of domination that absorbed all the subjectivity of the subordinate, such a relation has become, in this story, a normal and well-mannered piece of domestic machinery.

An odd legal distinction between *possession* and *ownership* is helpful in explaining the contradictions of these relationships. Legally, *possession* is a "state of fact" that generates certain advantages; hence, the adage that possession is nine points of the law. *Possession* is also legally a "source of rights," and is defined as actual control over property. When exclusive, it implies ownership, unless, in the words of the commentator Lightwood, "The apparent possessor holds only as a servant or bailiff on behalf of another."[14] This last reservation describes the governess's position rather nicely. She has complete control over all the other inhabitants of Bly, and since the uncle has renounced any exercise of the rights of ownership, her power seems to be exclusive. But it is only "apparent," since she holds only "on behalf of another."

This contradiction shapes the governess's relation to the children, whom she loves and must care for, but has no rights over. She needs their affection, and they are after all the only gentlefolk among her companions. But their relation to her is also one of combat. Although the governess is in "supreme authority" at Bly, it is the children who have been "put in possession" there (*TS*, 5). The governess and Miles outrank the other; each can lay claim to the highest position on Bly's social scale. At the same time, they are each totally dependent on the other: as the governess puts it, the children "had nothing but me, and I—well, I had *them*" (*TS*, 28). The children and the governess also serve each other as substitutes for the absent uncle. The governess is his direct deputy, but Miles is expected to "carry her away" (*TS*, 9), as his guardian did in London. For the governess, to hold onto the children is also to be held—taken up and taken care of—by the uncle. Thus, the typical relations of possession, through which the story directly represents social subordination, generate the story's initial indeterminacy—the indeterminate identity, displacement, and substitution that characterizes the governess's relation to the children. Before any ghost has appeared at Bly, the governess and the children have found in each other embodiments of the absent uncle.

The difficulties inherent in this position are demonstrated in the affair of Miles's dismissal from school. The governess cannot very well write to Miles's headmaster or investigate what happened at school; she has no rights in this matter. To ask questions the text does not invite, we might consider the problems she would face if she tried to put Miles into another school, or even to investigate which school might be appropriate. She cannot appeal for help to the uncle, who so breezily commands, "deal with him; but mind you don't report. Not a word. I'm off!" (*TS*, 10). The headmaster's letter is a deep embarrassment, because it delivers her over, before she ever meets Miles, to the tension between her apparent power and her real helplessness. This tension will, of course, grow more acute as Miles seeks to establish his own ascendency and demands to be sent away.

Leon Edel's interpretation of *The Turn of the Screw* suggests that James would have been especially sensitive to such contradictions and tensions while the tale was being written. Edel sees the story as an attempt to resolve the conflicts James felt over leasing Lamb House, his first permanent home since leaving America. James described himself as "coerced by some supernatural power" to sign the lease and feared that this provincial home would exclude him from his comfortable niche in London social life.[15] Indeed, James also addressed questions of ownership in "Covering End," a story that deals with the contradiction between owning a house and possessing it, and which was grouped with *The Turn of the Screw* for British publication. That volume was called, significantly, *The Two Magics.* Covering End, the property in question, is encumbered by mortgages, and only delivered to its rightful heir by an American widow's adept use of the second magic—money. She also inducts the heir into the real possession of his estate by teaching him to see it as a precious trust rather than a melancholy burden. This story is a rather simple and overt representation of a basic dialectic of possession: the possessor comes to be determined, restricted, and constrained by what is possessed. Some perception of this dialectic seems to have provoked James's anxiety about Lamb House, a property he was not to own for many years. And one of the first constraints imposed by his long-term lease was the need to pay for furnishings, which was the proximate cause of writing *The Turn of the Screw.*

With this understanding in mind, we can be more precise about the story's representation of possession. On the typical level, *possession* suggests a contradictory complement, ownership, while the indeterminate *possession* of the story suggests a less manageable complement, obsession. Thus, the text provides a nodal point connecting quite prosaic materials—mortgages, choice of a private school—with materials that, as Freud observed, are dangerous to the equilibrium of consciousness and cannot easily be represented directly.

The absent uncle is a key figure in both systems. He is, as we have said, the sole legitimate—we dare not say rightful—possessor in the text. But he tries to evade the dialectic of possession, to maintain control over Bly without becoming entangled in it or constrained by it. Thus, the most powerful figure in the story defines its terrain as a region of silence and absence, a region thrust into indeterminacy. The uncle's "main condition" for engaging the governess bears the mark of this contradiction in its very syntax, which pairs a proliferation of negatives: "That she should never trouble him—but never, never: neither appeal nor complain nor write about anything," with a matching series of global affirmatives, assertions of the governess's deputized authority: "only meet all questions herself, receive all moneys from his solicitor, take the whole thing over and let him alone" (*TS,* 6).

The Turn of the Screw is a variation of the familiar motif of the governess as median character.[16] She is caught between the gentility of her social origin and the subordination of her current class position; she represents the ambiguity of nineteenth-century attitudes toward children, who were to be tenderly protected, but also separated from the adult world—indeed, from civil society. As a median character, the governess has access to all the social regions of her complex household: above and below stairs, nursery and drawing room. Her experience, therefore, is a lens through which we can see the whole of this institution. In *The Turn of the Screw,* the ambiguities of the governess's situation are, of course, heightened by her isolation, which is a sort of ultimate extension of the Duchess of Malfi's project of creating a hidden domestic life.

But as we have seen, this "main condition" establishes an indeterminacy at the very heart of the story, an indeterminacy that becomes the fundamental condition of the narrative. No text is purely typical, and many stories about governesses resort to rather crude indeterminacies—consider the Gothic elements of *Jane Eyre* or *Villette.* But in *The Turn of the Screw,* the indeterminate elements carry the weight of the story. Those elements are derived from the contradictions of the story's typical relations, from the eerie doubling that short-circuits the relation between Miles and the governess into a confrontation of displaced images of the absent uncle. From this displacement further indeterminacies are generated: the ghosts, of course, and the governess's odd response to them, but also the complex beginning and ending movements of the story. Since we encounter the narrative frame first, let us begin our analysis of the story's indeterminacy there.

The induction to *The Turn of the Screw* presents the tale to us through a series of narrators, in what James called a series of "flights and drops" (*TS,* 6) sliding us by degrees into the narrative proper. In each of the frames, we hear repeatedly the syntax of negation, at first, unobtrusively enough, in the speech of the framing narrator, which is marked by rather ordinary negatives, and then more intensively from Douglas, who relates the tale to the audience stationed in the framing narrative. Having led his audience to beg for the tale, Douglas presents it to them through a series of negations:

> But it's not the first occurrence of its charming kind that I know to have been concerned with a child. (*TS,* 1)

> Nobody but me, until now, has ever heard. (*TS,* 1)

> It's beyond everything. Nothing at all that I know touches it. (*TS,* 1)

He seemed to say it wasn't so simple as that; to be really at a loss how to qualify it. (*TS,* 1)

I can't begin. *(TS,* 2)

It's in a locked drawer—it has not been out for years. (*TS,* 2)

Finally, when the narrator suggests that Douglas is telling his own story—that he is, in effect, a substitute for Miles, Douglas replies, "Oh thank God, no!" Through Douglas, we are introduced to the governess, and we see her, at first, as a creature of negation, a woman who hadn't told her story.

And so, waiting for a story that "*won't* tell, not in any literal vulgar way" (*TS,* 3), we are led to its initial negation, the uncle's "main condition" (*TS,* 5), and then immediately given its final negation, "she never saw him again" (*TS,* 6), an assertion we will probably have forgotten when, many pages later, we reach its proper temporal place in the narrative.

Indeed, it is part of the narrative frame's function to be forgotten. Nothing in the governess's tale will remind us of Douglas's reading voice, let alone the sociable fireside group or the bland, urbane, framing narrator. It is impossible to give full attention to Bly and simultaneously to recall this machinery. What, then, is the function of the frame? It has I think two effects, which correspond to the two uses of indeterminacy I mentioned earlier: it provokes our collaboration with the emotional world of the story, and it provokes and frustrates interpretation.

We can treat the first of these effects very briefly, since it is a truism that an introduction sets the mood of a story. One of the generic conventions of the ghost story is that it is often presented as a narrative event. Consider the following conventional opening of a popular thriller: "From within his evening dress Sir Jeffrey drew a cigar case, which faintly resembled a row of cigars, as a mummy case resembles the human form within. He offered me one, and we lit them without haste. Sir Jeffrey started a small vortex in his brandy glass. I understood that these rituals were introductory—that, in other words, I would have my tale."[17] The ghost story, here as in *The Turn of the Screw,* is itself an object of possession, a perversely desired gift. It is perhaps the single extended form of oral fiction that is still an element of mass culture, with its obligatory times and places: Halloween, campfires, slumber parties. In all these manifestations, the ghost story provokes a particular emotional response: delight in the gruesome, taking pleasure in fear, a complex emotion that is a poor relation to the painful pleasure of tragedy. The opening narrative of the ghost story schools us in that response, presenting us with both a sober narrator and an avid audience—in the case of *The Turn of the Screw,* the horrified Douglas and the audience that seeks to be horrified. James's rather special variation is the framing narrator, who is interested in Douglas, but affiliates with the audience's cultivation of the "kind of emotion on which our hopes were fixed" (*TS,* 4). The consciousness of this model, of course, must be discarded as soon as it emerges—we must forget that what we are reading has been labeled "ghost story," or we will not be frightened by it. The introductory signpost, the directional marking for the reader appears at the beginning of the story, to be immediately consumed and forgotten.

And then remembered again. Since James's story is more complex than Sir Jeffrey's narrative, it provokes a more complex response. Having read and having found the "kind of emotion on which our hopes were fixed," we find also something else, an inclination to question the text, to make it speak to us. Like the governess, we are looking for a confession. It is not surprising, then, that the critical controversy over this story, which we will analyze later, is a controversy over this nature of its guilty secret. Whether the text is read as a "Freudian" case study of sexual repression or as an allegory of original sin, it is understood as a veil of words. The interpreter penetrates that veil by interrogating the text until it admits its own guilt. The induction, a weak link in the story's presentation of itself, attracts hermeneutic suspicion. The chain of narrators, any of whom may be unreliable, the slippery elision of Douglas's introduction, even the generic cue "ghost story"—all appear as clues. And the fact that the induction has been forgotten in the act of reading only seems to confirm its usefulness as evidence. Interpretation is the act of a skilled reader, one who can discover things hidden from the naive eye. The concealment of the narrative frame at the very beginning of the story makes it a privileged text for such a reader.

The indeterminacy of the framing narrative inducts the reader into the indeterminacy of the tale proper. Before beginning a story about deputies and substitutes, we read an introduction in which the act of narration is triply deputized. We will read a story that turns on a search for confessions; in the introduction, we are invited to make such interrogations ourselves. The proper response to the story— recreational horror—has been demonstrated, but doubt was cast on its propriety by our narrator, who seeks sensations and scorns sensation seeking. And after alerting us, with its many cautionary signs and repeated negatives, to read the tale *as interpreters,* with a suspicious eye, the introduction immediately dissolves itself into the story proper and, after a decent interval, delivers us over to the fear that it promised and forbade. It is by means of the ghosts, of course, that

James keeps the promise and performs the transgression. Having sketched out the themes of displacement and substitution that mark the framing narrative, we can examine those themes in the story proper, in the matter of the ghosts and the governess's response to them. On the typical level, which marks the first two chapters of the governess's narrative, she is caught in a singularly frustrating position. Having installed herself at Bly in behalf of the uncle—now, significantly, referred to as the master, the governess begins to live out her isolation. She reconciles herself to loneliness with the promise of being "carried away" by the children, but they refuse to possess her and refuse her possession. Miles's damaging letter precedes him, compromising him and painfully emphasizing her own lack of authority. The governess is left, like the audience of the framing narrative, begging for a story, but Mrs. Grose, like Douglas, "won't tell tales" (TS, 12). The governess is thus doubly at a loss—her fidelity to the uncle renders her useless to Miles. The controlling relations of her world, possession by the uncle and possession of the children, become intolerably contradictory, and the governess cannot forget that, however much she may be in possession at Bly, she has no rights of ownership here.

The energy of possession thus is deflected into her obsession with the ghosts. They express, regulate, and contain the contradictions in the narrative. They represent the basic relations of possession at Bly in an indeterminate way, moving, as befits indeterminate creatures, among the levels of the narrative, appearing alternately as ghosts for us (representing our reading) and ghosts for the governess (representing her experience of possession). We move from the typical level, the level on which we beg for a story, to the indeterminate level, on which we forget that the fear we are experiencing is something we have sought out: we deliver ourselves over to the ghosts so completely that we forget that we have summoned them ourselves. And the governess, walking in the evening half-light, moves from the pleasant but contradictory world of the nursery to the haunted world formed by the gaze of Quint, a world that is anything but pleasant but that makes perfect sense. The ghosts watch the governess and, by performing the task of the absent uncle, give her a saving mission of her own. They are key elements in a very complex system of substitutions that the governess constructs. Silent, even passive, they are blank markers, place holders in the relations of possession and being possessed.

Their first function is substitution for the uncle, the master. Peter Quint wears the uncle's cast-off clothing, and when the governess first sees him, she mistakes Peter for the uncle, whom she had been hoping would visit. Quint, with all his ill-bred "familiarity," seems at first to belong to the typical register of the text—he is, at first, the uncle, then an unmannerly intruding tourist, a diversion from the real mystery of the story, the children's preternatural charm. But in the governess's hands, his very commonplace quality is invested with menace. Surrounded by withheld stories about the children, forbidden to tell their story to the uncle, the governess finds in Quint's breach of manners a story she can withhold and give:

> "I've been dying to tell you. But he's like nobody."
> "Nobody?" she echoed.
> "He has no hat." (TS, 23)

Thus, hedged about with negatives, the ghost is identified as the master's "own man," and the indeterminate register of the novella absorbs its play of substitutions and displacements.

The ghosts are called upon to effect further substitutions beyond that of Quint for the master, the most central of which is their substitution for the governess in relation to the children. If Quint watches over the governess as the uncle's deputy, then both Quint and Miss Jessel watch over the children as substitutes for the governess. In this relation, the governess's attention shifts from her own dilemma of being seen to the danger and scandal of the children seeing: " 'Two hours ago, in the garden'—I could scarce articulate—'Flora saw!' " (TS, 30). The ghosts explain by their very evil and horror the disturbing charm of the children, their having no faults, no history, "nothing to whack" (TS, 19), and thus eluding the governess's possession. If the children are not a care and a burden to her, then someone else must be taking care of the them. And the governess ascribes that role to the ghosts, who, like her, are subordinates of the uncle. She says of the children: "They haven't been good—they've only been absent. It has been easy to live with them because they're simply leading a life of their own. They're not mine—they're not ours. They're his and they're hers!" (TS, 49). By substituting the ghosts for herself, the governess consigns the children to the sphere of indeterminacy. Since they are not possessed by her, they must be possessed by somebody else—and, removed from the chain of ownership that the uncle has suspended through Bly, they do not really exist. They are, as the governess puts it, absent, and all their daily grace is to be scrutinized as evidence of their possession. Thus, in the final scene with Flora, the child's rejection of the raging governess, her denial that she sees anything, are ascribed to an "outside source."

Miss Jessel, acknowledged only by the governess, is made responsible for Flora's rebellion.

In the economy of the story's indeterminacy, substitution, unlike possession, is not an exclusive relation. Thus, while the ghosts substitute for both uncle and governess, the children can also substitute for the ghosts. The governess's project of saving the children rather quickly becomes a project of extracting from them some overt admission that they see ghosts. She justifies her unrelenting pressure on Miles; in the name of his own protection, he is continually expected to speak up—to name Quint, or his offense at school. There is always some secret to be surrendered, some "small shifty spot on the wrong side of it all [that] still sometimes brushed my brow like the wings of a bat" (*TS*, 35). The governess's overt questions to Miles become more intense and more devious:

> You must tell me now—and all the truth. What did you go for? What were you doing there? (*TS*, 47)
>
> What is it that you think of? . . . Of what queer business, Miles? (*TS*, 62)
>
> Tell me . . . if, yesterday afternoon, from the table on the hall, you took, you know, my letter. (*TS*, 84)
>
> What does it matter, now, my own?—what will he *ever* matter? *I* have you, . . . but he has lost you forever! (*TS*, 88)

But her most interesting questions are those she suppresses. She considers asking Flora to enter a typical sphere of intersubjective dialogue: "Therefore why not frankly confess it to me, so that we may at least live with it together and learn perhaps, in the strangeness of our fate, who we are and what it means" (*TS*, 42). But the governess also suppresses the triumphant aggression of: "They're here, they're here, you little wretches, and you can't deny it now!" (*TS*, 52).

In neither spoken nor unspoken questions is the governess really addressing the children; she is instead describing her own situation: she is someone whose survival depends on thinking through a set of relations that is always on the verge of becoming clarified, but that she never fully surrenders to understanding. The children, permanent repositories of this indeterminacy, are, like ghosts, bearers of the secret of Bly. Their real inadequacy to this role is revealed in Miles's final interview. There, he haltingly rehearses his offenses at school, the governess deploying incredible ingenuity to extract his confession,

sentence by banal sentence. Miles and Flora institutionalize the withheld story for the governess. In the indeterminate register of the story,
the withheld tale becomes one more representation of contradictory
possession: Miles's secret is a violation of the rights of possession. If
he did not "say things," then, according to the governess, he must
have stolen letters. To search for such a story is to give oneself over to
obsession, to become possessed by a negation—the unknown. As frail
vessels for explosive knowledge, the children, like the ghosts, can
permanently withhold their tale. They know nothing, or they do not
understand what they know, or they cannot explain what they understand. In a final flourish of this infernal structure, the governess displaces her constraint against speaking to the uncle, substituting a
constraint against speaking to the children: "I should indeed help
them [the children? the ghosts?] to represent something infamous if
by pronouncing them [questions about the ghosts], I should violate
as rare a case of instinctive delicacy as any schoolroom probably had
ever known" (*TS*, 53). The whole machinery of possession, substitution, and obsession is so finely balanced, its tensions so well ranged
against one another, that it can move at an accelerating pace through
the story, powered by the very force that should frustrate it, the
force of reason.

The Hermeneutics of Indeterminacy

Both the governess and the readers of her tale are caught in a style of
interpretation marked by aggression and interrogation rather than by
attention and disclosure. Both the reader and the narrator, in fact,
declare themselves enemies of the tale's indeterminacy. The difficulties of approaching the tale in this mood recall us to the need for a
hermeneutic more flexible and sensitive than the traditional opposition of appearance to reality. For the governess, the children's charm
is a delusive appearance, an emotional mirage to be dissolved by
reasoning about their collusion with the ghosts. Analogously, critics
of different persuasions tend to see the ghosts as delusive appearances,
to be exorcised by dissolving them into figures of sexual repression,
religious allegories, or conventional generic figures.[18] Consider the
following quotations:

> There are further, some arresting details in the description of
> Quint: "His eyes are sharp, strange—awfully; . . . rather
> small and fixed. His mouth's wide, and his lips are thin, . . . "
> These are unmistakeably the characteristics of a snake.
> (R. B. Heilmann in *TS*, 220)

In such a context it is no longer possible to be insensitive to the remarkable phonetical resemblance between the word "mast" and the word "master," which it cannot but bring to mind.[19]

Who is he? Mrs. Grose answers, "Peter Quint": some modern critics suggest, "The Devil": but in contemporary, realistic terms there can be only one answer to this question, "He is George Bernard Shaw."[20]

This tendency toward overstatement, this unscholarly decision of tone, demonstrates the power of the story's indeterminacy. So forcible is James's temptation to the interpreter than even a reader convinced of the multivalence of the story is likely to follow the trail of some association, suggestion, or echo, misled by the story's suggestion of its own awful coherence. Readers of *The Turn of the Screw* not only scare themselves; they also deceive themselves.

I have said that the typical world of Bly does not make sense, that its relations of possession are damaged by gaps and tangled in contradictions. The world of the ghosts fills those gaps and resolves the contradictions by permitting endless free substitution of persons in various roles of possession. It is a rational world, but a world that is also a temptation to reason. The governess is not delivered from that temptation. Neither, as we probe the story for its secrets, are we.

The agency of our entanglement, of our complicity in the indeterminate world, is abstraction. The story's indeterminacy is formed by abstraction from the myriad possessors and possessions to the basic relationship of possessing. This abstract reduction to essentials occurs more markedly in *The Turn of the Screw* than it did in *A Midsummer Night's Dream,* in which the force of passion flattens out individual differences and renders the young people interchangeable. In *The Turn of the Screw,* further, there is less tendency toward the impoverishment of categorical abstraction. Quint and Miss Jessel are not fully formed subjectivities any more than Lysander and Helena were, but unlike Lysander and Helena, they do not appear as reduced general images of "young man" and "young woman." In the ghost world of Bly, Quint and Miss Jessel represent relations rather than categories; they make available to us the constitutive qualities of possession: its exclusivity, its joint complementarity with ownership and obsession, its doubled quality—since the possessor can so easily become possessed—and its endless possibilities of substitution and displacement. To consider the ghosts is to write an inventory of all the forms of possession in the story: demonic possession, erotic possession, emotional possession, possession of a child, of a place, of oneself. But with that inventory, we have provided ourselves with a full description of the ghosts' functioning in the story. Like the children, they have "no history"; we know nothing of their prior lives and little of their deaths. There is nothing left over in them after the relations of possession have been accounted for. Further, this silence of the text is not an active silence—an absence that demands interpretation, like Miles's unnamed transgression at school. The ghosts are abstractions of the text's relations of possession: they present that relationship's dialectic exhaustively and exclusively.

The abstraction of the text is closely related to its negation, and negation is a consistent stylistic feature of the tale. Indeed, given Hegel's analysis of the relation between abstraction and negation, this association is not accidental. Hegel says:

> The action of separating the elements in analysis of an idea is the exercise of the force of Understanding, the most astonishing and greatest of all powers, or rather the absolute power . . . that an accident as such, when cut loose from its containing circumference,—that what is bound and held by something else and actual only by being connected with it,—should obtain an existence all its own, gain freedom and independence on its own account—this is the portentous power of the negative; it is the energy of thought, of pure ego. . . . It is this mighty power, not by being a positive which turns away from the negative, as when we say of anything it is nothing or it is false, and, being then done with it, pass off to something else: on the contrary, mind is this power only by looking the negative in the face, and dwelling with it. This dwelling beside it is the magic power that converts the negative into being.[21]

The *Turn of the Screw* can be read as a prolonged experiment in dwelling beside the negative, in thinking through the relations of possession—relations that, in lived experience, are always bound within a "containing circumference" of other relations and emotional forces. Finally, these relations, in all their unreality and negativity, are converted into beings—the ghosts, first of all, but still more magically, the being of the story. The "tale that won't tell" is in fact told.

We have said that possession structures the world of Bly, and that the story is predicated upon the master's evasion of the dialectic of possession. Thus, the overtly representative level of the story is already abstracted: it presents a world in which relations of possession play themselves out more explicitly and variously than they do in social life. But because of the uncle's absence, these relations are "cut loose" from their normal entangling circumstances—the governess will be left alone; she will contest for power with the children. In order to make the implications of these relations accessible, the text, having "looked in the face" its various negations (no story, no uncle, no history) produces from these very negations the images of the ghosts, images in which what would normally be invisible becomes concrete. And these images can do what the more conventionally typical—many-sided and realistic—characters of the story cannot do: they are able to render the world of Bly both rational and habitable. Rational, since the ghosts are encumbered by no disturbing individualities, since they are seen as nothing but ravenous wills to possession, to "get at" the children. Habitable, since only through the agency of the ghosts, with their endless capabilities for substitution, can all the work of Bly, all its labor of seeing and being seen, be carried out.

It is the very abstraction and negation of the ghosts, their indeterminacy, their lack of subjective density, that allows them to perform this function. The tale itself, in a sense, is wrested away from silence by indeterminacy; the story that "won't tell" can be kept secure in a locked box, preserved by Douglas's discretion. The ghosts, like the brothers in *The Duchess of Malfi,* deliver the heroine from banality, from inactivity, from domestic obscurity. The governess faced a prospect that recalls James's story *The Real Thing:* nothing might ever have *happened* to her, exiled out there in the country, entrusted with a mission that is both impossible and absurdly easy. The ghosts, in representing the controlling relations of this static situation, also reshape them into narrative, and thus form the plot. They give the succession of "flights and drops" a shape, a fictional form.

In moving the governess from stasis into narration, the ghosts expose the narrowness and constraint of her position. Their function is not only explanatory and representational but also critical. The horror that the governess faces is a very disciplined and directed horror, shorn of supernatural associations, of numinous romantic embellishments. This horror is rooted in reason—obsessive and misdirected reason, reason faced with the irrational and contradictory implications of possession in a world without equals. The ghosts stand, thus, as a kind of protest against this world, as if to say, "*This* is what it takes to make sense of such a mad system." The ghosts stand as emblems of the limits of ownership; they remind us that relations of possession cannot by themselves sustain an interior life, that to allow oneself to be controlled or exhausted by such relations is to become, in effect, a ghost.

The same movement that generates the novella's critical force generates its utopian moment. In the ghosts, *The Turn of the Screw* presents an image of social world in which none of the barriers of respectability that obtain at Bly have any force. Everyone is a potential erotic object, regardless of age or social class. Everyone can become someone else, take the place of the master, wear the clothing of another class or clothing that violates polite norms. No ties of family are honored; all constraints of class deference are dropped. Finally, in their power to return, the ghosts defy the absolute constraint of death. Even though they are dead, their death is not narrated; in terms of the story, with its economy of telling, they have not died.

But it is from the ghosts' thoroughgoing concentration of the relations of possession, from this "dwelling with the negative," that the story derives its power. As Hegel's reflection suggests, the final moment of such an investigation of the negative must confront the image of death. With this in mind, let us consider the closing of *The Turn of the Screw*.

The final episode of the novel complements its induction. Like the induction, it confirms connections between the narrative logic of the tale and the interpretive logic of the reader. Like the induction, it proceeds by "flights and drops" (*TS*, 6), and like the induction it combines global affirmations with global negations. What specially marks this final section, however, is the odd quality of its affirmations. They are, on their face, negations of the indeterminate world of the novel, refusals of its power. But examined more closely, these negations of the negative world express the governess's full collaboration with the dialectic of possession, her acceptance of the distorted norms of Bly as an intersubjective truth. She rejects the indeterminate world of the ghosts only because she has no need of it; the abstraction and negation of the indeterminate register have become the structuring principles of her intersubjective world. Death, the ultimate negation, now invades the social world of the tale. Instead of hearing a story about ghosts, the peculiarly fictional dead, we read now of a dead, quite material, child.

This final movement is opened by the governess's questioning, which elicits Miles's halting confession—a revelation, like the headmaster's letter, recalling the contradictions of the governess's position. Having sought so long for this surrender, the governess uncovers no diabolical secrets, only the mumbled admission that Miles "said things." In a sense, this anticlimactic admission shows that Miles has indeed violated the story's basic norm—"not telling." Miles had let loose the offense of speech, speech that can be repeated. The governess's response to this confession is characteristically doubled: she feels concern for the distressed child and displaces her aggression from him to the absent Quint:

> But the next after that I must have sounded stern enough.
> "What *were* those things?"
> My sternness was all for his judge, his executioner. (*TS*, 87)

The very epithet *stern* is displaced, since it suggests, by association, the judge. The governess's speech, then, is marked by a rhetoric of transference, as if she said, "I am being stern, but not to the child. I am being stern to the [stern] judge." A similar logic will shape her later identification of Quint as the "coward horror." Now, however, having invoked a deputy, the governess raises the ghost of Quint, which appears at the window.

Quint becomes a mediator between the governess and Miles. The governess's speech is addressed alternately to Miles and to Quint. Her first exclamation, "No more, no more, no more," seems to be for Miles, but is actually delivered to the "visitant." Thus, in the dialogue of this final episode, three motifs of the novella's indeterminacy are combined: negation, since what is said is negative; substitution, since what is said is not addressed to its ostensible audience; and possession, since the governess accompanies her speech by pressing Miles to her, claiming ownership of him. But at this moment, in this highly compressed atmosphere, the governess transposes the terms she had been using to understand Bly. She had explained her situation of not being possessed and not possessing by deflecting these themes to the children, seeing them as possessed. Now, claiming full possession of the child who has just surrendered his secret to her, she asserts that Miles has been delivered from all these contradictions, that he is free of the relations of ownership, possession, and obsession. His being grasped by her is his "liberation." Characteristically, this theme is first introduced into the text indirectly, as a way of indicating an absence: for Miles, as he searches for Quint, the window was "still to his own eyes free" (*TS*, 88). Miles's freedom, thus, is defined and conditioned by a narrative negation, the absence of Quint. It is not a sort of freedom that Miles had desired, the freedom to "see more life" (*TS*, 56). Miles has instead simply been handed over for a few days entirely to the governess, so that her rights over him are complicated by no other presence, neither that of Flora nor of Mrs. Grose nor of Quint.

To Miles's understanding, of course, this is no liberation. He traces from the governess's glance the unseen partner in her dialogue and searches, as the governess had searched, for some third party that would explain his odd contradictory place in these relations. To the governess's eyes, this search is a recognition of the children's status as objects, subalterns: she has him thinking that he is in store for "some sequel to what we had done to Flora" (*TS*, 88).

Miles's blindness to Quint is paired with the governess's sight of him; syntactically, Miles's experience of absence is connected to her experience of presence: "he was at me in a white rage, bewildered, glaring vainly over the place and missing wholly, though it now, to my sense, filled the room like the taste of poison, the wide over-whelming presence" (*TS*, 88). The governess is caught in a final radical denial. Face to face with the ghost who represents the inde-terminate relations of her world, able to experience and think of nothing *but* these relationships, she claims that she has been delivered from them at last. In proclaiming Miles's liberation, she claims her own mastery. Ironically, then, she triumphs in Miles's lack of vision just as she herself is most possessed by the sight of Quint. The govern-ess has imported the endless flexibility of the novel's indeterminacy into its typical register and brought the two worlds together in a quite audacious way. The ambiguities of possession are to be dissolved; negations give way, for the governess, to simple affirmative state-ments, statements that can be reduced to the iterated demonstrative *there*. The material world of Bly, the intersubjective and typical world, is presented as evidence that there is no indeterminacy, that the governess is completely in control. If the uncle asserts mastery by for-bidding speech, the governess compels speech, but forbids vision. In-determinacy, however, is not banished so easily. But I anticipate.

In the governess's final dialogue with Miles, she speaks entirely in the syntax of possession; their talk is literally an exchange, but an unequal exchange. Let us examine this passage closely:

> I was so determined to have all my proof that I flashed into ice to challenge him. "Whom do you mean by 'he'?"
>
> "Peter Quint—you devil!" His face gave again, round the room, its convulsed supplication. "*Where?*"
>
> They are in my ears still, his supreme surrender of the name and his tribute to my devotion. "What does he matter now, my own—what will he *ever* matter? *I* have you," I launched at the beast, "but he has lost you forever!" Then for the demonstration of my work, "There, *there!*" I said to Miles. (*TS*, 88)

The dialogue begins with an assertion of possession, the governess's decision to "have her proof." The proof she requests is that Miles name the antecedent of a pronoun, that he stop the whirling circle of substitutions, attaching meaning to a proper name: "What do you mean by 'he'?" she asks. Even though the question is hermeneutic in form, it is put in no understanding spirit, since the governess, "flashed into ice," has become a questioner who cannot be moved by any answer.

Miles's answer, of course, is a crux—one of the very rare cruxes in James, since he composed carefully, dictating punctuation as he went, and was not fond of verbal ambiguity.[22] Miles's answer, in fact, is a little masterpiece of indeterminacy. Let us rehearse the obligatory catalog of its possible meanings. Just as the name of Quint has escaped him, Miles entangles us in another ambiguous reference, since his "you devil" can refer either to the governess or to Quint. Further, this ambiguity does not strike the governess; it is an ambiguity for the reader, separating him or her from the governess at the very climax of her narrative, imposing a distance between *her* story and *the* story just when it is least convenient. Further, if "you devil" refers to the governess, it is an ironic expression, an irony that springs from Miles's manipulation of those rules of possession and substitution that have lately controlled his life. The governess has seen him as a fiend, has accused him of intercourse with a devil. Now, since his familiar is unseen, Miles turns that epithet against the visible possessor, the governess. She, however, interprets this very speech as a "tribute," an object of possession in itself.

Her reply to Miles's frenzied question, however, is still hermeneutic in form. She asks a question about meaning, "What does it matter now, my own?" "My own," of course, is scarcely a routine endearment in this charged context; it deflates all the intersubjective force of the governess's question. Her hermeneutic attitude becomes merely a rhetorical form, an alternate way of expressing the negative, "he is of no consequence." The governess's questions, delayed so long, have atrophied into gestures of possession. And in this question drained of meaning, I think, we can hear the sober echo of the governess's tragedy, of too long a labor at making sense of senseless social arrangements. The governess tried to subdue to intersubjectivity, to the language of the typical, relations and forces that denied her own subjective being. Her search for understanding in this hostile terrain freezes "into ice" and becomes a pretext for one more assault on the indeterminate, one more assertion of her right of possession.

And this final assertion presents the logic of possession in exceptionally pure form. The governess's claim of ownership is not addressed to Miles, but is flung out at Quint; it is "launched at the beast." The governess thus makes literally the claim that the story has already made in narrative form: if Miles loses Quint, the governess has gained him. The more insistent the governess's claim to have exorcised the ghost, the sharper is her invocation of its presence. Further, the governess's intention—to claim possession of Miles—is frustrated by the very form of her assertion. It is a claim made against a third party, and therefore an admission of a third party's rights. Just as the governess claims the boy as the fruit of her long struggle, she justifies this claim to an other. It is the situation of the headmaster's letter all over, but with the governess triumphant. Instead of being embarrassed by the silent watcher, she makes him her accomplice; she has a right to possess Miles completely because hers is a possession *against* the "beast."

The beast, the ghost, the watcher, the other, is invoked with the governess's repeated "there." This word, the governess's final reported speech in the novella, keeps faith with the tale's norm of silence. The governess's cry communicates as little as possible; and it gives no explanation for the holding and losing she has so triumphantly been proclaiming. Her demonstration—showing Miles as empty window—indicates the ghost by pointing at an empty space, reversing the relation that has held between indeterminacy and typicality in the tale. The ghosts had been representations of absence; now, absence is presented as a representation of the ghosts. The governess's cry and gesture invoke a prior understanding, an intersubjective agreement about what is to be seen "there" and what it means. But such an agreement could only have been reached in typical discourse, in which the governess and Miles would have learned "in the strangeness of our fate, where we are and what it means" (*TS,* 42). That discourse has been renounced, and so the governess's "there" refers to an absent context. She acts as if indeterminate language could be assimilated to the typical discourse of shared social understandings. She has fully conflated two worlds, so that for her the contradictions and limits of possession have vanished into the indeterminate structures of abstraction and free substitution. In the empty affirmation of her "there," the governess invokes an absolute negation.

There, Miles falls, into an "abyss," a vacancy, a space shaped entirely by his "loss"—a loss that, in the iron economy of possession, is the governess's gain. In this crisis, a final contradiction in the governess's project emerges. Gaining total possession of Miles, she abolishes him as an other; she absorbs him. But of course, it is impossible to possess what one has already incorporated, so that the governess's account of Miles's fall wavers in its voice—he is a creature who is hurled; he is the boy she catches. But the hurler and the grasper are the same; the abyss and the governess's arms have become alternate expressions for the same vacant place.

So the governess's gestures of possession seal Miles among those who alone can be fully possessed—the dead. Having become, finally, a fit object for possession, a "what," Miles is once again declared free, "dispossessed." In a final attempt to negate the negations of her world, the governess affirms her final isolation—"we are alone."

For the reader, the interpreter, the ending movement repeats, in compressed form, the doubled invitation of the story's induction: the invitation to be frightened, and the invitation to reflect. Like the induction, Miles's death seems to take place on a different plane from the other episodes in the narrative; *The Turn of the Screw* seems to be "about" ghosts and obsessions, not "about" death and material danger. Like the induction, Miles's death stands outside the text, commenting on the event it completes. It both confirms and closes the theme of negation that has marked the story as a whole—no further intensification of that theme can be expected.

The governess's "We were alone with the quiet day" is in its way as multivalent as Miles's "Peter Quint—you devil." She sees the dead child as a companion and so uses the plural *we*. Miles's death, restoring her sense of isolation, also fulfills his prophecy, given a few pages earlier, that "if we're alone together now it's you that are alone most." The absence of Quint is expressed in displaced and deflected terms: no "Quint was gone," but "we were alone." Finally, the adjective *quiet* modulates the theme of silence to an elegiac mood of closure.

That mood soon gives way to the desire for understanding and thus to the activity of the interpreter. Since Miles's death is not the ending we have been preparing for, it does not appear as a resolution of the story's problems. We want to know why Miles died, or how Miles died. Given the text's silence on these problems, our interest is soon displaced into questions about the governess's intentions, or the nature of the ghosts. At this point the reasonably reflective reader, the reader "not easily caught," moves to the induction, with its elusive web of narrators and its tantalizing information about the governess's later life. That information, as we have said, is given as a series of negatives: she never saw the uncle again, never married, never told the story of Bly. In trying to make sense of this information, and to relate it to the governess's tale, we join in her search for the "small shiftly spot on the wrong side of it all" (*TS*, 35).

In *The Turn of the Screw*, then, it is the indeterminate register that shapes the tale, that motivates our emotional response. This indeterminacy functions on several levels: on the level of framing narrative, within the plot, and on the level of style. The abstract and negative elements in the story provoke both our fear and our thirst for interpretation. Moreover, these responses reinforce each other. The more we are frightened by the story, the greater our desire for a resolution. We find then, in this tale, what James promised in his New York preface, "an annexed but independent world in which nothing is right save as we rightly imagine it" (*TS*, 119). But this tale never permits us to rest content with the rightness of our imagination.

3

TYPICALITY AND INDETERMINACY IN JACOBEAN CITY COMEDY

In my discussion of *The Duchess of Malfi, The Turn of the Screw,* and two of Shakespeare's plays, I have developed some primitive terms in the vocabulary of representation: dominance of the typical register, dominance of the indeterminate register, and representational strategy. In these somewhat schematic readings of renaissance plays and of James's novella, the social and ideological worlds of the text have pressed in on our explanation: in these readings, such ideological forms as the Tudor state, the royal body, and possession as legal relation and structure of feeling have emerged. Nor is this surprising, since the notion of representation is concerned with the connections and distances between the text and its world. I have also invoked other texts, referring to the conventions of tragedy and of the horror story, or to the tropes of narration. We are now prepared to consider these "extrinsic" forms explicitly. Since, under the rubrics of "social background" and "generic conventions," these topics have traditionally been used in criticism, my analysis of them will help to clarify the relation between the theory of representation advanced in this book and traditional mimetic or generic theories of literature.

Let us, then, seek out a manageable problem: to look at a compact series of texts related to a discrete range of social relations. Ignoring for a moment the methodological impossibility of establishing any limits to social relations, we can find such a problem in the city comedy, a subgenre of the Jacobean comedy that flourished from 1605 to 1630. Its most accomplished writers—Jonson, Middleton, and Marston—produced a limited number of "city" plays, distinct in tone and structure from older romantic treatments of the city such as Dekker's *The Shoemaker's Holiday.*[1] The city comedy, then, presents us with a limited series of texts, and the world to which they refer can be understood in limited terms: Jacobean London, a city whose economy, governing structure, and ideology had become sharply problematic.

Since we have defined the city comedy as a subgenre, some

initial remarks on generic theory are in order. Fredric Jameson has suggested how the notion of genre can be understood dialectically: "Dialectical thinking can be characterized as historical reflexivity, that is, as a study of an object (here the romance texts) which also involves the study of concepts and categories we necessarily bring to the object."[2] Thus, generic "forms" and "constraints," instead of being read as explanations of the text, can be seen as part of the act of reading and regarded by the hermeneutic interpreter with alternating piety and suspicion. Such an understanding of genre is especially appropriate in the case of city comedy, since this genre is a creature of critical reflection. While Jacobean dramatists wrote comedies, tragedies, tragicomedies, or masques and shared some understandings of these forms, they did not write city comedies, but only comedies that took "city matters" as their subject. The genre is an analytic tool, a way of grouping these texts together, separating them from earlier plays about gulling and swindling, like *Volpone.*

To read the city comedy as part of a genre, then, is to reread its critical history, a singularly compact one. Criticism of the city comedy has followed two lines of investigation, represented by Brian Gibbons's generic criticism and L. C. Knights's sociological criticism.[3] Gibbons notes in *Jacobean City Comedy* that the writers of the city comedy worked with a limited range of materials—satire, jest book, the Roman comedy—to form a rather stylized subgenre that celebrates trickery and swindling while castigating the greed that prompts them. Thus, city comedies are orthodox moral dramas—their corrective intent, perhaps, salted with ambiguity, especially in Middleton's plays. In Gibbons's treatment, city comedies can be explained simply by comparing them to other texts that resemble them. Complaints about the corruption of Jacobean London are referred to similar complaints about dissimilar cities. On the other hand, L. C. Knights in *Drama and Society in the Age of Jonson* ascribes the city comedy to specific changes in British society, citing the rise of the middle class and the commercial growth of London as its determinants. Within this context, Jonson appears as a guardian of traditional ethics and an acute observer of nascent capitalist relations. Middleton fares less well; Knights finds his satire diffuse and disconnected from the specific tensions of the period. Here, the text has been referred to its world, to its social background, even though this background is only known through these texts and others.

Recently, Margot Heinemann in *Puritanism and Theatre* has amplified L. C. Knights's understanding of the city comedy by looking closely at the relation between the political and ideological structure of the city and the plays of Thomas Middleton. The city comedy that emerges from her examination is a more complex genre than Knights's rather naive protest drama: Middleton's relation to the Puritan elite of London, and to the dominant Jacobean court, is shown to be contradictory, even (to use a word Heinemann would avoid) overdetermined. But while Heinemann's grasp of social history tells us a great deal about the world of the plays, some analysis of how that world is transformed by representation may yet be in order. It is not enough to say that "Middleton's city comedies, like much of the major drama of the period, present a society changing from one regulated by inherited status to one ruled increasingly by the power of money and capital."[4] Presented how, and to whom, and with what transformation? Mimesis explains the text for Heinemann, just as genre explained it for Gibbons: in both cases, the explanatory categories escape reflection.

Both of these lines of investigation—the sociological study that began with Knights and culminates in Heinemann's book and the generic study promoted by Gibbons—are, in more or less useful ways, circular. But in moving without reflection from text to text, they fail to achieve the balance of a hermeneutic circle. Gibbons, thus, threatens to divorce the city comedy from its specific historical situation; Knights and Heinemann dissolve the genre into that context. By seeing these plays as representations, and specifically by tracing the relations of typicality and indeterminacy in them, we can avoid this dilemma. By situating the plays, we can understand them as artistic responses to specific contradictions within the City of London's hegemonic ideology. The city comedy is an attempt to recover, by finding a new representational vocabulary for it, the harmony between the commercial and the communal organization of the city that chroniclers like Stow imaginatively portrayed as part of its recent past but which was compromised by the rapid growth, commercial development, and royal domination of the City during the Jacobean period. This search tended to focus on the marketplace, a central institution for preindustrial London, where the split between commerce and community, between a cash economy and celebratory space, was especially acute. And indeed, images of the marketplace recur within city comedies. But many traditional vehicles for presenting a harmonious relation between commercial and civic life—the language of politics, the ceremonies of the City—were also rendered indeterminate by the lived contradictions of the city's ruling ideology. The city comedy, I hold, was an attempt to work out representational strategies for reflecting on this indeterminacy, or for translating it into a typical register.

The Ideology of the City of London

Perhaps we can begin to reflect on this process by analyzing the ideological problem that London posed, beginning with the market-place as a place of both trade and celebration. The market, as secular space, locus of spontaneous public activity, has been most memorably characterized by Mikhail Bakhtin, in *Rabelais and His World:* "The marketplace of the Middle Ages and the Renaissance was a world in itself, a world which was one: all 'performances' in this arena, from loud cursing to the organized show, had something in common and were imbued with the same atmosphere of freedom, frankness, and familiarity. . . . The marketplace was the center of all that was un-official; it enjoyed a certain extraterritoriality. In a world of official order and official ideology, it always remained 'with the people.' "[5]

But just as the literal marketplace was, during the Jacobean period, becoming marginal,[6] slowly being replaced by the private shop, like Drugger's tobacco shop, so also the metaphorical arena of the marketplace, the arena of openness and play, outside the scrutiny of the church and the direct concern of the Crown, was being com-promised. This compromise, first, meant the transfer of the activity of the marketplace from governance by ideology of communal ex-change to the control of no law or custom other than the need to accumulate. Second, the older communal forms of city governance, forms expressive of the independent status of the city and of its organic ideology, succumbed to attrition and were replaced by more bureaucratic and official forms under direct royal domination. Thus, the marketplace is compromised both by becoming simply the loca-tion of exchange and profit rather than a gathering place, a common space, and also by being circumscribed more tightly by the "official order," by losing its "extraterritorial status" and becoming more in-tegrated with the central apparatus of the government—a process that of course also increased the access to power of the most wealthy merchants.

Thus, while Bakhtin's *Rabelais* can present the marketplace as the place where the rights of the "lower bodily stratum" are legiti-mated and where the popular subversive tradition of laughter, parody, skepticism, and utopian hope could be preserved, so straightforward a relationship to the marketplace was impossible for Marston, Mid-dleton, and Jonson. Their marketplace, their city, and their space of celebration were different.

We should notice that even as we tentatively probe this institu-tion, this image, our investigation has already become complicated, and the distinction between the world of the text and the world of texts has become problematic. The marketplace, surely, is part of the world; even today, it stands as a synecdoche for "worldly" activity. But the marketplace also gives out onto a collection of texts—fictions, of course, but also a whole series of other discourses not often admitted into the polite company of literature: curses, carnival songs, the cries and strategems of hucksters. These texts, further, enrich our sense of the text's background: no longer can we summarize that world under such reductionist rubrics as "the rise of the middle class." The text's world insists on itself as a determinate, everyday world, a world of bodies, a world with its own internal subversive structures.

Let us begin our discussion of the city comedy by trying to enter into that world, focusing on the contradictions between the ideology of the city of London and its economic and social functioning. Such an examination will lay the basis for our understanding of typical representation in the plays. We will, first of all, be locating the text in history, so that the distance and difficulty posed for an intersubjective understanding of the text is given its due. The text swims, as it were, in its own historical sea, carried by its own currents, competing with other indigenous flora and fauna. We approach it on this difficult ground, not to render it more exotic, but to do justice to its estrangement from us, the better to search out that common horizon of consciousness that Weimann has designated as the basis for a historicized—and therefore intersubjective—understanding of the text.

Further, we will be analyzing the terms available to Jacobean dramatists for thinking about the relations between individuals and groups, social parts and social wholes. By compiling a sort of Jacobean lexicon of social logic, we will be able, perhaps, to understand how dramatists used the structures of typical representation to rhetorically transform that logic. From the regularity with which Jacobean dramatists invoked city themes and the energy with which audiences responded to them, we can assume that images like the market, characters like the Puritan, and actions like gulling resonated with the common life of the city. But unless we investigate how language organized for consciousness that common life, we will get no further in our understanding than the barren recognition that London had markets, Puritans, and con men. Such observations will provoke—have provoked—the formalist rejoinder that since there are markets, religious dissidents, and con men in most cities, such themes only emerge in the city comedy because of a generic imperative unconditioned by history.

To investigate the governing structures of London during the Jacobean period is to uncover a structure of political representation as tangled as the plot of a Jacobean tragicomedy.[7] The archaic structure of city government, a web of institutions based on guild and charter, ward and parish, survived. That structure, theoretically, organized the political life, economic functioning, and social order of the city. And in theory, even during the Jacobean period, there was complete congruence between the economic functioning of the city of London and its political organization. To "take up the freedom of the city," to become a citizen, was to join one of the recognized city livery companies: those companies regulated the wages, hours, and production standards of the city, controlled the numbers of shops and the prices of goods, and had certain other legal powers. The Common Hall, in which all liverymen had votes, was responsible (again in theory) for nominating the lord mayor, the city chamberlain, and other officers, naming one of the two sheriffs. The aldermen themselves were closely linked with the twelve great companies. And the whole structure was regulated by a charter that set forth the relations between Crown and City as if they were not relatively simple relations between a sovereign and his subjects, but a freely undertaken compact between independent, if unequal, parties.

Whether this structure had ever worked in so organic a fashion is doubtful, but resolving that question is beyond the scope of this book. What is quite certain is that this structure had only the most remote relationship to life in the city during the Jacobean or Caroline period. Then, the rapid development of the city's liberties and outparishes, which were not under the jurisdiction of the guilds—or, for that matter, the central municipal government—placed most of the new craft and industry in the city outside traditional regulation.[8] The guilds continually pressed new tradesmen in the outparishes to "take up the freedom of the city," but since many preferred to avoid paying the fees required for guild membership, and the municipal government—which could have enforced such rulings—was extremely reluctant to take jurisdiction over the chaotic and ungovernable outparishes, the guilds' injunctions were largely unheeded. On the simple level of corporate and communal citizenship, then, the ideology of the city was visibly at odds with it real structure.

The institutions of city government faced certain pressures as a result of this dissociation. Common Hall decayed as an institution (although it would later be restored as a locus for antiroyalist agitation), and the Common Hall custom of nominating one of the London sheriffs devolved, by default, to the Crown. The Crown also intervened rather directly in the nominations of other officers of the city. After James, the charter functioned less and less as a compact; the levies and taxes imposed on London took the form of direct loans, extorted individually from the magnates of the London financial community.[9]

The commercial organization of the city itself was also changing. The old pattern of cloth trade with the Low Countries was disrupted, partly by royal intervention but more seriously by the religious wars. The traditional Merchant Adventurers, still the wealthiest of the London merchant companies, were being outdistanced by Indian and Levantine traders; both groups would be challenged, around 1640, by American colonial traders.[10] Although London's merchant class was not a stable formation—wealthy merchants normally retired to the country, while their ranks were replenished with rural gentry who entered trade—these shifts in relative power altered the fabric of London life, increasing the tension between the marketplace as the terrain of commercial enterprise and the marketplace as a public communal sphere. In the case of the East Indian and Levantine merchants, the magnates of these companies were divorced from any direct relation to a popular base: the East Indian and Levantine trade, unlike the western European cloth trade, was not connected to any substantial section of the London laboring population. Many Londoners were weavers, fullers, or tailors, and so had some stake in the activity of the Merchant Adventurers, but the East Indian and Levantine trade was largely a matter of importing spices and luxury goods, often for immediate subsequent export. Further, these "companies," unlike the more traditional guilds, did not include laboring people even formally among their members. Apprenticeship in the East India Company cost from £200 to £300 in 1640—in this company, the apprentice system was a method of training the sons of members to take their places as merchants and not of recruiting apprentices as permanent wage workers. Thus, the leading strata of London merchants had become divorced from the currents of popular life on two counts: their direct economic interests were only remotely connected with the basic activities of social reproduction, and they had no ties, not even formal ones, with laboring people in the city.

The American colonial traders challenged the communal structure of the city in yet another way. While the East Indian and Levantine traders were supporters of royal power, even at the cost of their municipal authority, the American traders were brought into contact with the insurgent aristocratic sponsors of Puritan colonizing and, as interlopers in a crowded mercantile field, had reason to resent royal monopolies and commercial interventions. Many of them, in fact, were rural MP's who invested in the American companies soon after entering Commons. For them, the marketplace was no longer a medieval or Renaissance place of celebration; as a physical space, it had been displaced and abstracted. These traders, further, might be expected to share the Puritan view of the market as a corrupt institution in a fallen world, the vehicle for efficient pursuit of one's particular vocation. Like Jonson's Puritan in *Bartholomew Fair,* they rejected the festal tradition; for them, commerce was more than lawful, but the fair itself was "no better than one of the high places."[11]

Given these contradictions between the political ideology of the city and its economic structure, we can expect that urban popular culture would express the difficulties of understanding the new relations between the city and its citizens. In fact, the city had a fairly well articulated ideology, expressing its communal and traditional structure in such forms as civic pageants, official histories, the lexicon of political relations, and popular dramatic celebrations of the city. All of these areas were vulnerable to the contradictions I have been describing; in all of them, images and relations that had been straightforward were becoming problematic. As a way of mediating between the political economy I have been discussing and the relatively autonomous theatrical world of the city comedy, I would like to examine three of these forms: the vocabulary of civic relations, official history, and the civic pageants.

In the language of the city, the contradictions between commerce and celebration can be traced in the development of two terms, *liberty* and *freedom. Liberty* did not, of course, carry its full range of modern political meanings, although it certainly did imply the freedom to do as one wished, or release from a personal or capricious rule. At the same time, this sense of release implied accepting the legitimate and often legally sanctioned domain of some person or corporation. Thus, the areas under the jurisdiction of the City of London, but not part of its official territory, were called "liberties," because they were "at liberty" from manorial or shire rule. However, the liberties—which were rather extensive during our period, including Blackfriars, Whitefriars, Greyfriars, Spitalfields, Southwark, the Tower Hamlets, the Inns of Court, and some other areas—did not come under the purview of the sheriffs of London, and hence were virtually ungoverned areas. (The Crown liberties, including Blackfriars and Whitefriars, were surrendered to the City in 1608, but this jurisdiction was exercised only halfheartedly.)[12] The liberties were without watch and ward, and perhaps enjoyed relaxed ecclesiastical government, since the wardmote and vestry may have been less developed in neighborhoods completely detached from the Common Council. They were theoretically under the authority of the City, but actually places of literal liberty opened within the city by the contradictions between its legal structure and its material life. Thus, liberties were places of refuge for festive activity—for theaters and markets (Bartholomew Fair was held in Spitalfields), for gaming and houses of resort.

Paradoxically, the liberties were also populated by many Puritans, who, I have suggested, were enemies of the traditional festive marketplace. The theater was not the only communal activity that sought the legal shelter of the liberties: lectureships, meetings, and other expressions of "Christian liberty" also found a relatively secure haven there. Thus, Dol berates Face as:

> A Whore-sonne, upstart, *apocryphall* capitayne,
> Whom not a puritane, in black-friers, will trust
> So much, as for a feather! [13]

Liberty, then, one of the central terms in the vocabulary of the city, a term with many resonances in the festal culture of the marketplace, was highly contradictory and overdetermined. It meant both freedom and constraint; it invoked both a specific urban jurisdiction and an area outside the law: liberties sheltered both refugees from the traditional celebratory marketplace and its Puritan opponents. Thus, a term that initially described the process of incorporating individuals into political groups, a term that had implied a transparent and "typical" relationship between social life and the political means of representation, had become indeterminate: it described a range of contradictory relations, and it referred to those relations in a contradictory way.

The term *freedom* also invokes many of these contradictions. To "take up the freedom of the City" denoted participation in the City's independence, in that communal existence legally recognized by the charter. But by the time of James, "taking up the freedom" was a purely commercial act, and as we have noted, not a very wise one at that. In *Michaelmas Term,* Middleton plays with these senses of the word, and also with the rather rare slang term *free-woman* for prostitute: [14]

> *Helgill:*   A woman's breaking sets her up.
> Virginity is no city trade
> You're out o'th'freedom, when you're a maid. [15]

And *freedom* was of course, like *liberty,* a central term in Reformation religious discourse in such usages as "free will" and "free election." A double sense of *freedom,* invoking both its meaning of independence and that of commercial empowerment, does not survive in today's use of the word. However, the contemporary term *franchise,* meaning both the right to vote and ownership of a Burger Chef, still carries the marks of some of the diverse pressures on this term. It reminds us of the difficulty of speaking clearly, during the Jacobean period, about communal and political relations that had become economic relations.

While single words are not representations, these terms suggest the ways in which conventionally typical means of representation had become indeterminate. *Liberty* and *freedom* had designated membership in a community: *liberty* now implied a marginal status in that community, and *freedom* denoted a release from traditional religious and sexual restrictions, a dispensation from mediating forms. We have seen, in our examinations of *A Midsummer Night's Dream* and *The Duchess of Malfi,* how institutions such as marriage and the church, mediating between individual passions and social order, lend themselves to typical representation. In the case of London, the language associated with these institutions had become indeterminate, an indeterminacy that dislocated the rhetoric of the text. The solidarity between performers and audience that was assumed in *The Shoemaker's Holiday* and parodied in the induction to *The Knight of the Burning Pestle* becomes, in the city comedy, an appeal to a fragmented and divided audience. Rather than harmoniously reinforcing each other, multiple meanings speak differently to different sections of the audience.

Since the rhetoric of the plays had become complex, the writers of the city comedy were prompted to a thoughtful and subtle treatment of the contradictions we have been discussing. They were writing for an audience that could appreciate both Malevole's freedom and his foolishness. Since Harbage's initial formulation of the differences between the public and private theaters, critics have held that private theaters encouraged more topical satire, more "literary" speech, and more borrowing from the conventions of the masque. However, as Gibbons has demonstrated, city comedies, especially after the beginning of the century, were sometimes performed in both public and private theaters and were adapted to the public stage when the private theaters declined in popularity after 1606.[16] The city comedy, then, played to a dual audience: that of the private theaters, including many Inns of Court men, to whom the traditional romantic images of the city were familiar but not convincing, and a broader public audience, who would not have accepted a purely satirical treatment of those images.[17]

Middleton's exploitation of the varied senses of *freedom* in

Helgill's *Michaelmas Term* speech, for example, permits him to assert an equivalence between commerce and prostitution, even as he denies that the city trades in virginities. Such simple indeterminacy, heightened by the problematic status of Helgill as a speaker, exploits the very currency of the official language of the city, its exemption from reflection. Language intended to express a mediation between the city and its citizens actually discloses the alienation of citizens from one another, the difficulty of effecting intersubjective understanding among them.

And it is perhaps because it was impossible to articulate these contradictions directly, the very language in which they might have been discussed having been compromised by them, that indirect and literary representations of these problems are among the most revealing. Let us look, then, at two examples of the "official art" of the City before turning to the city comedy: Stow's celebration of the communal past in the *Survey of London*[18] and Middleton's attempt to celebrate the commercial present in his civic pageants.

In keeping with Stow's self-description as an "antiquarian," the *Survey* is a record of customs, places, and usages that had already been transformed. And in recording customs, Stow places special emphasis on those promoting social solidarity or a communal spirit: the keeping of markets, the giving of alms, investitures in brilliant liveries, and the celebration of traditional holidays. Consider the following account:

> In the Moneths of Iune, and Iuly, on the Vigiles of festiuall dayes, and on the same festiuall dayes in the Euenings after the Sunne setting, there were vsually made Bonefiers in the streetes, euery man bestowing wood or labour towards them: the wealthier sort also before their doores near to the said Bonefiers, would set out Tables on the Vigiles, furnished with sweete breade and good drinke, and on the Festiuall dayes with meats and drinks plentifully, whereunto they would inuite their neighbours and passengers also to sit, and bee merrie with them in great familaritie, praysing God for his benefites bestowed upon them. These were called Bonefiers aswell of good amitie amongest neighbours that, being before at controuersie, were there by the labour of others, reconciled, and made of bitter enemies, louing friendes, as also for the virtue that a great fire hath to purge the infection of the ayre.[19]

As with the city's lexicon of political relations, so with traditional public feasts: a form that had expressed intersubjective understanding has become problematic. In this case the literal opening of interiority into public life has become a nostalgic ritual. In many of Stow's chapters—consider a title like "Sports and pastimes of the old time used in this Citie"—the account of the communal city is the tale of a lost city, an account infected with utopian longing. Stow loads and overloads the typical register of his narrative, connecting the city with the greater cosmographic whole, presenting an image of a city in which there is no need for division, envy, or bitterness, no need for barriers, since all men can feast in common, openly, at peace. But such an image of unmediated intersubjectivity cannot be read as an image of lived experience: so intense is the longing that suffuses this passage that we read it as an image of an impossible city, a desired and nonexistent city, a utopian city whose relation to any real society is problematic and indeterminate.

In the civic pageants written by Thomas Middleton during his term as city chronologer, we can find a similar overloading of the typical register, with important differences. In Middleton's practice, however, the vocabulary of the masque, a genre especially rich in expressions of group relations and especially intimate in its rhetorical structure, is used to celebrate the norms of commercial life.

Perhaps the most striking instance of this desperate endeavor is *The Triumphs of Truth,* a pageant prepared for the lord mayor's accession in 1613. At the climactic moment of the pageant, the mists of error vanish, and London is displayed in tableau, surrounded by Religion, Liberality, and Perfect Love. This last figure receives further elaboration: "on her left side sits Perfect Love, his proper seat being nearest the heart, wearing upon his head a wreath of white and red roses mingled together, the ancient witness of peace, love, and union, wherein consists the happiness of this land, his right hand holding a sphere, where in a circle of gold is contained all the Twelve Companies' arms, and therefore called the sphere of True Brotherhood, or *Annulus Amoris,* the Ring of Love: upon his left hand stand two billing turtles, expressing thereby the happy condition of mutual love and society."[20]

There is, of course, much more: a display of the recipients of the Grocers' Company charity, figures of Knowledge and Modesty, of Chastity, Fame, Simplicity, and Meekness, but more important for our purposes is the assimilation of cosmic imagery—the ring with twelve signs within a sphere—to the glorification of the twelve companies, and the pairing of this symbol with a symbol of political union (the two roses) and of sexual union (the billing turtles). It would be a mistake, of course, to demand discursive or philosophic justification for the symbols mobilized in a pageant: after all, symbols in need of such justification would not be very effective in a public celebration. However, the disproportion between the cosmic range of the symbol for the twelve companies and their virtual absence as a theme in the rest of the pageant suggests that this symbol is a somewhat arbitrary construction, suggested by the number twelve rather than by a serious belief that the great liveries really were like the all-encircling zodiac. This figure stands as evidence, perhaps, of the difficulty of celebrating a commercial activity that was no longer central to the communal life of the city. It was not possible for Middleton, as it would be for Dryden, to praise the city simply as a "great emporium"; in this pageant, the celebration of accumulation is only pronounced by a character named Error.

Middleton also attempted to dramatize the global scope of London commerce. In *The Triumph of Honor and Virtue,* he shows a black king and queen traveling to London in gratitude for the blessings of trade and Christianity—an outright borrowing from Jonson's *Masque of Blackness.* This episode does solve the problem of concretely representing the city's new trade. But since the merchants most involved with Asian and Levantine trade were not members of the twelve companies and had no direct role in the governance of the City, the spectacle honoring them floats free of the rest of the pageant and becomes, in effect, an antimasque.

The city pageants are allegorical images rather than typical representations; nobody is expected to take Religion, or the Ring of Love, or the Black King, as anything but a shadowy invocation of the abstraction it refers to. But in these figures, images, and characters, Middleton is invoking harmonious relations of individuals and groups, celebrating the ideological forms that were, for his audience, the bases of intersubjectivity. This pageant can be seen, then, as an allegorical, indeterminate version of the themes Stow presented typically. And just as Stow's typicality becomes indeterminate and utopian, Middleton's allegorical celebration of intersubjective life dissolves into a series of disparate images, failing to achieve the coherence of earlier civic pageants or of the most successful masques. In the pageants, as in Stow's history, indeterminacy and typicality do not enter into a dialectical relation. They are simply at odds with each other. No text, to be sure, is ideally unified or free from contradictions. But these invocations of the city of London are marked by contradictions they cannot express or examine.

We should now have a fuller sense of both the social and the literary contexts for the city comedy. London was a complex world with its own internal structures of representation, structures whose relation to social life is anything but straightforward. And that world was also rich in texts, all sorts of texts, that attempted to translate the contradictions of civic life into one of the languages of representation. We can make our understanding of the relations between London and its world of texts more precise, and move closer to the historical and textual situation of the city comedy, by examining some cultural forms closely linked to the genre, the institutions of celebration associated with the Inns of Court.

At the simplest level, the Inns of Court are biographically linked to the city comedy; Jonson, Marston, and Middleton, the major writers in the genre, all had connections with them. Marston studied in Middle Temple. Middleton married the daughter of a clerk of chancery and was involved in constant litigation with his stepfather. Jonson dedicated *Every Man out of His Humor* to the gentlemen of the Inns of Court and lived for a time in Blackfriars.[21] The Inns were marked not only by a lively literary and political atmosphere but by a rich tradition of feasts, of times of liberty. Bakhtin recognizes the close connection of such student festivals with the celebration of the marketplace: "We have already pointed out the importance of school festivals and recreation in medieval culture and literature. The schoolmen's exuberant compositions had already attained the level of great literature and played in it a substantial role. These recreational writings were also related to the marketplace. School parodies, travesties, *faceties* in Latin and in the vernacular, prove this relation and bear inner resemblance to popular forms" (*RW,* 156).

While the scattered surviving texts of the Inns of Court revels do not suggest that these "exuberant compositions" often "attained the level of great literature," they do suggest a very close relation between the feasts celebrated at the Inns and the popular feasts of misrule analyzed by C. L. Barber.[22] In the Inns's Prince D'Amour revels, for example, a mock ruler was brought to power in a mock coronation. The schedule of these revels, as reconstructed by Finkelpearl, suggests an alternation of popular festive events—gaming, dicing, a disorderly "inspection" of the kingdom, travesties such as the "Tufftaffeta Oration" and "Fustian Answer," sexually suggestive speeches—with more courtly entertainments, such as masques and barriers.[23] The Inns of Court at liberty, then, were the Inns of Court at celebration, a celebration whose forms suggested those of carnival, of the feast of misrule, a recollection of popular and secular celebrations in the marketplace. What had been serious was parodied and profaned—lawyers engaged in mock orations much as Bakhtin's clerics recited parodies of scripture and liturgy. The rights of the body were enforced and celebrated; normal forms of authority and order were ritually degraded—when the Inns of Court revelers came to visit the Court, they were so disorderly that they could not be received.

In his illuminating *Carnival in Romans,* [24] Emmanuel Le Roy Ladurie has shown how the archaic forms of carnival could contain and release the pressures of competing social classes, how they could alternatively be used by insurgents and established powers. In the texts associated with the Inns of Court, we can trace a similar deployment of indeterminacy, a use of representational forms that had become problematic to explore the possibilities of social discourse. The literature associated with the Inns sketches out, as it were, emergent forms of consciousness.

The Inns of Court, for example, fostered not only traditional celebrations but a literary form closely linked with them—satire. This genre enjoyed a tremendous vogue at the end of the sixteenth century and was linked, through Donne and Marston, with the Inns. In satire, the festive traditions of abuse, cursing, and debasement of official forms were preserved. The language of late Elizabethan satire is closely related to the "billingsgate"—the language of abuse, the language of the body—which Bakhtin identifies as the language of the marketplace. Consider these displaced versions of the traditional billingsgate image of excrement, from Marston's *The Scourge of Villanie:*

> My minde disdaines the dungie, muddy scum
> Of abiect thoughts, and Enuie's raging hate.

> O what dry braine melts not sharp mustard rime
> To purge the snottery of our slimie time? [25]

And in Marston's cadence, a fit object for Jonson's parodies, we can hear the echoes of "free speech" of the marketplace, a speech not yet subdued to the fluid rhythms that were to mark English verse, in which the traditional four-beat line of folk meter fights, unsuccessfully, the new five-stress iambic rhythm. [26] Bakhtin's account of the subversive quality of such speech might seem excessive, if we did not keep in mind official reactions to satire: *The Scourge of Villanie,* with other satires, was burned, and the genre was forbidden. Perhaps the bishops who had ordered this suppression would have agreed with Bakhtin:

> Abuses, curses, profanities, and improprieties are the un-
> official elements of speech. . . . These elements of freedom, if
> present in sufficient numbers and with a precise intention,
> exercise a strong influence on the entire contents of speech,
> transferring it to another sphere beyond the limits of con-
> ventional language. Such speech forms, liberated from norms,
> hierarchies, and prohibitions of established idiom, become

themselves a peculiar argot and create a special collectivity, a group of people initiated in familiar intercourse, who are frank and free in expressing themselves verbally.

(*RW*, 187–88)

The satirists were claiming a similar right to free speech, a form of speech that was transposed into dramatic dialogue after the bishops' suppression; Marston was especially explicit in this claim in *The Malcontent,* where Malevole says:

Well, this disguise doth yet afford me that
Which kings do seldom hear, or great men use—
Free speech; and though my state's usurp'd
Yet this affected speech gives me a tongue
As fetterless as is an emperor's.
I may speak foolishly, ay, knavishly,
Always carelessly.[27]

But as Malevole's disguise demonstrates, free speech could never be unproblematic, especially in a theater. The "fetterless" tongue is bound, first of all, by the exigencies of "affected speech," the need to give the indeterminate register of the play its due. For the Jacobeans, such a disguise could also be more than a dramatic imperative. Censorship by the Master of Revels was alert and active, if not especially acute, and political discourse, even of the most general sort, was discouraged. A dramatist drawn to the theme of the city, then, was well advised to disguise his unfettered speaker. Such a dramatist would not have been the first or last to use traditional themes and familiar stories to say what would otherwise have been left unspoken. Just as the political language of London had become so indeterminate that intersubjectivity could be achieved only by contradictory rhetorical negotiations, so also the traditional celebratory forms of the marketplace had to be translated, expressed, and refashioned. The genre produced by both of these rhetorical transformations was the city comedy.

Representational Strategies in the City Comedy: Middleton's Indeterminacy, Jonson's Typicality

The writers of the city comedy could take the part of neither the Prologue nor the Citizen in the argument that forms the induction to *The Knight of the Burning Pestle:*

Citizen: If you were not resolv'd to play the jacks, what
need you study for new subjects purposely to
abuse your betters? Why could you not be content,
as well as others, with *The Legend of Whittington,*
or *The Life and Death of Sir Thomas Gresham with
the Building of the Royal Exchange,* or *The Story
of Queen Eleanor, with the Rearing of London
Bridge upon Woolsacks?*

Prologue: You seem to be an understanding man: what would
you have us do, sir?

Citizen: Why, present something notably in honour of the
commons of this city.

Prologue: Why, what do you say to *The Life and Death of
Francis Drake,* or *The Repairing of Fleet-privies.*[28]

Rather, they handled the interrupted and discontinuous ideology of their city by invoking the tradition of festive liberty, of the
marketplace—those traditional plots and motifs "notably in honour
of the commons of this city." In the city comedy, two strategies
emerged for presenting this material: it was either circumscribed
ideologically or formally displaced. The first strategy, in which the
indeterminate register of the text is developed but finally subordinated
to the typical relation between the text and the world, is characteristic of Jonson. It is marked by invocations of royal authority or the
demands of reason and nature, concepts that, in Jonson's dramatic
practice, simultaneously mediated the individual and communal and
invoked an ideal, authoritative, and indulgent audience. The second
strategy, formal displacement, is more characteristic of Middleton.
Here, the indeterminacy of the text is both dominant and assertive;
we are presented with a dramatic world protected from the operations
of conventional morality, and we are reminded forcibly that this
world is artificial. Both of these strategies are quite complex; both of
them allowed the writers of city comedy to refashion the traditional
images of the marketplace by subduing the motions of trade to the
misrule of the feast. A writer could celebrate the freedom of exchange,
its endless circulation, its possibilities for rapid shifting of roles and
reversals of fortune, or he could use the norms of the festival as a
corrective to the norms of commerce—the voracity of misers and
usurers can be educated by the rule of the feast. Either method
allowed the writer to invoke the traditional ideology of the city
without nostalgia, to celebrate commerce as a part of the communal
life of the city without directly falsifying the contradictory relationships between communal and commercial life that were part of

the common experience and common sense of his audience. Thus, traditional ideology was refashioned dramatically; it was "let out at the seams" to accommodate the ever-shifting relations of a market controlled by the demands of accumulation. Typical forms that had been rendered problematic and indeterminate could be re-presented, their very indeterminacy rendering them dramatically interesting. What could only be invoked in allegorical or chronicle forms, forms in which the dialectic of typicality and indeterminacy was diffuse, could be investigated in the drama, a form that fostered dialectical tension. Traditional themes "notably in honour of the commons of this city," now distanced from daily life, could become once again dramatic. What had once been romance (*The Legend of Queen Eleanor*) and had become satire (*The Repairing of Fleet-Privies*) was finally comically transformed into a series of representations that moves with tremendous freedom among images of the city as it was remembered, experienced, feared, and desired. The rich vocabulary of dramatic framings, doublings, and disguises developed by Elizabethan playwrights was mobilized to present the relations of the market as relations of freedom and dramatic play. This sense of play simultaneously suggested a moral standard against which the norms of accumulation could be judged.

Let me examine some of these assertions. First, the city comedy invokes the tradition of festive liberty, but without nostalgia. Many of the city comedies are set within, or refer to, the city's liberties. *The Alchemist* is set in Blackfriars; *Bartholomew Fair*, in Spitalfields. The solemn entry of Michaelmas Term in the induction to Middleton's play, as he is received "with music" by the other terms, recalls a very ancient festival of another liberty—the staid dancing of "measures" at the Inns of Court during the Reader's Feast. *The Alchemist* is set in a very unromanticized Blackfriars, a neighborhood populated with prostitutes, Puritans, and young law students anxious for excitement. The play turns upon Face, Subtle, and Doll's immunity from normal legal surveillance. The neighbors may be suspicious of their house, but no ward government or vestry takes note of those suspicions; the watch comes only at Mammon's call. And *Bartholomew Fair* is similarly structured by its setting within a liberty, and a highly commercialized liberty at that. Moreover, the liberty is not invoked nostalgically; in *Bartholomew Fair,* we are reminded by Grace Wellborn that "none goes thither of any quality or fashion" (*Bartholomew Fair,* 1.5.122–29). In the comedies of Middleton, the liberties are less prominent, but the traditional *topoi* of the city's commercial importance are often invoked, if ironically, as in Sir Walter's promise to the Welch Gentlewoman, his mistress, that he will "turne thee into Gold Wench,"

> And make thy fortune shine out like your bright Trade,
> A Gold-Smithes Shop sets out a Citie Mayd.
>
> (*A Chaste Maid in Cheapside,* 1.1.105-6)

And in *Michaelmas Term,* the commercial privileges of citizens are introduced in traditional terms: they are means of binding together the inhabitants of the city, signs of communal responsibility. But those terms are deceptive; in this play, the traditional relations of cosigners and sureties, presented as expressions of custom and mercy, are traps to cozen Easy out of his inheritance. The traditional communal ideology has been invoked, but not validated. Even the obligation of guildsmen to attend the funerals of their members becomes an occasion for deception: Quomodo engineers a bogus funeral to see how his death will be mourned and how his inheritance will fare. Such a subversion of communal norms, however, is not dramatically presented as reprehensible. Quomodo is as clever as he is rapacious, and his dream of landed wealth is by no means as repulsive as Overreach's dream of social status in *A New Way to Pay Old Debts.* Who, after all, can entirely hate a character who parodies Falstaff? "Stay, hah! Hast thou that wit, faith? Twill be admirable. To see how the very thought of green fields puts a man into sweet inventions!" (*Michaelmas Term,* 4.1.78-80).

The city comedy also makes use of the traditional elements of marketplace festivity. Two of these elements deserve further mention: billingsgate, or the language of abuse, and the motif of resurrection, of triumph over time and death. I have already mentioned the historical link between satirical abuse and the city comedy, and illustration of such language in the plays would be an exhausting, if interesting, procedure. Jonson, of course, was most fertile in the dramatic rendering of this language, most capable of endlessly modulating its tone. Marston and Middleton were more likely to assign billingsgate to a single character, like Cocledemoy in *The Dutch Courtesan,* or to an episode, like the christening scene in *A Chaste Maid in Cheapside.*

The motif of birth, death, and rebirth is also quite common. Characters rise from pretended death in *A Chaste Maid, Michaelmas Term,* and *The Dutch Courtesan;* are threatened with death in *The Dutch Courtesan* and *A Mad World, My Masters;* and confront the daily presence of death in *The Alchemist.* Moreover, in the city comedy we find frequent images of pregnancy and birth, including the stubborn fertility that populates *A Chaste Maid in Cheapside* with so many infants, and the figure of great-bellied Win wandering in *Bartholmew Fair.* And in both *Michaelmas Term* and *A Chaste Maid in Cheapside,* the mock funeral is a prelude to a marriage, and a forbidden marriage at that. To read such images as Christian allegory, I think, is to lose the extraterritoriality from traditional morality that the plays work to achieve. Rather, such images can be read as instances of the festive celebration of the body, seen as a secular expression of the transformative power of time, of the openness and penetrability of human beings, of the fragility of the boundaries among them and between them and nature. In Bakhtin's phrase: "The unfinished and open body (dying, bringing forth and being born) is not separated from the world by clearly defined boundaries; it is blended with the world, with animals, with objects. It is cosmic, it represents the entire material bodily world in all its elements. It is an incarnation of this world at the absolute lower stratum, as the swallowing up and generating principle, as the bodily grave and bosom, as a field which has been sown and in which new shoots are preparing to sprout" (*RW,* 27).

Since our investigations of London's ideology and social structure have shown that the traditional communal organization of the city was contradictory to its emerging commercial organization and that this contradiction created severe ideological strains, the city comedy's ability to combine traditional motifs with new themes cannot be taken for granted. Indeed, rather complex representational strategies were employed by the dramatists. Let us examine these strategies—the typical strategy of establishing the ideological boundaries of the text and the indeterminate strategy of exempting the dramatic world from conventional morality—beginning our examination with the indeterminate strategy. In *Michaelmas Term,* by presenting Quomodo's subversion of the traditional ideology of exchange and his blatant use of that ideology as a tool for deception, Middleton is handling dangerous material: he assumes unbridled accumulation as a commercial norm and refers to the compromised traditional institutions of the city. But Quomodo's behavior is rendered less problematic by the nature of the world in which he operates, a world in which the passionate behavior of Jacobean tragicomedy has been localized, rendered homely and ultimately harmless. In Quomodo's London, many have his greed, few have his charm, and none is above reproach. Thus, the play preserves the unsanctioned and subversive values of festive space as a point of reference. Any direct invocation of conventional moral values would call into question the legitimacy of the norms of the marketplace, a strategy Shakespeare may have been pursuing in *Measure for Measure*. But a writer who, like Middleton or Marston, was interested in using the values of festive space as a tool for asking questions had to open a dramatic space for these values, even if that space existed only between parentheses. One way of drawing in such parentheses was to create a world in which moral judgment was so overloaded that it was no longer a reliable way of organizing subjective experience; the audience is then thrown back on aesthetic criteria, which always favor the creative and playful virtues of the marketplace. This strategy, I think, provides some explanation for the unmotivated conversions in Middleton's plays— the insertion of anomalous and incomprehensible good behavior into the naughty world of the plays further upsets the equilibrium of conventional morality.

Jonson's typical approach to the problem of representation is characteristically straightforward. He ratifies the action of the play by invoking royal license or the needs of fallen human nature. Thus, in his 1616 dedication of *Every Man out of His Humour* to the Inns of Court, Jonson recommends the play to the gentlemen of the Inns: "Yet, I command, it lay not in the way of your more noble, and use-ful studies to the publike. For so shall I suffer for it: But when the gown and cap is off, and the Lord of liberty raignes; then, to take it in your hands, perhaps may make some Bencher, tincted with humanity, reade: and not repent him."[29]

Such an apologetic dedication recalls the fifteenth-century circular letter justifying the Feast of Fools associated with the Paris School of Theology and quoted by Bakhtin. There, such feasts are excused as concessions to "that foolishness, which is our second nature and seems to be inherent in man" and which must "freely spend itself at least once a year" (*RW,* 75). For Jonson, however, play is a concession, not to foolishness, but to a delicately ambiguous "humanity," implying both "human frailty" and "humane" (rather than "noble and use-full") study.

The values of the festive marketplace—escape from official power, freedom, secularism, and skepticism—have been consigned to the indeterminate gaps, the blank spaces left unoccupied by sanctioned work. Under the sign of indeterminacy, these values are subordinated to the official values of "noble and use-full study," but they are also ratified, preserved, and, as "humane" studies, reconciled to intersubjectivity.

A second version of this strategy is the invocation of royal authority. The Crown was the main political opponent of the City's traditional governance, but celebration of royalty was also an element in the traditional glorification of the city—as in Thomas Deloney's novels, with their nobles disguised as shoemakers and their great feasts given to kings by the guilds. A typical instance of Jonson's deployment of these themes is the epilogue to *Bartholomew Fair;* there, Johnson makes poetic license part of the king's prerogative. The king knows:

> the scope of writers, and what store
> Of leave is given them, if they take not more
> And turn it into licence: you can tell
> If we have us'd that leave you gave us, well:
> Or whether we to rage, or licence break,
> Or be profane, or make profane men speak?
>
> (Epilogue, 3–8)

Here, *licence* is used twice, first as synonomous with "abuse of liberty," and second as synonomous with "royal permission." The king is the ultimate source of the play's license; the writer appeals to him against the "envious few." Thus, the king's presence and implied permission is an assurance that the liberties taken in the play have been placed within a limited context, and those limits are constructed from the traditional ideology itself. Royal permission licenses license.

The Function of the City Comedy: *Bartholomew Fair* and *A Chaste Maid in Cheapside*

Clearly, the writers of the city comedy did not go to the trouble of inventing such complex representational strategies, of invoking such problematic themes, of reviving such compromised traditions, only to puzzle future critics. We come, then, to the question of the function of the genre, which I hold to be the translation of the relations of exchange and accumulation into the language of the feast, so that these relations could be discussed, whether that discussion was a celebration of the relations of exchange or a criticism of them.

Thus, many city comedies present an image of a world organized around accumulation and raise serious questions about this world, without focusing the audience's attention on accumulation or greed, without losing the comic tone of the play or its contact with the traditions of the popular feast. The play develops *through* unbridled accumulation, as various characters try to outwit and swindle each other; it is a transparent assumption of the play. Thus, greed may be posed as the central ethical problem of the play, but the con-

ventional answers—charity and contentment—press upon our attention less than the play's image of the lavish and carefree material life
of the festive marketplace. In *The Alchemist,* for example, although
all the characters are motivated by a desire for money, the only
characters we experience as greedy are the dupes—Mammon, the
Puritans, Drugger. When accumulation is successful, as with Doll,
Subtle, Face, and ultimately Lovewit, we experience it as cleverness
rather than greed. Similarly, in *Michaelmas Term,* it is the rapacity
and lust of Gruel/Lethe, seasoned with gratuitous cruelty, that we
condemn, rather than Quomodo's simple acquisitiveness. The desire
for money is presented as a grotesque, but simple, extension of the
pride in wealth and in astute dealing that marks Middleton's civic
pageants; in his travesty of the official forms of livery organization,
Quomodo is still close to the festive tradition. Quomodo's greedy
actions—his inveigling Easy into signing the note, or lecturing him for
having given his signature lightly—are never heavy-handed; they carry
neither the intensity nor the ambiguity of Barabas gleefully poison-
ing a convent in *The Jew of Malta.* While Quomodo—and certainly
Subtle—are not just goodhearted rascals, their cozenings are presented
in a festive spirit: Quomodo's bogus funeral, his final attempt to
preserve his wealth beyond the grave, is also an invocation of the
festive tradition of mocking death, of seeing in death itself an occasion
for rebirth, and in this case, a rearrangement of lands and spouses.

Such plays present us with images of accumulation phrased in
terms of the festal tradition of the marketplace. Accumulation and
greed are never allowed to enter the typical register of the play: they
connect with other elements of the text, like cleverness or lust, rather
than suggesting a connection between the text and its world. In *The
Dutch Courtesan,* for example, the larceny and gulling of the trick-
ster Cocledemoy are justified—in a flood of billingsgate—as correctives
to Mulligrub's commercial greed. They are seen as mere transformations of each other: "To wring the wither of my gouty, barm'd,
spigot-frigging jumbler of elements, Mulligrub, I hold it as lawful as
sheepshearing, taking eggs from hens, caudles from asses, or butter'd
shrimps from horses—they make no use of them, were not provided
for them" (3.2.39-44). Similarly, in *The Alchemist,* the confederate
tricksters parody and reverse more conventional strategies for accumulation. Mammon the projector is confounded by Subtle's
alchemic projections; the greedy and hypocritical Puritan sect is out-
witted by a conspiracy of equally greedy pretenders; Drugger the
tobacconist is gulled by retail, by degrees, with small purchases of
magic.

In these plays, as in other city comedies, trade and industry are given very direct representation. But these social relations are incorporated into forms associated with festal tradition: abuse, confrontation with death, magical rebirth, and (most happily in *A Mad World, My Masters*) celebratory feasting. Accumulation becomes, like the festal forms, a metaphor; as a metaphor, it can enter into the discourse of celebration without endangering its equilibrium.

In Jonson's comedies, this strategy was especially successful, given the security of the plays' typical grounding in structures of acknowledged authority. Consider, for example, *Bartholomew Fair*, a play in which the festival elements of celebration of the body, skepticism, billingsgate, and festal abuse, are mixed with the business of buying and selling, whether the commodity is gilt-gingerbread, roast pig, or a judge's wife. Two great-bellied women, emblems of the "lower bodily stratum," preside over the play: pregnant Win, longing for roast pork, and fat Ursula, whose pig stall is "the very womb and bed of enormity" (2.2.107). The relation between these women is entirely commercial, a relation of exchange:

> *Ursula:*   Look, who's there, sirrah! Five shillings a pig is my
> price, at least; if it be a sow-pig, sixpence more;
> if she be a great-bellied wife, and long for't, sixpence
> more for that.   (2.2.110–13)

But their enormous vitality links them with a tradition of marketplace festivity that, even in debased and commercial form, is preferable to the snobbishness of Grace Wellborn. Their accumulation is playful, the temporary hoarding of "fairings" rather than the serious accumulation of capital.

Thus, the play is performed within a series of brackets. Jonson insists on its typicality, on its reference to a particular time and place, as if to bracket away any more abstract or general interpretation. The first set of brackets, as so often in Jonson, is the acknowledgment of royal authority, an acknowledgment made directly, both in the prologue and in the epilogue we have already discussed. These speeches circumscribe the play's "license" and indicate the correct attitude toward its action:

> These for your sport, without particular wrong
> . . . The maker doth present.
>
> (Prologue, 8, 11)

But if the wrong perpetrated by Jonson's satire is not particular in the sense of being individual, the target of his attack is quite specifically designated: "your land's Faction," the Puritans. In this prologue, specifically intended to introduce the play to a privileged audience, we are directed to use a typical hermeneutic interpreting it. We will understand its characters as representations of social groups; we will read these representations best if we see them from the vantage of the "vex'd" king, for whom the play will turn the frustrations of faction into release and sport.

The second bracket is provided by the Stage-keeper's Induction, a complaint against the play as a representation: it does not catch the spirit of the fair, and it violates the conventions of the Elizabethan comedy. The Stage-keeper quarrels with both the typical and indeterminate registers of the play, as it were, when he complains both of the lack of animal prodigies that were associated with the fair and of the absence of a traditional fool. In this complaint, the play is distinguished from the festal tradition of the marketplace, but that tradition is firmly invoked. The Stage-keeper's complaint locates the play in time and space: it is an inventory of commonplaces associated with a particular fair, and of their traditional comic treatments. While he warns us that the play we will see is a "conceited scurvy one," the Stage-keeper also provides us with a review of the representational forms that shape its world of texts.

This relationship becomes explicit with the imposition of the third, and most complex, bracket. The Scrivener proclaims a compact between author and audience, an agreement that borrows the norms of the market to regulate the audience's participation in the festival of the play:

> It shall be lawful for any man to judge his six pen'orth,
> his twelve pen'orth, so to his eighteen pence, two shillings,
> half a crown, to the value of his place.
>
> (Prologue, 85-90)

The abstraction and irrationality of the cash economy are here made accessories in the traditional rhetorical agreement between author and audience. Having concluded so much, Jonson's compact with the audience takes up more explicitly the question of representation. *Bartholomew Fair* undertakes to offer substitutes for the traditional characters associated with the marketplace: instead of an ape, for example, we will see a justice of the peace. But we are cautioned against interpreting the play allegorically, or against asking "what great lady" was meant by the pig woman. The norms of accumulation presented in the play, then, are to be read as the rules for a particularly strenuous amusement—or "sport," as Jonson would have it. This sport translates archaic forms into the language of Jonson's present, transforming cash relations into traditional decorous structures and borrowing legitimacy from the king's indulgence.

So strong are these typical structures that Jonson can afford to toy with marked indeterminacy. There is, first of all, the dizzying complexity of its plot, overgrown even by Jonson's standards, refusing to resolve itself into "main" and "sub" plots in any secure way. The liberty of the fair, further, is a liberty from the constraints of the self. Consider the following stage directions:

> The JUSTICE comes in like a porter.   (5.2)
>
> QUARLOUS in the habit of the madman is mistaken by
> MISTRESS PURECRAFT.   (5.2)
>
> BUSY scents after it [the steaming pork] like a hound.   (3.2)

Zeal o'the Land Busy's hypocrisy is only an especially acute version of the unstable subjectivity that afflicts so many characters in the play; those who are stable, like Wasp, are likely to be reduced to abstract humors, or, in the language of the play, vapors. Finally, the play parodies all attempts at translation or interpretation—and its own project of translating traditional forms—when, in the final puppet show, Hero and Leander are presented as plebeians of Puddlewharf and Bankside and enter into a burlesque dispute with Busy.

In this play, accumulation and greed, extensions or distortions of the normal commercial relations of the city, have been naturalized into some harmony with the norms of the festive marketplace. Bracketed within contexts of licensed festivity, collaboration with the author, and translation of traditional modes, the commercial rogues of *Bartholomew Fair* allow the exchange relations of the city full entry into the arena of communal celebration. Buying and selling, living by one's wits, changing one's social role in pursuit of gold, become new skins for the old wine: celebration of the body, of the cycle of birth and death, in a space outside the direct control of laws and hierarchy.

But certainly other city comedies, such as *The Dutch Courtesan*,[30] give this celebration a critical edge. The relations of accumulation can be discredited by being translated into the norms of the festal marketplace. We read not so much a renovation of archaic norms as a confrontation with the limits of the new ones. Cocledemoy's festive greed, for example, *corrects* Mulligrub's commercial greed. The critical edge of city comedy, however, is sharpest in the exploration of the relations between sex and money. This relation

allows the values of the festal marketplace to be most overtly counterposed to the values of accumulation. I will end this rapid examination of the city comedy with an analysis of how the sex-money relation
is deployed, concentrating on *A Chaste Maide in Cheapside.*

Sometimes, the equation between sex and money is presented
in the city comedy as a normal feature of festive liberty. Prostitutes
are obligatory characters in city comedies;[31] they suggest personal relations controlled directly by cash, and they often parody normal
commercial life, with abundant puns on *wholesale.* These puns, and
such lines as Helgill's "virginity is no city trade," subvert the official
language of the city just as the con games of *The Alchemist* subvert
normal commercial practices. The traditional relations of corpora-
tions, guilds, and tradesmen are "thrust down," as Bakhtin would
put it, into a "lower bodily stratum." But such abuse is part of the
normal repertoire of travesty that characterizes the festive marketplace, celebrating commercial norms more than correcting them. It
certainly has that function in *Bartholomew Fair,* when Justice
Overdo's discovery of his wife in whore's clothing reminds him that
he is "but Adam, flesh and blood" (5.6.100) and would do well to
invite everyone to dinner. And in *The Dutch Courtesan,* the "whole
argument" of which is the difference between the love of a wife and
the love of a prostitute, the satire is directed more against the prostitute than against the twelve companies.

Fairly often, then, talk about prostitution is of a piece with
other "low talk": it provides a technical vocabulary, based on sex,
for discussing new relations, based on cash. But in *A Chaste Maid in
Cheapside,* the equation between sex and money becomes obsessive,
and forms the basic structure of the play. Commerce controls sex,
not only in prostitution but in all erotic relations. In one family a
"citie mayd" is sold for marriage to Sir Walter Whorehound; in
another, his willing cuckold declares of Sir Walter: "in his gold I
shine" (1.2.41). A loving couple parts, since they cannot afford
children, and a barren couple quarrels, since they will be disinheri-
ted. Even a christening feast is an occasion for the greedy consumption of sweet wine and sugar plums and for cynical commentary on
that consumption. Middleton's strategy of presenting a world alienated from conventional ethics and marked by indeterminacy produces
a play that reverses the conventional evaluation of love and money—
no important or persuasive character permits sentiment to stand in
the way of profit. So obsessive is this structuring equation that the
play becomes an abstracted, indeterminate examination of the ways
that subjectivity can be bought and sold: fathers sell daughters; hus-
bands, their wives; married couples connive at prostitution; young

men make their way by it. We cannot read the play as a direct image of social life; its patterns of repetition call for an interpreter and warn us that the play is an abstraction we must make sense of.

Within this context of indeterminacy, the traditional norms of the feast are first debased and then preserved. If the traditional wedding or christening feast becomes an excuse for accumulation, the traditional "city" topics also sanction Yellowhammer's sale of his daughter. The festive world of the marketplace suffers from its subordination to the norms of accumulation, and we are to read in these images of debasement, I think, an index of the corrupting force of those norms. The universal translation of sexuality into a commodity in *A Chaste Maid in Cheapside* directs the play's satirical edge, not at the easy target of prostitution, but at the more central problem of the development of an urban society that could no longer be ordered by traditional norms, in which the fairy-tale plot of marriage between a tradesman's daughter and a gentleman had become a story of greed rather than of love triumphing over rank.

Middleton is able to restore the play to the context of the festival, and to preserve its indeterminacy, only by an audacious shift of tone in the final scene, when a bogus funeral leads to weddings, reunions of estranged spouses, and a feast. The play's final image of the resurrected lovers preserves the celebratory tone of the festal marketplace; it is a utopian image of communal re-creation, of the pretense of freedom so intensely experienced that it becomes real:

> *Touchwood Sr.:* I cannot thinke, there's any one amongst you
> In this full faire assembly, Mayd, Man, or
> Wife,
> Whose Heart would not have sprung with
> joy and gladness
> To have seene their mariage day?
> *All:* It would have made a thousand joyfull Hearts.
> *Touchwood Sr.:* Up then a pace, and take your fortunes,
> Make these joyfull Hearts, here's none but
> Friends.
> ⟨*MOLL and TOUCHWOOD JUNIOR rise from the coffin.*⟩
> *All:* Alive sir? ô sweet deere Couple.
> (*A Chaste Maid in Cheapside,* 5.4.24–31)

This moment stands as an invocation of the communal festive marketplace, to which all now come as celebrants, and as a critique of the commercial marketplace, to which all had come as commodities.

Middleton, more than other writers of city comedy, and more acutely in this late play than in his early work, understood the tensions between these two forms of common life. But all the writers of city comedy allowed themselves to be perplexed by the questions this contradiction posed in the official ideology of their city.

What has this investigation told us about the connections among representations, social relations, and questions of genre? Not surprisingly, as we have moved beyond individual texts, our understanding of the relations between typicality and indeterminacy has grown more complex, so that in asserting the dominance of one register over the other, we can speak more concretely of a representational strategy in which one register brackets or encloses or subverts the other.

Further, our investigation of city comedy also violates some conventional expectations about the relation between "realism" and social commentary. For a critic like Lukács, typicality, by linking the text with the world, prompted the writer to a progressive, or at least critical, commentary on social life. As veteran readers of postmodernist texts, we are perhaps not surprised when Jonson's use of typicality, by linking his plays firmly with the world he lived in, allowed him to confirm and celebrate the basic social relations of that world while taking into account all sorts of deviant material.

Still less are we surprised when a writer in the same genre, Middleton, committing himself to the most audacious indeterminacy, produces plays that are deeply critical of emergent social relations. Indeed, both the world of the text and the world of texts surrounding the city comedy are marked by nobility: the single play can be read as a momentary resolution of evanescent social images, some of them literary, others drawn from the repertoire of "common sense." And this is perhaps the most striking result of our investigation: at this level of close examination, the world of the text and the world of texts tend to merge. The social world of the play consists of relations formed by texts; texts appear as alternate forms of social relations. The task of the hermeneutic interpreter is not to privilege one world over the other, but to invoke the shadowy images of received ideas, stereotypes, popular texts, and transformed literary texts that hover about the work, so that the text appears as a commentary on them. Raymond Williams's notions of "emergent" and "residual" structures of feeling (*Marxism and Literature,* 123–27) provide us with conceptual tools for sorting those images out; an understanding of the dynamic of representation helps us to understand how they come together in a text.

If we look at a less compact genre, one that does not merely respond to a historical moment and a body of discourse but also in-cludes its own history, our investigation will become still more com-plex. The world of texts will include, for the author as well as the reader, a body of formal criticism and interpretation. Let us confront this complexity by turning to the bildungsroman, a genre with its own history, linked since its inception to the norms of typical representation.

4

THE HERMENEUTICS OF THE BILDUNGSROMAN: THE INTERPENETRATION OF TYPICALITY AND INDETERMINACY

The Bildungsroman and Self-conscious Representation

In this book so far, we have worked through a series of readings integrating increasingly complex and more highly determined elements of the writer's situation into our understanding of the text's dialectic of representation. The final step in such a process, appropriately enough, is reflexive: I will try to take into account some of the ideas about representation, typicality, and indeterminacy that shaped a major genre, the bildungsroman. Unlike the city comedy, the bildungsroman was and is a self-conscious genre; the first bildungsroman, Goethe's *Wilhelm Meisters Lehrjahre,* was widely imitated in Germany, and was a central text for many Victorians. The novel of education or self-formation has been popular for British and American writers, although the Anglo-American tradition does not recognize the exfoliation of subgenres (such as *Erziehungsroman* and *Entwicklungsroman*) accepted in Germany.[1] And, while French critics usually acknowledge very few novels as examples of the French bildungsroman, these are among the most generically sophisticated we have: Flaubert's *L'éducation sentimentale* and Stendhal's *Le rouge et le noir.* The knowledge that one is reading or writing a bildungsroman, therefore, becomes an element in the dialectic of representation.

Early practitioners of the genre, however, shared yet another set of concerns. They were quite interested in problems of representation, and especially in a range of issues—the relation of individuals to groups, questions of reference and intersubjectivity—that we have been grouping under the topic of the typical. These questions, further, were often seen in social as well as aesthetic terms. Let us look at two levels of generic consciousness, then—ideas about representation in general and about the bildungsroman in particular—and consider their implications for the task of interpretation.

In German intellectual circles at the beginning of the nineteenth century, the topic of representation was not a simple aesthetic matter—if aesthetics can ever be simple.[2] As deployed by Friedrich

Schleiermacher, sometimes held to be the father of modern hermeneutics, representation was a utopian theme, recalling the most intensely felt claims of enlightenment: "Thus there dawned on me
what is now my highest intuition. It has become clear to me that
every man is meant to represent humanity in his own way, in a special
combination of its elements, so that it may reveal itself in every
possible way, and that in the fullness of infinity everything that can
come forth from its womb may become reality."[3] The logic that
supports this passage is not new for us: the one stands for many, not
because it is average, but because it is individual. The individual is
special precisely because of his or her situation in universal history.
For Schleiermacher, history and subjectivity were linked by the relation of representation, and representation meant typicality.

For British writers, matters were not much different. For
example, G. H. Lewes, one of the most influential Victorian critics,
wrote in the introduction to his own novel of formation, *The Apprenticeship of Life* (1858): "To make my hero understand life I am
forced to make him pass through all the great typical dilemmas of
life so that at the close we may say of him, as of the 'many wandering and many-teared' Ulysses . . . 'He learned from all he suffered.' "[4]
Typicality is here the vehicle that locates a character in a web of
social relations, including a relation with a reader. It is a matter of
contradiction and consciousness, of dilemmas and learning from
them, rather than a simple abstraction or an average instance. These
relations give the work its intersubjective force, as Lewes was later to
comment on Charlotte Brontë's novels: "From out of the depths of
a sorrowing experience, here was a voice speaking to the experience
of thousands."[5] Lewes was abreast of Continental philosophy and
could easily have derived these categories from the Germans. But he
need have looked no further afield than Coleridge's *The Friend:*
"Never let it be forgotten that every human being bears in himself
that indelible something which belongs equally to the whole species
as well as that particular modification of it which individualizes
him."[6] The link between an individual and the universal species is
again a matter of representation, an "indelible something" that marks
us in the most interior parts of ourselves. Even individuality is only
a modification of this interior commonality. It follows that the most
subjective, interior narrative will represent what is most widely
shared—a basic assumption of typical representation.

As a critical term, however, *typical* could be double-edged. In
a comment on Dickens, Lewes begins and ends by invoking the
intersubjective, universalizing power of typicality, but drifts into the

reductive traditional sense of a "type character" in the middle of the paragraph:

> It was this which made him a creator, and made his creations universally intelligible, no matter how fantastic and unreal. His types established themselves in the public mind like personal experiences. Their falsity was unnoticed in the blaze of their illumination. Every humbug seemed a Pecksniff, every nurse a Gamp, every jovial improvident a Micawber, every stinted serving wench a Marchioness. Universal experiences became individualized in these types; an image and a name were given, and the image was so suggestive that it seemed to *express* all that it was found to *recall,* and Dickens was held to have depicted what his readers supplied.

Lewes was to remain uncomfortable with this aspect of Dickens, which he referred to as his "hallucinatory" power.[7] His discomfort with distorted, expressive, or grotesque versions of fictional individuality echoes Schiller's lament on the forms of subjectivity available in specialized modern society: "Everlastingly chained to a single little fragment of a whole, man himself develops into nothing but a fragment. Thus little by little the concrete life of the individual is destroyed in order that the abstract idea of the whole may drag out its sorry existence."[8] The logical relations are the same as those Schleiermacher celebrated, but the tone is quite different. Hallucination, negation, abstraction—these are themes I have been locating in the indeterminate register of representation. And indeed, conventional criticism, especially in Victorian England, has never been much at ease with indeterminacy, as we shall see when we return to Lewes's treatment of Dickens. But I should note first that in these quotations, the logical structures of typicality—the one as the representation of the many, intersubjectivity, universality, and particularity—are presented as analogues to the process of self-formation. The potentialities latent in universal humanity can be realized in the life of an individual, but only if they are arranged in an orderly series. The individual, then, undertakes a labor of self-culture that invokes the course of universal history. The formed life is a privileged juncture of meanings and relations, one that becomes fully significant because of its relation to other lives. It is not surprising that the plot of the bildungsroman so often suggested a broader historical plot, a telos of history, when, as Kant put it, "all the seeds which nature has planted can be fully developed, and the human species can fulfill its destiny on earth."[9]

The nineteenth-century concern for self-cultivation and its interest in dialectical logic, as well as the habit of seeing representation as a basic relation of social life, made the bildungsroman a natural topic for literary critical reflection. And indeed, in the first significant critical discussion of the bildungsroman, Wilhelm Dilthey wrote of *Wilhelm Meister:* "Goethe's work shows human formation in various stages, shapes, epochs of life. It pleases because it does not depict the whole world together with its deformities and the struggle of evil passions for existence; the brittle material of life is separated out."[10] Here, *shows* is a central word; human self-formation will be made presentable by being doubly transformed. Life is to be divided into epochs and stages, and its "brittle material" is to be abstracted out. The process of self-formation cannot be described directly; the bildungsroman is not conceived as an unmediated record of experience. It must be shaped and abstracted; it will therefore require interpretation.

But like the broad theme of representation, the project of the bildungsroman could be interpreted in either an optimistic or a pessimistic tone, as a confirmation of human possibilities or as a meditation on the difficulties of achieving understanding. William Thackeray's *Pendennis*,[11] for example, opens with an assertion of the author's determination to write about "a Man" (xviii), with all his weaknesses, in the hope of reconciling estranged generations. But in the same novel, the narrator later reflects:

> How lonely we are in the world! How selfish and secret, everybody! You and your wife have pressed the same pillow for forty years and fancy yourself united.—Psha, does she cry out when you have gout, or do you lie awake when she has the toothache? . . . Ah, sir—a distinct universe walks about under your hat and under mine—all things in Nature are different to each—the woman we look at has not the same features, the dish we eat from has not the same taste to the one and to the other—you and I are but a pair of infinite isolations, with some fellow-islands a little more or less near to us.   (1:149)

Here, the language that normally expresses commonality—"universe," "Nature," and "infinite"—invokes separation, alienation, and the impossibility of establishing any secure relation between discourse and referent. The Victorian lexicon of typicality has been raided and placed at the service of indeterminacy.

And in fact, indeterminacy was the great scandal of representa-tation for Victorian critics. We have already mentioned Lewes's dis-comfort with Dickens "hallucinatory" vividness; he later apologizes for applying so derogatory a term to such a sound writer: "Let me say that I am very far indeed from wishing to imply any agreement in the common notion that 'great wits to madness nearly are allied;' . . . and further, that I have never observed any trace of the insane tem-perament in Dickens' works, or life, they being indeed singularly free even from the eccentricities which often accompany exceptional powers; nevertheless . . ."[12] Nevertheless, Lewes continues, there is something unreal in Dickens's vividness of presentation. Dickens's ability to write novels that draw readers into the act of interpretation, that prompt them to negate conventional categories for understand-ing experience, to construct images that challenge by their lack of reference to unmediated experience—all these qualities, which we would analyze under the topic of indeterminacy, were simply embar-rassments for Lewes. In Victorian literary theory, the early bildungs-roman was simply a typical representation; readers and writers were troubled by the genre's collusion with indeterminacy, but their critical methods and structures of feeling were not adapted to understanding the interdependence between typicality and indeterminacy.

That interdependence is quite acute in the case of the bildungs-roman, and we must now leave the framework of nineteenth-century theory to analyze it. We will then consider the hermeneutic situation we have constructed for ourselves, as readers who share certain assumptions with some nineteenth-century audiences but are at odds with them in others.

Indeterminacy is asserted by the baldest possible statement of the theme of the bildungsroman—conscious human self-formation. The project of the novel's protagonist must necessarily be reflexive: he forms himself as a subject; he works on forming himself as an object. And so the most typical of logical structures, in which an individual stands for a group, generates the most indeterminate of narratives, in which a protagonist is alienated from himself in the very act of achieving self-consciousness. This alienation, of course, need not be a misfortune: if Hegel speaks of works of art as objecti-fications or alienations, he does not intend us to dislike art for that reason. All forms of labor imply some degree of alienation. But if self-objectification is not a misfortune for the protagonist of the bildungsroman, it is certainly a problem for the reader. Max Beerbohm was one of many readers who thought Wilhelm Meister's self-formation mechanical and sterile. Equating Goethe with his protagonist, Beerbohm wrote: "Of Goethe we are shy for such reasons as that he was never injudicious, never lazy, always in his best form—and always in love with some lady or other just so much as was good for the development of his soul and his art, and never more than that by a tittle."[13] Indeed, Goethe seems to recognize this difficulty, and to integrate an image of it into the final chapters of *Wilhelm Meisters Wanderjahre.*[14] The novel ends with a tableau of Lucindor and his beloved Lucinda embracing. Lucindor, joyful and incredulous, watches this embrace in a luminous mirror, framed against a country landscape. Here, the natural and the artificial are indistinguishable; the image is artifical precisely because it is a direct record of an actual event, like a television camera engineered by some deranged optician. The image is splendidly indeterminate because it is ingeniously typical, and this interdependence stems directly from the problems posed by the project of self-cultivation: Is the final embrace of the rhyming pair sincere and spontaneous or calculated and suspect?

The problem of interiority and spontaneity, of the self as subject and object, is also phrased in a second form in this genre: Is education an interior process, or a matter of negotiating with external forces? The meeting of Lucindor and Lucinda has been carefully managed by the Society of the Tower. Is the meeting a full, adequate expression of their inwardness or the triumph of an external plan? The issue, clearly, is meant to lie open, but even to pose this question requires the bildungsroman to mobilize both typical and indeterminate registers of representation. We can understand something of this dialectic by considering how the process of self-formation might be represented in only one register.

If, on the one hand, the bildungsroman were to be written as a purely typical narrative—assuming that such a thing is possible— the protagonist's interiority would translate directly into intersubjectivity; it could only be expressed by being shared immediately; there would be nothing secret or inexpressible. Everything external to the protagonist, then, could appear in the text as "nature"—the same force that shapes the protagonist manifesting itself in a different, unconscious and objectified, form. There would be no real tension or difference between the interior and the external; they would be differently modulated expressions of the same kinds of experience, the experience of intersubjective understanding. *The Prelude,* in fact, is as close as we can come to a narrative of self-formation in the purely typical register, and a puzzling work it is for audiences who expect to read it like a novel.[15]

On the other hand, if only the indeterminate register were available in the bildungsroman, everything interior could only be expressed by being alienated from both the protagonist and the reader. The fact that a subjective state had been given objective expression would deprive it of any authentically interior quality.[16] And since the interior is the unknown, in a totally indeterminate bildungsroman the external world would consist of a series of deceptive surfaces, distanced and distorted clues to other subjectivities as unknowable to the protagonist as his or hers is to us. In a representation confined to indeterminacy, there can be no tension between the interior and the external, because the two modes are so radically separated that they have no contact with each other. Joyce's *Portrait of the Artist as a Young Man,* with is succession of mutually negating attempts at an accommodation between inner and outer, is a text consumed by indeterminacy—and a puzzling book it is for an audience that expects a bildungsroman.

The two contradictions we have been considering—between the self as subject and as object and between the interior and the external—were seen by German classical theorists as two expressions of the same duality. Friedrich Schiller, in his eleventh letter on *The Aesthetic Education of Man,* distinguishes something in man "that endures, and something that perpetually alters," which he designates as persons and their conditions.[17] Person is free and grounded in it-self; condition is grounded in time. If he integrates changing conditions into his subjectivity, man succeeds in maintaining a "never-changing ego," a project that can be accomplished by organizing a world of perception and form. In this way, influenced by art, the fragmentary and specialized individuality of modern culture can be transcended. Here, the self as object is located in time; the self as subject, elevated above it. The world is simultaneously a simple field for subjective cre-ativity and, as the ground of conditions, the determiner of subjectivity.

For the bildungsroman, such a discursive resolution of the con-tradictions between subject and object, interior and exterior, is im-possible. And so certain thematic clusters have served as pretexts or occasions for re-presenting these contradictions, and these clusters of themes, as ways of phrasing the relations between individuals and groups, between individuals and history. They include the familiar exigetic categories of this book: the family and the state.[18] The state was an important theme for Schiller, and Goethe also investigates it in *Wilhelm Meister.* Later English writers like Disraeli and Bulwer-Lytton would signal the successful completion of the hero's educa-tion by having him stand for Parliament, taking his place in the ruling circles of the state and becoming literally "representative." Similarly, the themes of choosing a vocation and establishing a family join the interior and the exterior, allowing the writer and the interpreter to establish a relation between the typical and the indeterminate registers of the novel. What distinguishes the use of these themes in the bildungsroman from their appearance in Shakespeare's history plays or in *The Duchess of Malfi* is that for the bildungsroman, these themes are generally reflexive. The bildungsroman's treatment of the state is not only a discursive investigation of political forms but also an investigation of a fundamental problem posed by all relations between individuals and groups, the problem of social and textual representation.

This reflexivity can be most conveniently demonstrated by looking at the theme of memory, which figures prominently in many of the novels we will discuss.[19] While not usually cited as a concern of the bildungsroman, the theme of memory implies strong connections between the objective and the subjective; it is a theme that invites the conjunction of the typical and the indeterminate registers. By means of memory, history is domesticated and becomes available to subjectivity: consider the authority of the "eyewitness account." But like all other narratives, memory is a fallible abstraction from the irreproducible variety of the lived world. As record of and judgment on the lived world, then, memory mediates the typical and the indeterminate registers of the text.

For the Victorians, the central text on memory was *The Prelude*. While German theorists continued to pose the contradiction between person and condition as a fundamental question of narrative, a question of how the seriality of plot could express the simultaneity of consciousness, British writers tended to mediate this contradiction by allowing a protagonist to experience himself as a constant witness to his own constant change.[20] The hero, in short, remembers.

And memory, of course, had been for the romantics the crucible for transforming emotion into art. Memory would ensure continuity of the personal subjectivity that changed and developed, and it provided a vehicle whereby history could be understood and interiorized. For memory is not simply an image of one's own life; it is also an individual appropriation of the historical world, since a novelist describes characters' subjectivities by recording their reactions to the lived world. Such reactions can only mean anything to us if we compare them to our own representations of a remembered world.

Strategically located between the objective world and subjective understanding, memory is also crucial for the bildungsroman because it corresponds to the subject-object relations of self-formation. Memory provokes emotion—nostalgia, regret—and identification. But the theme of memory also allows a narrator to become a spectator. Such detachment may be deliberately cultivated, as when Stendhal's Henry Brulard excuses his cynical narrative of loves past: "I am trying to destroy the spell, the dazzling character of events, by thus considering them in military fashion."[21] Any act of recollection will provide two locations in the text for the reader, two choices for emotional identification or distance. We can identify with what is remembered or with the act of remembering. The first location, which asserts a relation between the text and the world, corresponds to the typical register of representation; the second, which implies alienation and abstraction, to the indeterminate. Given this dual relationship and the corresponding close articulation of typicality and indeterminacy in the bildungsroman, it is not surprising that memory should be a recurring theme in the genre. Later in our analysis of the bildungsroman, we will discuss the significance of memory in *David Copperfield,* Stendhal's *La Chartreuse de Parme,* and Doris Lessing's *The Four-Gated City,* but we might also have invoked the retrospective structure of *Jane Eyre,* the problem of suppressed memory and regression in *Great Expectations,* or the codification of memory into ritual in *Wilhelm Meister.*

If we shift our focus from the fine structure of the bildungsroman to the global problems it addresses, however, the theme of memory, like those of family, state, and vocation, becomes a way of investigating the relations between individuals and history. It is part of the genre's power, I think, that in these novels, issues of representation are so closely linked with the novel's meditation on social life. This most typical of questions, a question about relations between individuals and groups, suggests in the bildungsroman two indeterminate kinds of answers: socially critical answers, in which the individual attempts to transform or transcend social relations, and utopian answers, in which social relations are beneficently arranged to foster the growth of the protagonist. Both criticism and utopia are modes of indeterminacy, suggesting as they do that things could well be otherwise, and both operate through negation and abstraction. And the bildungsroman has traditionally been a critical genre; Wilhelm Meister's self-culture is the first of many to begin with a rejection of the middle class: "I know not how it is in foreign countries; but in Germany a universal, and if I may say so, personal cultivation is beyond the reach of anyone except a nobleman. A burgher may acquire merit; by efforts he may even educate his mind; but his personal qualities are lost, or worse than lost, let him struggle as he will."[22] But if it begins in criticism—criticism oddly directed against the victims of class divisions rather than their beneficiaries—*Wilhelm Meister* ends with the utopian machinery of the Society of the Tower, just as *Jane Eyre* ends with the utopian assertion, "Reader—I married him!" and *The Way of All Flesh* ends in a secular utopia of wealth and cultivation.

Indeed, the elementary structure of a novel of self-formation fosters both critical and utopian impulses. The protagonist must define himself against social relations, but his very project of self-formation implies a certain openness of history. The protagonist is an exceptionally swift runner along a historical path, a telos that culminates, as Tennyson put it, in a "crowning race"

> Whereof the man, that with me trod
>   This planet, was a noble type
>   Appearing ere the times were ripe. [23]

We have become thoroughly entangled in the ideology of the bildungsroman: even while we suggest that it might be transcended, we invoke a classic apology for the ideology on which it is based. Perhaps, then, it is time to consider our hermeneutic situation in relation to the genre. How can we in the twentieth century read the bildungsroman?

To understand this genre, we can no longer afford the fiction that typicality and indeterminacy are tools of interpretation—objects independent of the text and reader, self-subsisting, and technically adapted to the task of interpretation. For, as a series of assumptions about the relations of individuals and groups and as a series of interpretive canons that codify the representative power of individual lives, typicality is in these texts as much as it is for the reader. (Or perhaps, since it is for the reader, it is in the text.) In fact, since both the assumptions and the canons of typicality are called into question by the novels themselves, typicality—or one of the topics we have subsumed under that term—is likely to be an explicit theme in the novel. Thus, the bildungsroman initially appears as a direct reflection of one of our central interpretive categories, as a genre that explains itself. We begin to suspect that this congruence of categories is too neat, and that when a text offers itself to us so easily we are consuming it rather than interpreting it.

Indeed so. For, if the theorists of the bildungsroman were concerned with questions of typicality, they were embarrassed by questions of indeterminacy, although in the texts themselves, as we have been discovering, indeterminacy and typicality are very closely linked. Moreover, nineteenth-century critical theorists might use *typical* to refer to the traditional type character, as Lewes did, or to invoke biblical types, as in the Tennyson quote. On both counts, nineteenth-century notions of typicality tended toward rationalism and objectivism, as if, in the typical, a whole range of experiences were not merely invoked and made available to interpretation but had become—or should become—really present, and transparently accessible to the reader. To value the typical was to value those experiences.

The bildungsroman, then, does not simply reflect our interpretive categories back to us. It provokes and fosters an interpretive reflection on the basic relations of representation, a reflection it cannot limit or control. In reading a history play, we are invited to consider certain political and subjective relations, but we will not take up that invitation in the play's own terms; we will not reflect soberly on the foolishness of violating primogeniture. In reading a bildungsroman, to be sure, the temptation is much more to replicate the logical structure of the text in our interpretation of the protagonist's life. If the text invites a reflection on subjective self-formation and history, it is likely to invoke at the same time an operative structure of feeling that prompts us to see these two processes as metaphors for each other and links them both by notions of progress or utopia. Indeed, we were just so entangled in the categories of *In Memoriam* a page or so back. The net of social life still binds us to the characters of the bildungsroman, to its initial audience, to its writers. They are our past, or they are no one's.

But the representational categories of the bildungsroman do not confirm such easy affirmations. On the simplest level, we may be put off by the details of plotting—Dickens killing off Dora's dog to heighten the pathos of her death. Or we may need to abstract from the novel in order to manage our identification with the protagonist: we may read Jude's exclusion from the university as an image of other forms of class exclusion. And as interpreters, we do not wholly share the nineteenth-century uneasiness with hallucinatory images, its belief in the historical plot that would eventually justify individual lives, or even its familiarity with scriptural modes of figuration. In short, our reading of the novels' representational structures will value their indeterminate registers more than the initial authors or audiences would have liked. For them, the bildungsroman was an attempt to subdue the "brittle material of life" to the forms of typicality; we are not so likely to be convinced of the success of that struggle.

Our relation to the bildungsroman, then, is dialogic. The texts' original categories call out to us; the net of social life still binds us to this audience, only a few generations removed from us. But we also read their demands for affiliation as statements about their historical situation and our own past or as questions about the categories we have brought to the act of interpretation. Even in our desire to give the indeterminacy of these novels its due, then, in our desire to listen to their muffled voice of abstraction and negation, there is an intersubjective and dialogic interest.

And, finally, we confront in the bildungsroman not just "this text," but always "these texts," a series of novels that comment on one another, influence one another, and question one another's assumptions. Least of all here, then, can we see ourselves as objective critics, inspecting a reified formal structure. We are working with a series of mutually exigetic texts; we stand beside them, not in them or away from them. We are caught in a web of commentary that we are ourselves helping to weave.

David Copperfield and the "Normal" Bildungsroman

Let us use, then, the traditional exigetic method of close reading and consider a canonic bildungsroman, *David Copperfield,* beginning with the first sentence of the text. We shall then turn to some later novels that call into question the relation between typicality and indeterminacy asserted in a "normal" text like *David Copperfield.* Our interest is not in composing a history of the genre, although we will work chronologically, but in analyzing a number of representational strategies that confront, in one way or another, its formal and ideological limits.

With its first sentence, *David Copperfield* is projected as a presentation, a "showing" of the narrator's life for which no reductive formula can substitute: "Whether I shall turn out to be the hero of my own life, or whether that station will be held by anybody else, these pages must show."[24] The re-presentation of the narrator's life is given dramatic shape—it may have a plot; it must have a hero. The novel's opening implies that the ideal life is fully shaped and formed, that the narrator would do well to be artificial. At the opening of the novel, then, the narrator is situated outside of his own life. He takes up a station with us to watch that life unroll into the future, even though his is the privileged vantage of a spectator who knows the ending of the story.

The self is thus both subject and object of the narrative, and this dialectical relation structures the novel's basic mode of representation. The novelist repeatedly refers to his relation to the reader and to the life he narrates, installing the reader as his judge, so that David's life is seen as a blank or vacancy only realized when it is inscribed in a text: "Looking back, as I was saying, into the blank of my infancy, the first objects I can remember as standing out by themselves from a confusion of things, are my mother and Peggotty. What else do I remember? Let me see" (*DC,* 12). The narrative prompts memory, rescuing mother, Peggotty, and David's infancy from oblivion. We seem, in this passage, to be witnessing the actual birth of a consciousness, although we are in fact witnessing the fictional birth of a narrative. But throughout this novel, the narrator's struggles with the tale are offered us as an analogue, or even a substitute, for the protagonist's struggle with his life. Indeed, the narrative and David's life are both surrounded with dreams and shadows:

> I lay in my basket, and my mother lay in her bed; but Betsey
> Trotwood Copperfield was forever in the land of dreams
> and shadows, the tremendous region whence I had so lately
> travelled.   (*DC,* 11)

> O Agnes, O my soul, so may thy face be by me when I close
> my life indeed; so may I when realities are melting from me,
> like the shadows which I now dismiss, still find thee near me,
> pointing upward!   (*DC,* 751)

The author is not only divinely omniscient, he is also divinely creative, plucking his life's story and significance out of an original chaos, dismissing Betsy Trotwood, his feminine double, into oblivion in the first chapter of the story, only to produce her as his daughter in the last. Even when the narrative—and our attention—are absorbed in the objectified image of the young and victimized David, or the foolish and adolescent David, his own narrative voice establishes him as a fully self-possessed subjectivity.[25] Indeed, as these two quotations illustrate, the narrator is most subjectively powerful when the protagonist is most objectified: as David the character meets the limits of birth and death, the narrator appears as the lord of these limits, able to transcend normal human experiences.

But if Dickens's narrative strategy permits David Copperfield to take both sides in the subject-object dialectic, it also produces some problems in the text. Sometimes, it is only a matter of which verb tense to use: "As I *walked* to and fro daily between Southwark and Blackfriars, and lounged about at mealtimes in obscure streets, the stones of which may, for anything I know, *be worn* at this moment by my childish feet, I *wonder* how many of these people were wanting in the crowd that used to come filing before my eyes in review again, to the echo of Captain Hopkins's voice" (*DC,* 145, my italics). Here the ambiguous "be worn" transfers the text from the past to the present, and shifts the narrative from the typical register, which absorbs us in David's London life, to the indeterminate, as we take our place beside the observing and reflecting narrator.

But often, the shift between subject and object is harder to negotiate. Early in the first chapter, David describes the sale of his caul: "I was present myself, and I remember to have felt quite un-comfortable and confused, at a part of myself being disposed of in that way" (*DC*, 2). This sale foreshadows David being "disposed of" when he later becomes inconvenient to the Murdstones; it also re-minds us of Schiller's distinction between person and circumstance. The caul is, on the one hand, intimately a part of David—it is, literally, his birthright. But it has long been separated from him, and, auctioned, bartered, raffled, and misunderstood, it is subject to all the vicissi-tudes of commerce. David's qualm here is a reaction to the ojectifi-cation of his self, to its subjection to an eccentric cash nexus. In the final chapter of the novel, we will find this uneasiness subdued, and the objectified self given a natural, beneficent incarnation: "I find it very curious to see my own infant face, looking up at me from the Crocodile stories; and to be reminded by it of my old acquaintance, Brooks of Sheffield" (*DC*, 748). David has managed to transmute the objectified image of himself from a withered caul to a living infant, to cast off those parts of his person that where shaped by circum-stance, while keeping hold of some essential ego.

On the level of plot, this project is represented by the tension between interior and exterior sources of self-formation. The prob-lem David faces in the novel is simultaneously to discipline his un-disciplined heart and to make his own way in a world of inadequate schemes for ordering his life. David must evade the "improvements" of the Murdstones, who have a plan for him, but he must also fight free of the neglect and formlessness that is most acute at the ware-house, but also shapes his life at Salem House, the disorderly school, and during his sleepy tenure at Doctor's Commons. What David must win, by long and solitary journeys, is a place in which spirit and form, interiority and activity, the self and the communal, can begin ade-quately to join. Such a place can be found, in his youth, in Betsy's eccentric household; in his maturity, in his own establishment with Agnes. In contrast with David, two of the presiding spirits of the novel represent rigid externalized formation and simple self-indulgence—Uriah Heep and Steerforth. Heep, product of the institutionalized culture of the workhouse, learned there to turn humility into a tool of unenlightened self-interest: "Father and me was brought up at a foundation school for boys; and mother, she was likewise brought up at a public, sort of charitable, establishment. They taught us all a deal of umbleness—not much else that I know of, from morning to night. We was to be umble to this person, and umble to that; and to pull off our caps here, and to make bows there; and always to know our place, and abase ourselves before our betters. And we have such a lot of betters!" (*DC*, 649). And Heep ends the novel in the grips of a second institution, the prison, in which he is appropriately kept in solitary confinement, drenched in spleen, saying that the world would be a better place if we could all be made to come to prison.

But Heep's opposite number, Steerforth, is in all things indulged. His mother explains why he was put to school at the disreputable Salem House: "It was not a fit school generally for my son, far from it; but there were particular circumstances to be considered at the time, of more importance even than that selection. My son's high spirit made it desirable that he should be placed with some man who felt its superiority, and would be content to bow before it; and we found such a man there" (*DC*, 253). The humility of the Heeps is reflected in the arrogance of the Steerforths; the Heep's corruption of the upper-class Wickfield mirrors Steerforth's seduction of the lower-class Emily. And while Heep profits from his proudly displayed re-formation in prison, Steerforth dies in a sea storm, suggestive of disordered passions, face to face with a man he had never permitted himself to see: Emily's lover Ham.

Heep and Steerforth are both warnings and temptations for David. He is in danger of being trapped by his cavalier distaste for Heep or of being seduced by Steerforth and can only negotiate these dangers by schooling his conscious perception, learning to "penetrate the mysteries of his own heart" (*DC*, 890). For David, such an education is undertaken by writing. In writing, he objectifies himself, and this objectification is liberatory: the narrator will care for and deliver the fictional David, who has been neglected and put at risk. The objectified self formed in writing also signifies his self-understanding; it redeems the errors of his youth. And David's self-understanding connects his life to other lives, so that he grows in his appreciation of characters like Traddles, Aunt Betsey, and the Micawbers, and eventually, as a distinguished author, finds himself a sort of official repository for intersubjective sympathy. Such a solution to the problem of self-objectification, such a mediation of the interior world and external reality, is of course firmly within the bounds of mid-century common sense, wedding as it does the subjective values of romanticism with a stabilizing recognition of the claims of public life. But in many ways, Dickens simply uses the common-sense solution of the disciplined heart, orderly family, and commitment to a vocation as a kind of ideological scaffold to support some rather audacious experiments in representation and some unconventional perceptions about the difficulties of self-cultivation. A consideration of the theme of memory in the novel is a convenient way of analyzing these experiments.

An interest in memory is implicit in David's presentation of himself in the text. Unless the narrator remembers, there is simply nothing to tell. But the theme of memory is also made explicit in the novel, and it becomes almost obsessive. We are often reminded that the whole novel is a heroic act of recollection. "This narrative," says David at the end of the novel, "is my written memory" (*DC,* 889). Memory mediates what is interior and what is exterior in the narrative; David recounts a series of experiences peculiarly his own, but the narrative constraint that he leave no gaps in his story appears as an external rule to which he only reluctantly submits. This constraint is especially strong in the chapter recounting David's stint in the London warehouse. There, memory is unbearably vivid: "They are all before me, just as they were in the evil hour when I went among them for the first time, my hand in Mr. Quinion's" (*DC,* 132). But because memory is so immediate, it can hardly be expressed: "The deep remembrance of the sense I had, of being utterly without hope now; of the shame I felt in my position; of the misery it was to my young heart to believe that day by day what I had learned, and thought, and delighted in, and raised my fancy and my emulation up by, would pass from me, little by little, never to be brought back any more, cannot be written" (*DC,* 133). And indeed, beneath the rhetorical flourish of this passage, the tangled layers of memory and hope are not at all amenable to the sequencing conventions of a normal plot. Instead of serial development, we are confronted with an inchoate mass of possibilities—David as beloved child, David as lost child, David as "learned and distinguished man," David as "little laboring hind"—all of them inhabiting the same narrative space, as unexpressed memories of a prematurely abandoned hope.

It is this sense of remembering lost potentials—or potentials that seem to be lost—that gives *David Copperfield* much of its emotional power. We see David emerge, as it were, from the crowd of other people he did not become, starting with Betsey Trotwood Copperfield and ending with the man who could never tell Agnes he loved her. Dickens is therefore able to save Copperfield from that cold-blooded rationality that annoyed English readers of *Wilhelm Meister:* his hero survives, but it is only an accident. And this structure also preserves the indeterminacy of the text. David's life is not a carefully planned trajectory; he does not put everything, even his mistakes, to good use. Indeed, his childhood experience in London cannot be made use of; it must be temporarily forgotten if David is to become "a passable boy yet" (*DC,* 196). Only in the narrative is it remembered; no other character ever refers to it directly. It is a discarded scrap of time, and only in the novel can it take its place in the whole of David's life.

But if memory preserves indeterminacy by recording unrealized possibilities, it is also a vehicle of typical intersubjectivity. David's remembrance of his past—how that memory replicates, within the text, the gesture of sheltering an abandoned child—absorbs the indeterminacy of the narrative. We are to believe in its referential power because we have allied ourselves with the narrator; our intersubjective tie with him numbers us among the emotional rescuers of that child. The close articulation of typicality and indeterminacy in this text, then, which allows us to identify with David both as subject and as object, also allows the novelist to project a very complex picture of how subjectivity and social life interrelate. We do not trace a unitary path through limited possibilities, as if the protagonist were formed by a mechanical accretion of experience, but rather confront a very subtle and complex representation of averted disasters and decisions made in passing, a representation in which other lives and other worlds are always tempting our glance, like the spot under a rushing wing that the governess in *The Turn of the Screw* can never quite bring into focus.

Let us turn, then, from David's memory to what David remembers, since it is here that both the critical and the utopian aspects of the novel are located. David's prototypic experiences of peace and harmony are those of infancy. Such events as his long evening's talk with his mother and Peggotty when he returns from school and his walks on the beach with Emily seem to take place outside time. David tells Emily that "my mother and I had always lived by ourselves in the happiest state imaginable, and lived so then, and always meant to live so" (*DC,* 84), while his courtship of Emily is uncomplicated because "we had no future. We made no more provision for growing older, than we did for growing younger" (*DC,* 87). Dickens surrounds these recollections with portents and foreshadowings of disaster, making them seem rarer and sweeter. No later happiness will evoke from David language quite as intense as that of the Yarmouth chapter, nearly every paragraph of which is marked by such words as *delight, intimacy, charmed, perfect, good-natured, innocent,* and *angel.* Indeed, for David to achieve a "disciplined heart," he must consign these events to memory and overcome his desire to return to Emily, to be cared for by his mother, and must instead accept the strenuous effort associated with Agnes. It is no accident that after he and Agnes declare their love for each other, they do not sit comfortably by the fire, but wander out into a bitter, brilliant, winter night. The past of childhood, then, the most intensely felt utopia of the novel, is a sheltered and inaccessible place.

Childhood is not simply a utopia of perception and sentiment: the early chapters of *David Copperfield* do more than translate into prose the Blest Babe sections of *The Prelude*. Rather, they present, in temporary resolution, some of the basic thematic tensions of the novel, those associated with class divisions and with power in the family, themes that mediate interior subjectivity and exterior circumstance. In the Pegotty household and in the early family of David, his mother, and Peggotty, we find family groups that cross class boundaries, that substitute relations of generosity and mutual affection for those of wage labor and paternal authority. In fact, no biological father is present in either household; in an Oedipal dream, David can take that desired role while remaining a treasured and protected child. Similarly, he can be friends with Peggotty, friends with Emily, friends with Ham, treating them all as equals of some sort, while retaining the privileges of his gentle birth. The novel opens with an image of a world in which the two great forces of division—paternal authority and social class—have become entirely beneficent. These chapters establish, for the rest of the novel, a utopia that is a hope for something that has already been.

Such a displacement into the past has two functions in *David Copperfield*. It quarantines much of the novel's political criticism, and by underscoring the centrality of writing in conserving utopian vision, it legitimates David's self-formation. By locating two dreams—intimate friendship among classes and nonrepressive family life—in the past, Dickens withdraws them from the realm of political desire. Already accomplished, they are not available for anyone's agenda; they are sacred memories rather than programs for social reform. This withdrawal, perhaps, accommodates conservative sentiment, but it also protects the utopian force of Dickens's vision. In *Theory of the Novel*, Lukács said that an authentically utopian vision cannot realize itself in normal time and space;[26] just so, Dickens's utopia is estranged, not by barriers of oceans or mountain ranges, but by being placed "back there," in the privileged location available to all novels of self-formation.

Further, if utopia is a matter of past experience, the writer who remembers is its preserver and agent. It is by writing the novel that David attains the status of hero of his own life, and this achievement is at once modest and triumphant. But David the agent of utopian consciousness is also David the unwitting social critic, since he has found no one, in all his youth, more heroic than his own unassuming self. This criticism is deep, but it is diffused by a badly conceived idea of the transformative power of labor.

The chapters that recount David's sojourn in the warehouse can be taken as paradigmatic of the novel's social criticism. We take David at his word when he describes the misery of this experience, especially since we know that Dickens was bitter about his own stint in a blacking factory. But in many ways, London seems better than the claustrophobic home David has just left. We need only remember the interminable afternoons under Miss Murdstone's eye, or her brother's sadism, or the suppressed hysteria of David's mother being "taught firmness," to feel a clear sense of relief at David's escape into the slipshod, good-humored Micawber household. Not improving company, perhaps, but much more cheerful. Yet David clearly sees this exile as the worst of Murdstone's offenses against him, worse than being beaten, worse than being estranged from his mother. Why?

In the Murdstone house, David is subjected to cruelty; in London, he undergoes neglect. At the Rookery, the dream of the fatherless house becomes a nightmare, but in London, the fantasy of being at one with the working class turns into a terrifying reality. He is part of business as usual, one of a crowd of "little laboring hinds" who are being brutalized by the routine daily work of industrial capital. The acuteness of the narrator's understanding of the waste and shame of ordinary wage labor is an index, I think, of the depth of his social criticism. Rather than sending David to toil in the coal mines or cotton mills, or even to scrape out a living as a pickpocket, Dickens simply gives him a steady job and marginally satisfactory lodgings. Nobody abuses David; he is likely, in fact, to meet with casual kindness. But he is utterly forgotten, and in danger of forgetting himself.

In the London chapters, we read a representation of the basic relations of emerging industrial capitalism: reduced, abstracted, quite vivid, sentimentalized, but not at all melodramatic. Like most wage earners, David stretches his salary from week to week, is at his employer's disposal, and tries to find some corner for himself in the lives that have been connected to his own. These routine operations are deeply indeterminate in this novel, first, because of their abstraction: David pockets his shilling, buys his puddings, pawns the Micawber silver, and does very little more. His life is reduced to a series of cash transactions. But the London narrative is also indeterminate because of the odd defamiliarization and distortion of having a child live out the "normal" activities of work and consumption. Even as David is most typical, as his life is absorbed in the relations that determined many other lives, he is most indeterminate in his displaced presentation of those relations. The force of the account, I think, is much deeper than the narrator, with his casual dismissal of laborers and debtors, intends. To read these chapters seriously is to call up David's image of all those hurrying London crowds, and to read in all those laboring lives, unremembered and unrescued, a story of the systematic organization of suffering and waste. David makes his way in life accompanied not only by the ghosts of all the people he did not become, but also by figures like Mealy Potatoes, who has no eccentric aunt to be his witness, remember his name, or see him as a boy rather than as an employee.

David's world and David, then, are both reduced to representations of what we might call the capacity for abstract labor, the expenditure of human energies organized so that they can easily be equated with one another. Marx, who saw abstract labor as the basis of capitalist production, held that it is expended indiscriminately, wherever wages are to be earned, and that in this alienation of the worker from his productive activity and its organization are to be found the deepest sources of oppression in capitalist society.[27] In the laborer's inability to determine the direction, conditions, or compensation of his work, Marx located the precondition of commodity value, of the deceptive appearance of human relations as relations among products. In the interchangeability of laborers, he saw a counterpart of the universal interchangeability of goods. By subjecting a sensitive and imaginative child to these relations, Dickens was able to distance them, deprive them of their appearance of inevitability. By recording that child's verdict on a life shaped by such relations, Dickens was able to express their deep inhumanity: "I am solemnly convinced that I never for one hour was reconciled to it, or was otherwise than miserably unhappy" (DC, 139). But to stop here is to write an unproblematic text by a prematurely Marxist author. There is another side to Dickens's social criticism and to his utopian vision; David Copperfield also celebrates the new forms of labor that it criticizes. At a crucial juncture in the novel, David praises himself for diligence and punctuality in a rare instance of explicit self-congratulation: "whatever I have tried to do in life, I have tried with all my heart to do well; . . . whatever I have devoted myself to, I have devoted myself to completely; . . . in great aims and in small I have always been thoroughly in earnest" (DC, 518). This celebration of labor is militantly indiscriminate. Effort is to be lavished on "great aims and small," on learning parliamentary shorthand and writing novels. It is, the narrator says, the one gift he has not abused, the ability to pour out attention and labor. Dickens invested David with so much of his own history that we are not surprised that this quality was one that Dickens prided himself on. As he put it in a letter to his wife justifying his obsessive attempts to cure a young woman's hallucinations: "the intense pursuit of any idea that takes complete possession of me, is one of the qualities that makes me different—sometimes for good; sometimes I dare say for evil—from other men." Here again, indiscriminate labor, abstracted from any aim or value—and here, more clearly, aggressive self-assertion: in his letter, Dickens closes the topic with, "This is the plain truth, and here I leave it."[28]

Labor is magic, and the ability to labor is a gift like the gift of a fairy godmother. It cannot be explained or altered. It is not a talent, but it is the precondition and ground of all talents. It will determine the hero's fate, like a talisman that only gradually reveals its powers. And indeed, in this novel, the narrator's vocabulary of labor recalls the utopian world of romance. David's willingness to work hard never goes unrewarded: because of it, he achieves Aunt Betsey's protection, Dr. Strong's patronage, and Agnes's love. Indeed, his self-formation could be economically described as a slow renunciation of the utopia of freedom, fraternity, and self-indulgence that formed David's childhood in favor of strenuous labor and delayed gratification. But other characters are equally fortunate in the fruits of their work: Agnes is rewarded for her patient labor when Heep is miraculously exposed by Micawber. Even Micawber, incorrigible voice of the pleasure principle, will be reborn into solvency in Australia when he learns to work. Perhaps most striking is the transformation of Mr. Dick, Aunt Betsey's addled lodger. He feels the bracing effects of work immediately upon beginning to copy for a piece rate: "never, while I live, shall I forget his going about to all the shops in the neighborhood to change this treasure into sixpences, or his bringing them to my aunt arranged in the form of a heart upon a waiter, with tears of joy and pride in his eyes. He was like one under the propitious influence of a charm, from the moment of his being usefully employed" (DC, 452). David Copperfield's affinity with the romance has often been noted,[29] but the particular quality of this romance, I think, is a wholehearted assent to the ideology of industrial labor. All exertion will find its reward; the organization and goal of labor matter less than its intensity; in earning and spending, we do not merely sustain ourselves but justify ourselves. As social theory, this ideology is disastrous; as a utopian image, it suggests a hope that the enormous labor that supports our lives will not be wasted, and that such labor might become a means of self-formation. Insofar as this hope forgets the neglected, overworked child in favor of the beloved, productive author, it compromises the memory that is so central to the novel and abuses the indeterminacy that engages us so powerfully. But it also expresses a wish that labor might become a bond and a ground of common life. If in the bildungsroman one life speaks for thousands, David's labor speaks for millions. As a report, it speaks deceptively; as a hope, it is not a simple lie. For Walter Benjamin, the utopian consciousness understood that every moment of historical time is "the strait gate through which the Messiah might enter."[30] For a Victorian at mid-century, that gate was formed by labor. It was strait indeed, and badly constructed besides. But it was open.

Much more could be written about *David Copperfield*, but we would perhaps do well to step back from this text and reflect on the genre we have taken it to represent. And, while it is in many ways a unique novel, in its treatment of the four topics we have just been examining—the self as subject and object, the tension between interior and exterior formation, the theme of memory, and the close articulation of self-formation with utopia and social criticism—*David Copperfield* is entirely representative of its genre. The same material is treated with subdued, almost elegiac complexity in *Great Expectations,* a novel in which the protagonist does not become the hero of his own life, but does face a similar tension between exterior and interior promptings to self-formation, similar problems of correctly ordering memory, and similar problems of negotiating the dialectic between self as subject and as object. And in *Jane Eyre,* the protagonist wrests her subjectivity from an external, mechanical set of limits, and then faces the problem of finding norms, or as she calls them, "laws," to which she can wholeheartedly assent. Or we could look at Butler's *The Way of All Flesh,* which has been called an "evolutionary case study,"[31] as an instance of calculated typicality in the bildungsroman. A more interesting and useful course, however, would be to move from these "normal" novels of self-formation to examine a number of works that approach the limits of the genre, either by subordinating the theme of self-formation or by taking a failed, blocked, or deflected life as their subject.

To that end, let me begin with *La Chartreuse de Parme.* Stendhal's novel, of course, is not a bildungsroman in the same sense as *Wilhelm Meister* or *David Copperfield.* Conventional lists of the genre usually cite, as the sole French examples, Stendhal's *Le rouge et le noir,* Flaubert's *L'éducation sentimentale,* and perhaps Stendhal's *La vie de Henry Brulard.*[32] But for our purposes, perhaps Stendhal's idiosyncratic *La Chartreuse de Parme* is an interesting limiting case, since it includes as one of its major plots the story of Fabrice's self-fomation, and since it situates that plot in a world where the openness of history, which is so essential an assumption of the normal bildungsroman, is blocked. The novel concerns itself with what happens to a young hero as he grows under the eyes of adults in a world empty of possibilities.

La Chartreuse de Parme: Bildungsroman as Subplot
***

If the protagonists in *David Copperfield* and *Wilhelm Meister* faced the problem of reconciling their subjective impulses with an external plan for their education, Fabrice in *La Chartreuse de Parme*[33] faces wandering subjective impulses and a vacuum of real external directions. Society is highly stratified, but none of its institutions is invested with enough authority to seriously challenge Fabrice's allegiance; Fabrice may be imprisoned, but he cannot be made to feel guilty, as David Copperfield was. Stendhal's metaphor for this situation is the game of whist—structured, open to chance but not improvisation, entirely a matter of external behavior. Fabrice finds that police or clergy or courtiers expect certain behavior of him, but they are not concerned with his interior life, or with the course of his development. The nickname of the cell where he is imprisoned—the "passive obedience"—could stand as the motto of all the social structures that Fabrice encounters.

Given the strong teleology inherent in a novel of formation, the historical setting of *La Chartreuse* during a period of reaction allows Stendhal to manipulate our expectation that Fabrice's maturity will somehow represent an opening of historical possibilities. Our expectation of such typical norms of representation allows Stendhal to deflect us into a world of doubling and repetition, a world of indeterminacy. The novel, then, is a representation contested between typicality and indeterminacy.

La Chartreuse de Parme is set in the post-Napoleonic reaction. In this world, where the direction of history has been reversed and where all youthful hopes are betrayed, personal self-formation has become acutely problematic. The historical telos cannot be taken for granted, and so personal life must somehow become a vehicle for those utopian hopes and possibilities that were invested in the public sphere. This is not an easy transposition, since simple survival in a period of reaction requires such resources as irony, duplicity, patience, and the willingness to cut one's losses—"if not the red, then the black." This is not the stuff of which utopia is made. The problem of maintaining the self as subject and object sharpens as the problem of mediating internal and external impulses to self-formation becomes more acute. Public life threatens to become a fully objectified performance; private subjectivity takes on a manic intensity.

We should not be surprised, then, that utopian impulses in *La Chartreuse de Parme* are totally detached from such questions as work or the choice of a vocation. Rather, they take refuge in the innermost recesses of the private—in memory and passion. Passion—Mosca's passion for Gina, Fabrice's passion for Clélia, Gina's passion for Fabrice—seems to be untouched by the reactionary structures of repetition that form its context. The beloved is always unattainable, always free, always on the verge of leaving or constrained by a vow or about to drink poison, so that passion seems to be a door out of the wandering passageway of reaction, and the protagonists to have one foot out in the free air. But of course, Stendhal allows no such easy escape; passion brings Gina to the ridiculous principality of Parma and leads her to bring Fabrice to join her. It sets the Prince against Mosca and makes Clélia unapproachable for Fabrice. Passion, then, appears in both the typical and the indeterminate registers of the novel. It makes the main characters seem "like us," even when they are made republican outlaws or cultivated ministers of state. Passion appears as a humanizing explanation of historical events— kings and princes are motivated by desire and jealousy, just as we are. But since it has no explicit ideological content—it is not a programme or a manifesto—passion can function as the best of all refuges for an insurgent spirit, a refuge of indeterminacy and multiplied meanings, of negations that somehow function as triumphant affirmations. Thus, Mosca and Gina seem to feel that there is something Jacobin about their relationship, and Fabrice pours all the fervor he had felt for Napoleon into his love for Clélia. We can see these relationships as reductions of a historical impulse. And in a way, they are miserable substitutes for the consciousness of the Enlightenment, a conscious- ness that had aspired to a self-representation that would be typical in its force, to a generous invocation of the ties among human beings, to a depth of subjectivity that would indeed allow one to speak for many. Such a consciousness, confined to the utter privacy of passion, becomes, as it were, its own ghost. Indeed, the melancholy that sur- rounds Mosca and Gina in this novel would support such an interpre- tation. But we are also likely to see Fabrice, Gina, and Mosca as characters who conserve the insurgent impulses of their youth, not as matters of opinion or political activity—irony and self-delusion con- trol these spheres of activity—but because of their feeling for one another. This most private of practices is all that remains of their earlier experience of a world from which all that was "vieux, dévot, morose" had been exiled, a utopia of the expansive gesture, where an epigram or a caricature could penetrate the consciousness of a whole city. That world was one in which intersubjective understanding, seemingly unconditioned by customary forms, emerged suddenly, as a new possibility, as an enlightenment, a promise of fraternity. That even a reduced image of such a world, the most public and rhetorical of utopias, could be preserved in Parma, in that community of three, is remarkable.

Such a preservation underscores the role of memory in *La Chartreuse*. Reactionary periods attempt to erase the official memory of the revolutionary periods that precede them, so that even history becomes an affair of individual recollection, taking refuge in the private and indeterminate, surviving the hegemonic amnesia in a series of unauthorized versions, each with its own idiosyncratic emphasis. Napoleon was kind to my husband, Gina says; he wanted Italy to have its own king, remembers another character. Memory, then, must hold together a subjective vision and an intersubjective experience. It conserves the past for both public and private spheres. The tension of this dual role, I think, flavors with bitterness the memories of both Mosca and Gina. They possess and are possessed by a living memory of Napoleon, and of the old culture his army, to their great relief, displaced. So they are aware that what they are doing is nothing new, that their tragedy is being staged according to the conventions of a comic opera. As Gina declares in frustration: "What a miserable stupidity! To come and live in the court of an absolute monarch! A tyrant who is personally acquainted with every one of his victims!" (*CP*, 295). Mosca and Gina, caught in a world where public events are manipulated, try to manage private history. Gina moves heaven and earth to sail with Fabrice on a lake, as she had in her youth. But these attempts at sentimental restoration are not often successful. The mature characters of the novel frequently, and always with great relief, declare themselves restored to youth, but each of their new beginnings, burdened with more knowledge and less hope, seems costlier and more desperate.

In a sense, the main characters of *La Chartreuse de Parme* adapt themselves to reaction by becoming technicians of representation. They learn a series of strategies for translating their experiences and aspirations into subjectively intelligible language, and they also learn to multiply meanings, to protect themselves with indeterminacy.

We watch Fabrice learn these arts. He begins the novel as a youth unable either to express himself or to dissemble, a clumsy reader of omens and auguries. In prison, he learns a series of alphabets, systems of representation he uses to communicate with Gina and Clélia. Each interlocutor demands a separate system: for Clélia, letters scratched out in charcoal; for Gina, a coded system of lights and numbers. With Clélia, Fabrice faces the problem of distracting her from discourse about his situation as a prisoner, and opening discourse about his subjectivity, while the Countess must also be distracted from planning his escape, but from her his subjectivity must be concealed. These constraints produce dialogue marked by non sequiturs, as when Fabrice answers Clélia's frenzied message about poison, cords, and chocolate, a message delivered under cover of an operatic recitative, with his hastily scribbled declaration: "I love you, and life is dear to me only because I see you. Above all things, send me some paper and a pencil" (*CP,* 345-46). Fabrice can seldom indulge in such frankness, however; as a well-brought-up girl, Clélia will not listen to a declaration of love from a political enemy of her father's. In order to express himself to her, then, Fabrice must consent to talk of something else: his love speech is a displaced and indeterminate representation: "With the high wind blowing today I can only catch very faintly the advice you are so kind as to give in your singing; the sound of the piano drowns your voice. What is this poison, for instance, of which you speak?" (*CP,* 346). Such a strategem is worthy of the man who later, having become a famous preacher, keeps a prayer to the Virgin by him in the pulpit, so that he will not be without resources if the sight of his beloved in the congregation should strike him dumb. Indeed, for Fabrice multivalent speech defends the public self against the threat of passion. Thus it is also a defense of the private, allowing it indirect expression while concealing and protecting it.

Fabrice's language, with its dual function of concealment and disclosure, indicates his uneasy resolution of the tension between interior and exterior forces, between the self as passionate subject and as politic object. *La Chartreuse de Parme* links together extremely heterogeneous materials, under extremely adverse conditions. For this reason alone, it demonstrates some of the basic assumptions of the bildungsroman: the interdependence between self-formation and historical openness in the genre, its strong utopian impulse, and its tendency to concentrate social relations in individual characters. In *La Chartreuse,* we see what happens when these assumptions become problematic, when history is closed, utopia compromised, and individual lives limited to a private sphere. The basic premises of the bildungsroman have been called into question; the novel of self-formation is inserted into a novel of romance and intrigue, and the interpenetration of indeterminacy and typicality in the normal bildungsroman becomes an uneasy and unresolved contest between them.

But the bildungsroman is not lost in this struggle. Rather, the ending of the novel, with its dedicatory epigraph "To the Happy Few," signals the beginning of a new text, and releases the problem of self-formation from the confines of the novel to visit it on us, the readers. We may understand the "happy few" as the passionate characters of

La Chartreuse de Parme, or as Stendhal's passionately desired future readers, who find in this novel the prefiguring of their own joys. But of course, most of us will direct the dedication neither backward nor forward, but will see the happy few as the elect group of those who have spent some afternoons with the three remarkable protagonists of the novel. The happy few, then, are, at least in one sense, the reader and the narrator, united by their gaze at the fading images of the novel. The final dedication, then, places us in a reflexive position very like that which David Copperfield occupies at the end of his novel. Stendhal, rather than enclosing the indeterminacy of this self-reflection within the typical relations of the novel, has given the last word in the text to us. In *La Chartreuse de Parme,* the plot of self-formation is situated within a novel of intrigue, but the dialectics of representation enclose both of these plots within a broader discussion of education and maturity, a discussion in which we as readers—having claimed a place among the "happy few"—inquire of ourselves and the times in which we live whether our lives will justify a claim to happiness or whether they will present only its appearances. We are invited to participate in the distanced reflection, the almost satirical analysis, that has been the controlling tone of the novel's last chapters. We join Stendhal's final celebration of esprit as the source of intelligence, mobile wit, and the willingness to imagine that things could be different. Such a celebration might seem to be a final descent into cynicism and privacy. Not so; not quite. In this novel, esprit is the first cousin to Jacobinism; by privileging this faculty, we return in spirit to the revolutionary Milan of the book's opening chapters, a Milan awakening from centuries of boredom to laugh and to think. We have been returned, then, by a circuitous route, to history, the history within which our own self-formations must be carried out.

Stendahl's novel, then, was an early recognition that the process of self-formation may not be successful, that history is not always open. Such a possibility was not normally represented in English bildungsromane until the end of the century, when Thomas Hardy wrote, in *Jude the Obscure,* a story of failed or deflected self-formation with none of Stendhal's lightness of touch. This bildungsroman, rather than manipulating our generic expectations, turns them against us. Here, the normal vehicles of self-formation—marriage, education, the choice of a vocation—become engines for deforming and repressing any authentic subjectivity. Jude's marriages are galling bonds; his education puts him at odds with any conventional social role and his chosen vocation is a source of misery, since he never enters the ranks of the clergy. Hardy disappoints our expectations on other levels, too. The novel's pattern of representation is quite irregular, since it opens with audaciously overdrawn episodes like Jude being hit in the face with a hog's penis and moves into a world where the conventions of realism simply collapse. For example, when Jude's child, whose unlikely name is Little Father Time, kills himself and the other children, Hardy comments: "On that little shape had converged all the inauspiciousness and shadow which had darkened the first union of Jude, and all the accidents, mistakes, fears, errors of the last. He was their nodal point, their focus, their expression in a single term."[34] Hardy's language here invokes typicality—the child expresses a range of experiences—but what is being represented typically is itself fictional: the protagonist's two marriages. And the aspects of those marriages that the child represents are contingent and negative; he himself is an abstract "expression in a single term." Both typicality and indeterminacy are being deployed self-consciously, as if this episode, so improbable and so moving, must be explained away. Here, then, the bildungsroman, which began its classical period by assuming that the individual human life had unique representative power, knitting the notion of the typical into the very fabric of its plot, prepares to enter the twentieth century with the admission that something else is needed, that there are elements in social life that cannot be mediated by a growing subjectivity, but must be otherwise represented.

The Four-Gated City: A New Canon of Representation?

One attempt to work out such a strategy of representation can be found in Doris Lessing's *The Four-Gated City,*[35] a novel that ends with madness, the spread of telepathy, and worldwide ecological disaster. Here, as in *Jude the Obscure,* our sense is that the basic assumption of the bildungsroman, that one life can speak for many, no longer holds. Lessing finds that the story of Martha Quest's growing up, a story she has been wholeheartedly narrating in the four previous volumes of *Children of Violence,* can no longer adequately describe the relation of the heroine to the world. In *Children of Violence,* the assumptions of the bildungsroman are revealed as they collapse. One of the earlier volumes of the series, *A Ripple from the Storm,*[36] which can be taken as a modern example of a normal bildungsroman, is an extremely perceptive account of the protagonist's involvement with the Communist party of Zambesia, a fictional African state. In this account, the basic assumptions of the normal bildungsroman are mobilized: Martha's life, even in remote southern Africa, is profoundly affected by the events of World War II. Her politicization, her daily struggles, her love affairs can thus be taken as representations of a series of "questions": the woman question, the question of wartime radicalism, of communism. Simultaneously, in the growth of Martha's consciousness, in the insistent subtlety with which she perceives the behavior of her group, we are given access to the particularity of her quite unusual situation—a woman who has left her husband and daughter, a member of an ill-assorted Communist party in a marginal British colony, involved first with a British airman, then with a German refugee. In *A Ripple from the Storm,* then, the typical register, perfectly balanced between universality and particularity, predominates. Indeterminacy enters this narrative only indirectly, in the form of dreams or reveries. One of the themes of the book, for instance, is the resistance of human suffering to conventional political analysis. Such a theme is not adapted to typical representation: what is presented typically must seem intersubjectively intelligible rather than unknowable. Lessing develops this theme indeterminately, but it is a sort of note written in the margins of the text—striking, impossible to ignore, but unintegrated with the flow of the narrative. For example, Martha has a fever dream in which she sees the "head and shoulders of an immense saurian that had been imprisoned a thousand years ago in the rock," and thinks "It's alive. . . . It's alive after so many centuries. And it will take centuries more to die. Perhaps I can dig it out?" (*Ripple,* 85). The dream lizard is forgotten when her fever is cured, but the rest of the novel stands judged by this image, in which Martha renders a verdict on the project of putting an end to suffering by reordering society.

In *The Four-Gated City,* on the other hand, both Martha's self-development and the course of history have become more problematic, and the narrative, not surprisingly, becomes more indeterminate. The book begins during the postwar British reaction. Martha, who has immigrated to London, is working as editor and housekeeper to Mark Coldridge, an author. Her self-cultivation, for most of the novel, consists of trying to regain her memory. She spends hours of each day trying to remember her past, to regain possession of herself as a person who exists continuously in time. And she tries to avoid what she calls "having to do it over again" (*FGC,* 203), the involuntary repetition of past experiences. So far, we are well within the bounds of ordinary typical representation.

Toward the end of the novel, however, the narrative takes a sharp turn into indeterminacy. Martha moves from her upper bedroom to the basement where Mark's mad wife has been living, to enter the world of insanity, lying on the floor and listening to voices in her head. This ultimate turn toward subjectivity is also a particularly brutal objectification of the self. Martha coolly catapults herself into madness through starvation and sleeplessness; it is a sort of bad transcendence of the subject-object dialectic. Martha also wrestles with the contradiction between interior and exterior, and we can see her experiment as proposing a series of extreme solutions to this problem: What if the world of others could just come inside our heads? What if the world of others comes from inside our heads in the first place? Martha is presented as a person on the edge of evolution, discovering new mental powers. She sees visions, foretells the future, learns to control abnormal mental states. What is striking, and unsettling, is that Lessing renders all of this indeterminate matter—talking chairs, TV sets in the mind—as if it were ordinary, typical, plotty incident. She presents Martha in the familiar language of German romanticism: "And it was precisely this quality at work everywhere, the lively yeast, which made Martha hold on to that prime thing she had learned in her life . . . that if she was feeling something, in this particular way, with the authenticity, the irresistibility, of the growing point then she was not alone, others were feeling the same, since the growing point was never, could never be, just Martha's, could not be only the property or territory of one individual" (*FGC,* 512).

The process of self-cultivation is still imagined in reference to a universal humanity, as a situation of the individual in history. But in the world of this novel one life cannot speak for thousands in any ordinary language; we are too constantly aware of the failures of intersubjectivity, the sharpness of the alienations that separate us. Nor is this world one in which history, in any ordinary sense, can be seen as telos: it is a world in which ecological disaster presses in upon the imagination. But so powerful is the mandate of the genre—and the momentum of the four volumes that precede *The Four-Gated City*—that the novel maintains both intersubjective force and a sense of the openness of history, awkwardly and uncomfortably translating these typical motifs into its indeterminate register. If Martha cannot be shown in any harmonious relation to her closest friends, or be comfortably situated in some understanding community, she will understand the telepathic voices that pour into her head. If she cannot be engaged in the history of her generation, she can be given a crucial role in an improbable history of the future, when the Sahara is melted to glass and the Thames is choked with weeds.

Such an ending coheres with a novel with no more illusions that history implies progress. We might recall, from *A Ripple from the Storm,* Anton's triumphant assertion of the intelligibility of history, and of the individual capacity to make a place in it: "Comrades, this is the dawn of human history. We have the supreme good fortune and the responsibility to be living at a time when mankind takes the first great leap forward from the barbarity and chaos of unplanned production to the sunlight of socialism—from the boyhood of our species to its manhood. Upon us, upon people like us all over the world, the organized members of the communist party, depends the future of mankind, the future of our species" (*Ripple*, 53). Against ths triumphant vision of typicality, we must place the indeterminate image of the world Mark Coldridge fashions in his study, tracing and marking on maps the patterns of bombs, germ weapons, chemical weapons, psychoactive drugs, pollution, "War, Famine, Riots, Poverty, Prisons," and eventually mental illness, social decay, and all the other topics under which a general collapse can be investigated. This room, in which empirical evidence is arranged in "an almost metaphysical or medieval way" (*FGC*, 297), is, like the room in the cellar where the mad wife listens to her voices, an extreme image of the exhaustion of classical self-cultivation. The study, traditionally that most private of spaces, reserved for interiority, is invaded by an exterior world that can no longer be understood, that is no longer useful as a tool for self-formation.

The novel, then, has worked itself into a tight spot, simultaneously affirming the values of the classical bildungsroman and developing a narrative line that subverts them. And, it must be said, Lessing's resolution of this dilemma is not very satisfying. She simply projects the generic mandate of typicality onto a character, or set of characters, the "new Children" born after the ecological disaster, who are posited as fulfillments of the mandate that one life should speak for many. "They are beings who include . . . history in themselves and who have transcended it" (*FGC*, 647). We never meet any of these children; in this novel, we are not even asked seriously to believe in them. But, as the last motif in a series of novels that had confronted so steadily the tensions between the interior and the social, so cavalier an assertion that these tensions can be transcended, such a thin and forced utopian image, is deeply disappointing.

But before we become energetic in our disappointment, we should perhaps remember the late Lukács, patiently analyzing the contradictions of late capitalism in all their complexity and then petulantly wondering why contemporary novelists did not write like Balzac. In the bildungsroman, we have seen how realism becomes a disclosure of the limits of the real, and finally of the limits of literary disclosure. Nor can we forget that Lessing's is the bildungsroman that we, as readers, have evoked, a novel for which we bear a special hermeneutic responsibility. It is woven into the web of our situation; whether its limits will be happily transcended is a problem that lies in our hands. That solution may not be a matter for literary criticism, but it will have much to do with the choices we make in constructing our common representation of reality.

CONCLUSION: THE PUBLIC, THE PRIVATE, AND THE DIALECTICS OF REPRESENTATION

In nearly all the readings in this book, the notions of public and private have appeared. It is appropriate to end by retrieving these concepts, foregrounding them, and using them to reflect on the central concern of the book: the dialectics of representation.

The main locus for discussion of the public and the private in contemporary socially critical discourse is feminist theory. Indeed, it was through the feminist slogan "The private is the public" that this opposition emerged into political discourse. For feminists, *private* is closely associated with *female* and invokes all those activities traditionally assigned to women: the creation of domestic life, care of children, even emotion and subjective life in general. *Public* refers to the themes traditional in masculine political discourse: parties and alliances, candidates and programs, economics and foreign affairs. To treat any of these questions is to enter "public life"; to focus on domesticity is to "live privately." The great power of feminist critique has been to show the profound connection between these two seemingly independent spheres, enabling materials and themes that had been frozen into privacy to enter public discourse.

The feminist treatment of the division between public and private runs at a bias to the other canonical analysis of the public and private within the radical tradition: the Marxist and socialist analysis of the contradiction between the public, socialized production of wealth and the private appropriation of profit. Here, *public* implies activity across social boundaries, involving large numbers of people, broadly influential in its effects on social relations. The sphere of the public is ruled by forces outside any individual control. *Private,* on the other hand, implies self-sufficiency, control by a single person or by a corporation that is responsible only to its stockholders: what is central in the private for Marxists is not the intimacy or interiority of the feminist *private,* but the lack of accountability that Marx referred to as the anarchy of capitalist production. It is not surprising, then, that the force of the Marxist critique of the division between public and private has not been to move material from the private sphere to the public, but to subdue both the disordered power of the public and the individual anarchy of the private. This summary, of course, ignores a great deal of a more subjective Marxism's analysis of consciousness; it should be taken as a crude boundary marker for the paradigmatic senses of public and private in the socialist tradition.

Both of these oppositional notions of the public and the private play off the original sense, in our culture, of how these terms are related. Richard Sennett has formulated the primary sense of "the public" as "a life passed outside the life of family and close friends," while "the private" constituted a domain of nature, of natural feelings and natural ties. [1]

Sennett's extensive treatment of the traditional understanding of *public* and *private* shows that their underlying metaphoric structure was drawn from the terrain of re-presentation and performance: what happened in public was understood by analogy to theatrical performance. Public life, Sennett says, was organized as a deployment of signs, rather than of symbols: the public, as it was originally constituted, was a location from which indeterminacy was banished, in which conventions had been secured, and for which no interpreter was required. The private, originally coextensive with the family, was seen as the domain of straightforward "natural" emotions to which all men were subject. (We have seen, however, that this conflation of privacy with the family was itself a modern creation, a modification of the earlier notion that located the private in relations of friendship.) Sennett understands the theatrical/natural disjunction between public and private, a creation of the ancien régime, as an essentially beneficent, even liberating, structure. It was disrupted during the nineteenth century, when private life was conflated with truth, specifically the truth about individual personalities. Not only did this transformation complicate family relationships, but it also could not be contained within the sphere of the private, and so was also always disturbing the equilibrium of public life. For the nineteenth century, then, public life was enmeshed in indeterminacy, and produced anxieties that could only be contained by strenuous efforts to preserve decorum.

While Sennett's romanticization of the ancien régime is not very credible, his analysis of the way that the public and the private were understood in the eighteenth and nineteenth centuries reveals some submerged senses of the terms. If we combine the organization of the public and the private in the two periods Sennett has studied with the feminist and Marxist sense of the terms, it becomes clear that these concepts are not only themselves contradictory; in them, contradictory strata of meanings coexist uneasily. Public and private are concepts organized by opposition, but what is opposed changes radically with different historical periods and theoretical frameworks.

Moreover, all of these oppositions imply a dialectic of concealment and disclosure, a dialectic of representation. For Marxism, for example, the disorder of social relations is a representation of the chaos enforced by individual ownership; for some feminists, the intimacy of domestic life is a representation of the utopian possibilities of a transformed public sphere. And the dialectic of representation also shapes the relations between the strata. What Sennett broadly called the ancien régime is not something over and done with: these relations still exist in residual forms, and emerge not only at events like street fairs and costume balls but within official structures like those of university governance. Various senses of the public and the private, then, will be activated as our investigations move into different areas. This stratified structure of the public and the private is reflected in my own use of these concepts. Public and private have both emerged as composite and contradictory ideas, whose content changes at different social and historical junctures. It is the very contradictory force of the public and the private that makes them useful for analyzing representations, which also tend to be complex and contradictory. But if we cannot define a "real" sense of the public and the private, an authentic meaning that should control our use of these notions, how then can we think critically about their use in reading? How can we use the public and the private as interpretive categories? We can begin by looking at how these terms are deployed, and we see that their rhetorical force is often moral. This rhetorical bias toward moralism both reveals and blocks the representational movement of the public and the private. Let us look at a series of illustrative quotations, some of which have already been cited.

> Why should the private pleasure of some one
> Become the public plague of many moe?

> Shakespeare . . . intuits that order depends, not on concepts
> of hierarchy and degree, but on the fabric of personal and
> social relations, which is woven by ties of marriage, kinship,
> and friendship, by communal interests and ideals of loyalty
> and trust.

> This mass [of the extraparliamentary bourgeoisie] that every
> moment sacrificed its general class interests, that is, its political
> interests, to the narrowest and dirtiest private interest, now
> moans that the proleteriat has sacrificed its ideal political in-
> terests to its material interests.

> With settling judgements now of what would last
> And what would disappear; prepared to find
> Ambition, folly, madness, in the men
> Who trust themselves upon this passive world
> As rulers of the world; to see in these,
> Even when the public welfare is their aim,
> Plans without thought, or bottomed on false thought
> And false philosophy.[2]

For all of these writers, the fundamental superiority of one sphere over the other is a moral axiom. We have a moral duty to value either the public or the private; morality, in fact, consists in the rejection of a "dirty" private or a "false" public.

But even in the syntax of these moral assertions, we can find traces of the dialectical logic of representation. For the consequences of an individual mistake in the valuation of the public and private are not limited to a compromise of personal integrity, but also include dangers to the security of the whole society—a "public plague," an erosion of public order. Precisely because these moral valuations require individual assent at the risk of social disorder, they assume a close relationship, indeed, an interdependence between the spheres of the public and of the private. Further, that relationship of interdependence assumes the possibility of material being translated from one sphere to the other: the rage of the moralist, in fact, is excited by failed or inappropriate translations. The rape of Helen made a private passion into a public calamity; the French bourgeoisie abandoned their public role for private gain; the politician substitutes false worldly thought for settled and private judgment. Or conversely, a happy translation between public and private draws moral approbation; a well-ordered family implies political order.

This interdependence, however, is recognized only implicitly. The quotations I have chosen overtly assert a simple disjuncture between the public and the private. And although we have seen that the public and the private are composite ideas, in which various historical senses are preserved, the moralistic use of these terms assumes that they are univocal. Everyone already knows what Lucretia's or Marx's *private* means: the term becomes a simple category marker. An interpretive approach to the public and the private will reverse these two assumptions: the public and the private will be seen as an interdependent pair and they will be located in history. For such an approach, there can be no absolute boundary between the literary deployments of the public and the private and their use in other forms of discourse, including political theory, popular culture, and everyday language. For although the notions of the public and the private in this book have been put in aid of the investigation of literary representations, not all representations are literary, and I assume differences in degree rather than kind between the processes that produce novels and those that produce fantasies or Western movies. What our sketchy investigation of the public and private suggests is that these other representations can also be read dialectically.

The public and private, then, can be assimilated into a hermeneutics of social representation, as an attempt to understand the ways in which lived experience is made intelligible, codified in "common sense," criticized and transformed. The public and the private appear as translations of one another; the dialectic of representation, with its figures of transformation and reversal, organizes that translation.

An example of the hermeneutic use of the notions of public and private for interpreting social representations is Jürgen Habermas's analysis of the public sphere in late capitalism.[3] The state, as we have seen, is virtually a constituting category for the public, and so politics can easily assume the status of a paradigmatic public activity. Habermas questioned this assumption by examining the effects of advanced communications, cybernetics, and social scientific methods on political life. He found that they transform political questions into technical problems, so that the sphere of the public is diminished and fragmented. Here, social representation has been called into question. Habermas asked what kind of social problem has, in fact, been realized as a political question in modern society, rather than allowing the normal categorization of political problems to pass unquestioned. His analysis traced the submerged translation of a broad range of issues from the public sphere into the domain of bureaucratic function. Although Habermas's analysis of the public sphere has moral force, in his analysis neither the public nor the private is a preferred term. Rather, what is at issue is the translation of social relations between public and private, and their use in organizing social representations. What had appeared as direct and obvious is shown to be problematic and subject to change. Brecht presents the same process dramatically:

> But all this I yielded up to astonishment
> Even the most familiar part of it.
> That a mother gave her child the breast
> I reported like something no one would believe.[4]

It would be interesting to follow the trail of representation down these broader paths—to ask, for example, how the representations formed by common sense differ from those of literature or how changes in social representation are disseminated. But it is more appropriate for this book to return to literary representation, and to make a few final remarks about how the public and the private operate in that context. We can identify two major ways. The public and the private can be used to understand literary representations referentially, so that the work can be said to be about relations between the two spheres. Or the public and the private can function reflexively, as a commentary on the act of reading. We can ask of a representation, then, how it divides social life into public and private spheres, or how materials are translated from one sphere to another, or how those translations change over time. Or we can see the public and the private as enabling motions, the movement between them referring to less easily represented interdependencies or functioning as a pretext for examining the transformations and reversals that mark all representations. Such an interpretation works against the moralistic grain of the notions of public and private, although it may respond to moral categories of its own. But rather than valuing either the public or the private, a hermeneutic use of these concepts will question their natural appearance, their transparency, their historical particularity, or the unproblematic conventions that permit easy translations from one sphere to the other.

Several of the readings in this book use the notions of public and private referentially: a work is seen as a fictional investigation of the relations between the two spheres, and of their transformation. In my reading of *The Duchess of Malfi,* for example, the family is seen as moving from the public to a private sphere, while in *Richard II,* a new form of private subjectivity can be identified, emerging just as the formation of an omnicompetent state radically changes the structure of public life. Such readings have exploited the similarities of movement, structure, and relation between the public and the private and the central dialectical pair of this study, typicality and indeterminacy, since each pair alternately offers and frustrates an intersubjective bond to the reader. In these referential readings, the historical specificity of the public and the private does not call into question the general movement of the dialectics of representation, but instead exploits that movement to work out a different opposition between the hidden and the manifest. A text that is concerned with the public and the private, then, is not simply "about" a specific institution, such as the family or the state. It is also a representation of social movement and the forces that block such movement, of the preservation of social relations through changes in their specific structure, of the transformation of social relations as their context changes. What is represented in the work, then, is not simply a record of a specific social experience, but the basic dialectical forms that compose our understanding of history.

More reflexive treatments of the public and the private use the intensely contradictory relations between them to show other kinds of change and contradiction, including those internal to the representational strategy of the text. The text's treatment of the public and the private becomes a vehicle for thinking about concealment and re-presentation. The translation of materials between public and private indicates other kinds of translation, indeed the whole activity of preserving the signified while changing the signifier. In Middleton's city comedies, for example, we find a deployment of the public and the private that can be analyzed reflexively. By seeing traditional forms as manifestations of norms of accumulation, Middleton opens to investigation, first, the use of money as a universal means of representation, and second, the representational strategies, including the dramatic strategies, that had organized the ideological life of the city of London. Although Middleton's plots, characters, and theme are not original—close analogues can be found in other city comedies, or in the work of other Jacobean dramatists—he is especially audacious in his reflexive use of the categories of public and private, categories that are simply accepted by a writer as penetrating as Ben Jonson. In *A Chaste Maid in Cheapside,* the public and the private are used both referentially, to call into question the structures of social relations, and also reflexively, to question the representation of those relations in social life and in the play's own practice.

We have already spoken of Middleton's use of the indeterminate register, and indeed this reflexive use of public and private as interpretive categories is a peculiarly indeterminate strategy. But the typical register can also be used to translate between the public and private spheres. Doris Lessing's *The Four-Gated City* can stand as an example of this project. Its stated theme—changes in public opinion seen as relations between historical change and changes in consciousness—in many ways simply transposes into contemporary terms the typical equation between the individual and the community that was, as we have seen, axiomatic for the bildungsroman. In another sense, Lessing's is a profoundly different investigation, an investigation of a subjectivity that confronts mass media, a developed apparatus for controlling public opinion, and various psychological technologies. If Habermas, analyzing similar forces, developed a theoretical critique of the public sphere, Lessing develops a literary critique of the private. To be sure, not all the formal problems implied in such a project are solved in *The Four-Gated City:* to question subjectivity, a basic category of the novel, is not easy, especially in the typical register that dominates this book. I have already spoken of the awkwardness of some of Lessing's solutions, of the unsatisfying literalness of her ending. But what is remarkable about this book is its willingness to work through the contradictions between advanced capitalist society and the presuppositions of typical representation: intersubjective connection, relation to history, the tension between individual identity and group inclusion. Lessing is unwilling to block the translation of disorder and the dispersal of meaning from the public sphere to the private, and in performing this translation, she moves the traditional themes of typical representation to an indeterminate register. The public and the private are used, here, to organize a critique of social representation that breaks loose and becomes a reflection on the representational norms of the novel, moving it outside the trajectory of *The Children of Violence,* a series that had been bound for the normal elegiac close of an extended bildungsroman.

The public and the private, then, can be read as representational structures, and also as ways of reflecting on strategies of representation. Their presence in so many of the readings in this book is not accidental; as tools for social reflection, they recall some of the underlying concerns that motivate the literary reflections in this book. But of course, it is not a matter of simple congruence. The notions of the public and the private, like the notion of representation, are contested ideas. My conclusion could be fruitfully placed over against the critique of subjectivity in the writings of Derrida and Foucault, for whom the topics associated with the public and the private—interiority, individuation, passion, reason—are so many symptoms of logocentrism, of belief in the metaphysics of presence, or of the ideological delusions of humanism. But this book proceeds from different axioms and is formed by a different tradition.

My attempt throughout this book has been to knit together texts and readers, not to preserve a unitary culture, but to link together specific locations of the past with audiences and problems of the present. The movement of concepts through history is discontinuous, as the example of the public and the private illustrates. Therefore, I have felt no license to consign anything to the past, but only to listen, to translate, to yield the work "up to astonishment." In this interpretive act, I do not hope to recover the subjective experiences of past audiences in all their dense immediacy. I can only seek mediated, that is, labored-over, understandings of how past experiences were composed, of how they changed. To understand and recognize the dialectic of representation helps us see how we confront and compose representations in our experience of social relations, and helps us to come to terms with the possibilities of changing both representations and experiences. Such a project, such a practice, is not a search for the essential truth of history. It is rather a way of keeping in mind the possibility that every moment of historical time, including even this present, is the strait gate through which a messiah might enter.

ABBREVIATIONS

Works cited frequently have been identified in the text by the following abbreviations:

AR   Paul de Man. *Allegories of Reading: Figural Language in Rousseau, Nietzsche, Rilke, and Proust.* New Haven: Yale Univ. Press, 1979.

BI   Paul de Man. *Blindness and Insight: Essays in the Rhetoric of Contemporary Criticism.* Theory and History of Literature, vol. 7, 2d ed., rev. Minneapolis: Univ. of Minnesota Press, 1983.

CP   Stendhal. *La Chartreuse de Parme.* Paris. Garnier Flammarion, 1964.

DC   Charles Dickens. *David Copperfield.* Edited by Nina Burgis. Oxford: Clarendon Press, 1981.

FGC   Doris Lessing. *The Four-Gated City.* 1969; reprint, New York: Bantam, 1978.

HF   Karl Marx. *The Holy Family.* Translated by Richard Dixon and Clemens Dutt. Pp. 5–212 in *Karl Marx–Frederick Engels: Collected Works,* vol. 4. New York: International, 1974.

PU   Fredric Jameson. *The Political Unconscious: Narrative as a Socially Symbolic Act.* Ithaca, N.Y.: Cornell Univ. Press, 1981.

RW   Mikhail Bakhtin. *Rabelais and His World.* Translated by Helene Iswolsky. Cambridge, Mass.: MIT, 1968.

SER   Georg Lukács. *Studies in European Realism.* Translated by Edith Bone. New York: Grosset and Dunlap, 1964.

TS   Henry James. *The Turn of the Screw.* Edited by Robert Kimbrough. New York: Norton, 1966.

NOTES

CHAPTER 1: THE DIALECTICS OF REPRESENTATION

1. Paul de Man, *Blindness and Insight: Essays in the Rhetoric of Contemporary Criticism*, Theory and History of Literature, vol. 7, 2d ed., rev. (Minneapolis: Univ. of Minnesota Press, 1983). Subsequent references are given parenthetically in the text.

2. Fredric Jameson, *The Political Unconscious: Narrative as a Socially Symbolic Act* (Ithaca, N.Y.: Cornell Univ. Press, 1981). Subsequent references are given parenthetically in the text.

3. Paul de Man, "Dialogue and Dialogism," *Poetics Today* 4, no. 1 (1983), 104.

4. Paul de Man, *Allegories of Reading: Figural Language in Rousseau, Nietzsche, Rilke, and Proust* (New Haven: Yale Univ. Press, 1979). Subsequent references are given parenthetically in the text.

5. Denis Donoghue, "Deconstructing Deconstruction," review of *Deconstruction and Criticism*, by Harold Bloom, Paul de Man, Jacques Derrida, Geoffrey Hartman, and J. Hillis Miller, and of *Allegories of Reading*, by Paul de Man, *New York Review of Books* 27, no. 10 (June 12, 1980), 40-41.

6. Jürgen Habermas, *Reason and the Rationalization of Society*, vol. 1 of *The Theory of Communicative Action*, trans. Thomas McCarthy (Boston: Beacon, 1984), 50; Mikhail Bakhtin, *The Dialogic Imagination*, trans. Caryl Emerson and Michael Holquist (Austin: Univ. of Texas Press, 1981), 281-82.

7. George Kennedy, *Classical Rhetoric and Its Christian and Secular Tradition from Ancient to Modern Times* (Chapel Hill: Univ. of North Carolina Press, 1980), chapter 2. See also George Kennedy, *The Art of Persuasion in Greece* (Princeton: Princeton Univ. Press, 1963), chapter 2.

8. See, for example, de Man, *Allegories of Reading*, 53, 67, 110, 115, 205.

9. For modern formulations of the hermeneutic circle see Martin Heidegger, *Being and Time*, trans. J. Macquarrie and E. Robinson (New York: Harper and Row, 1962), 194-95; Jürgen Habermas, *Knowledge and Human Interests*, trans. Jeremy Shapiro (Boston: Beacon, 1971), chapter 8; and Hans-Georg Gadamer, *Truth and Method* (New York: Crossroads, 1982), 235-40. For recent applications of hermeneutic theory to aesthetics, see Richard E. Palmer, *Hermeneutics: Interpretation Theory in Schleiermacher, Dilthey, Heidegger, and Gadamer* (Evanston, Ill.: Northwestern Univ. Press, 1969); David Couzens Hoy, *The Critical Circle: Literature, History, and Philosophical Hermeneutics* (Berkeley and Los Angeles: Univ. of California Press, 1978; and Josef Bleicher, *Contemporary Hermeneutics as Method, Philosophy, and Critique* (London: Routledge and Kegan Paul, 1980).

10. De Man, *Blindness and Insight*, chapter 2.

11. Alexandre Kojève, *Introduction to the Reading of Hegel*, trans. James Nichols (Ithaca, N.Y.: Cornell Univ. Press, 1969), 202–3.

12. Gilles Deleuze and Félix Guattari, *Anti-Oedipus: Capitalism and Schizophrenia*, trans. Robert Hurley, Mark Seem, and Helen Lane (New York: Viking, 1977); (Minneapolis: Univ. of Minnesota Press, 1983); Michel Foucault, *The Order of Things: An Archeology of the Human Sciences* (New York: Vintage, 1970), 383; Louis Althusser and Etienne Balibar, *Reading Capital*, trans. Ben Brewster (London: NLB, 1970), 180; Balibar, *Reading Capital*, 252.

13. Althusser, *Reading Capital*, 142.

14. Max Horkheimer and Theodor Adorno, *Dialectic of Enlightenment*, trans. John Cumming (New York: Seabury, 1972), 144.

15. Theodor Adorno, *Negative Dialectics*, trans. E. B. Ashton (New York: Continuum, 1973), 312, 46.

16. Georg Lukács, *The Young Hegel: Studies in the Relations between Dialectics and Economics*, trans. Rodney Livingstone (Cambridge, Mass.: MIT, 1975), 285–95.

17. See Terry Eagleton, "The Idealism of American Criticism," *New Left Review* 127 (May–June 1981), 64–65, and Edward Said, "Opponents, Audiences, Constituencies, and Community," in *The Politics of Interpretation*, ed. W. J. T. Mitchell (Chicago: Univ. of Chicago Press, 1983), 22.

18. Raymond Williams, *Marxism and Literature* (New York: Oxford Univ. Press, 1977), 101, provides an excellent compressed history of the term.

19. N. G. Chernishevsky, "Life and Aesthetics," trans. S. D. Kogan, *International Literature* (June 1935), 51–53.

20. Hippolyte Taine, "Balzac," *Noveaux essais de culture et de l'histoire* (Paris: Hachette, n.d.), 1–94. Reprinted in *Documents of Modern Literary Realism*, ed. George J. Becker (Princeton: Princeton Univ. Press, 1963), 108.

21. G. W. F. Hegel, *Logic, Being Part One of the Encyclopedia of the Philosophical Sciences*, trans. William Wallace (Oxford: Clarendon Press, 1975), 226. Other analyses of part-whole logic can be found in Hegel—see, for example, *Science of Logic*, trans. W. H. Johnson and L. G. Struthers (London: Oxford Univ. Press, 1929), 219. The *Logic*, for that matter, demonstrates that these relations are subject to transformation. I am working with the formulation in *The Logic* because it seems to have provided a vocabulary for later writers, and because it corresponds to the problems this book addresses.

22. Hegel, *Logic*, 227.

23. Ibid.

24. Ibid.

25. G. W. F. Hegel, *Aesthetics: Lectures on Fine Art*, trans. T. M. Knox (Oxford: Clarendon Press, 1975), 79, 81, 83.

26. G. W. F. Hegel, *The Phenomenology of Mind*, trans. J. B. Baillie (New York: Harper, 1967), 382–89.

27. Victor Hugo, *William Shakespeare*, trans. Melville B. Anderson (Chicago: A. C. McClurg, 1887), 224.

28. Karl Marx, *The Holy Family*, trans. Richard Dixon and Clemens Dutt, in *Karl Marx—Frederick Engels: Collected Works*, vol. 4 (New York: International, 1974), 5–212. All subsequent references are given parenthetically in the text.

29. Karl Marx, *Grundrisse*, trans. Martin Nicolaus (New York: Random House, 1973), 100–101.

30. Ibid., 100.

31. Wilhelm Dilthey, "Briefe von und an Hegel," *Archiv für Geschichte der Philosophie I* (1888), quoted in Michael Ermarth, *Wilhelm Dilthey: The Critique of Historical Reason* (Chicago: Univ. of Chicago Press, 1978), 263.

32. Wilhelm Dilthey, *Gesammelte Schriften*, vol. 5 (Stuttgart: B. G. Teubner, 1957). In this discussion, I am drawing heavily on Rudolf A. Makkreel, *Dilthey: Philosopher of the Human Sciences* (Princeton: Princeton Univ. Press, 1975), 240-42.

33. Dilthey, *Gesammelte Schriften*, 5: 279, 250, in Makkreel, 240, 241.

34. Georg Simmel, "How Is Society Possible?" in *On Individuality and Social Forms*, ed. Donald Levine (Chicago: Univ. of Chicago Press, 1971), 10-11; Max Weber, "'Objectivity' in Social Science and Social Policy," in *The Methodology of the Social Sciences*, trans. and ed. Edward Shils and Henry Finch (New York: Free Press, 1949), 90.

35. Georg Lukács, *Studies in European Realism*, trans. Edith Bone (New York: Grosset and Dunlap, 1964), 6. This statement is fairly representative of Lukács's use of *typical*. However, since Lukács's writings span half a century, and for much of that time *typical* was a central term in his work, its sense changes somewhat. Moreover, the rhetorical interests motivating different monographs often led to changes of emphasis in works that were almost contemporary. It might be helpful then to supply some representative uses of the term in Lukács.

In the very early *Soul and Form*, first published in 1910 (trans. Anna Bostock, Cambridge, Mass.: MIT Press, 1974), *typical* appears, but not in the sense it would later acquire for Lukács. In critical dialogue on *Tristram Shandy*, one of the characters criticizes Sterne's "humour" characters: "The 'humour' is a mask left over from an ancient, still wholly allegorical culture when life and drama were personified by types: a culture in which the whole nature of a man was compressed into an epigram, an inscription; for as long as the play continued, he could never, not even for a moment, be anything but true to type" (134). Lukács maintained his distrust of the allegorical, which became a stalking-horse for Znadovism in his later work. But, after his engagement with Marxism, typicality came to have a positive, dialectic force in his aesthetic theory. For the early Lukács, however, the central term was *totality*, and the representation of history was the central question. For a useful study of this period, focusing on *Theory of the Novel*, see J. M. Bernstein, *The Philosophy of the Novel: Lukács, Marxism, and the Dialectics of Form* (Minneapolis: Univ. of Minnesota Press, 1984).

In *The Historical Novel*, written in 1936, one of the most achieved of Lukács's anti-Stalinist generic studies, the typical is specifically associated with totality, but that association is weighted in the direction of artistic selection and particularity (*The Historical Novel*, trans. Hannah and Stanley Mitchell [London: Merlin, 1962]). Further, the typical is used analytically rather than evaluatively: the novel and the drama realize typical representations in distinct ways: "It is clear, however, that if this world [in the novel] is to evoke a totality, if a restricted circle of people and a restricted group of 'objects' are to be portrayed in such a way that the reader has the immediate impression of an entire society in movement, then some form of artistic concentration is again necessary and any straightforward copying of reality must be resolutely abandoned. Accordingly, the novel, like the drama, must give central place throughout to all that is typical" (139).

In a contemporaneous work, "The Intellectual Physiognomy of Literary Characters," Lukács extends his analytic use of the typical. But there, the concept also bears the scars of a prolonged confrontation with hagiographic notions of realism. (The essay is collected in *Writer and Critic*, ed. and trans. Arthur Kahn [New York: Grosset and Dunlap, 1970].) Lukács begins by distinguishing the creation of the typical from empirical observation and connecting it to the writer's definition of the "basic issues and movements of his time" (158). In that sense, Lukács says, "Don Quixote is one of the most typical characters in world literature," since in the major scenes of that novel the author has intensified basic social contradictions, exacting their last ounce of expressive capability. But precisely because the typical situation is so extreme, the typical character must be realized, as Lukács says, on a "high intellectual level," so that his understanding of his situation can render it plausible. Lukács's intention here was probably to make a case for novels that focused on intellectuals, rather than workers or peasants. He has also redefined the typical as the heroic.

In later works, the connection of typicality with intellectual power would be transferred from the character to the writer. To create successfully typical characters, the author must be able to foretell the future. As Lukács put it in "Franz Kafka or Thomas Mann?" (collected in *Realism in Our Time: Literature and the Class Struggle*, trans. John and Necke Mander [New York: Harper, 1971]): "For a typology can only be of lasting significance if the writer has depicted the central or peripheral significance, the comic or tragic characteristics of his types, in such a way that subsequent developments confirm his portrait of the age" (29). Thus, we prefer—or ought to prefer—Balzac and Tolstoy to Ibsen.

The post-Stalin Lukács interpreted typicality very differently. Let us look first at a topical discussion of the term in his 1964 essay on *One Day in the Life of Ivan Denisovich* (in *Solzhenitsyn*, trans. William Graf [Cambridge, Mass.: MIT, 1969]). Lukács begins by praising Solzhenitsyn for concentrating the "typical behavior of millions" into the focused narrative of his novella. Such concentration, says Lukács, is anything but naturalist. Lukács then elaborates the notion of typicality in two directions: he criticizes the instrumental and purely political deployment of the typical, and he opposes to such instrumentality the "human essence" of the character: "In literature, the concrete and individual character is primary—the beginning and end of the creative process" (18). It is as if Lukács opposed to political dogmatism a dogmatism of character, dazzled by the representational power of the realistic novel into believing that it created real individuals.

Let us end our treatment of Lukács's typicality with a very late use of the term, in the 1967 preface of a volume of selected writings, *Muvészet és tásadalom* (Art and society), in *New Hungarian Quarterly* 13, no. 47 (Autumn 1972), 44-56: "The aesthetic type, therefore, in which particularity is most artistically manifested signifies the road of concrete fulfillment of human existence as a species. It is the central category of artistic creation because it is through it that artistic creation becomes the sensually unfolded and united concrete reflection of the embodying of a stage in the great road of the human species seeking and finding itself" (54).

The constraint that the typical be able to predict the future remains, but it is distanced—we read of a reflection of an embodiment of a stage—and softened by the final utopian evocation. Further, the sense of artistic production as a practice that engages the senses, missing from Lukács's middle work, reemerges. What is missing, however, is precisely the strength of his use of typicality in that period: a sense of the typical as a concrete analytic device for the interpretation of specific texts.

36. W. K. Wimsatt, "The Concrete Universal," in *The Verbal Icon: Studies in the Meaning of Poetry* (Lexington: Univ. Press of Kentucky, 1954), 69–83.

37. Ibid., 82.

38. "On the Question of the Literary and Art Treatment of the Typical," editorial, *Kommunist*, no. 18 (December 1955). Reprinted and translated in *The Current Digest of the Soviet Press*, vol. 8, 3, pp. 11–15. It is interesting to note that this discussion was published two weeks before the opening of the Twentieth Party Congress.

39. One such instance is Stefan Morawski's introduction to his *Karl Marx and Frederick Engels on Literature and Art* (New York: International, 1974).

40. Jürgen Habermas, *Knowledge and Human Interests*, trans. Jeremy Shapiro (Boston: Beacon, 1968), 179–180.

41. J. Hillis Miller, *The Form of Victorian Fiction: Thackeray, Dickens, Trollope, George Eliot, Meredith, and Hardy* (Notre Dame, Ind.: Univ. of Notre Dame Press, 1968), 53–93.

42. Karl Marx, *Economic and Philosophic Manuscripts of 1844*, trans. Martin Milligan (New York: International, 1964), 139–41.

43. The thesis that Shakespeare's history plays were recensions of the orthodox Tudor worldview becomes central to the critical response to the plays with E. M. W. Tillyard's book *Shakespeare's History Plays* (London: Chatto and Windus, 1944), closely followed by L. B. Campbell's *Shakespeare's "Histories"* (San Marino, Calif.: Huntington Library, 1947). This view continues to generate critical studies, including R. B. Pierce's *Shakespeare's History Plays: The Family and the State* (Athens: Ohio Univ. Press, 1971), which argues for the organic connection of familial harmony and justice in the state. The Tillyard-Campbell thesis has, however, generally attracted revision or criticism from recent writers. There is a substantial literature that broadens the scope of "orthodox" ideology, either by access to additional sources or by more extensive analysis of the layers of the historical tradition. This trend can be traced to I. Ribner, whose *The English History Play in the Age of Shakespeare* (Princeton: Princeton Univ. Press, 1957), is broadly supportive of Tillyard. David Bevington, in *Tudor Drama and Politics* (Cambridge, Mass.: Harvard Univ. Press, 1968), establishes the plays as generally orthodox, but not specifically partisan to the Tudors. And H. A. Kelly, in *Divine Providence in the England of Shakespeare's Histories* (Cambridge, Mass.: Harvard Univ. Press, 1974), argues for layers of orthodox opinion in the chronicles. The well-developed literature on Machiavelli was applied to this controversy by W. Sanders, in *The Dramatist and the Received Idea* (Cambridge: Cambridge Univ. Press, 1968), to support the thesis that the plays explore the boundaries of the politically permissible. This thesis is also argued, in a very different tone, by Jan Kott in *Shakespeare Our Contemporary* (Garden City, N.Y.: Doubleday, 1964), an absurdist and existential reading of the histories. M. Manheim, in *The Weak King Dilemma in the Shakespearean History Play* (Syracuse, N.Y.: Syracuse Univ. Press, 1973), argues for a virtually antipolitical, transcendent vision of statecraft: the weak king is here virtuous and therefore a good king. In a similar vein, Robert Rentoul Read's *Richard II: From Mask to Prophet* (University Park: Pennsylvania State Univ. Press, 1968) is a competent example of the critical lineage, stretching back to Swinburne, that reads the play in terms of the development of the deposed king's subjectivity. Robert Ornstein's *A Kingdom for a Stage* (Cambridge, Mass.: Harvard Univ. Press, 1972) holds that Shakespeare

"places as great a value on the sanctity of personal relations in the History Plays as in the tragedies, because he intuits that order depends, not on concepts of hierarchy and degree, but on the fabric of personal and social relations which is woven by ties of marriage, kinship, and friendship, by communal interests and ideals of loyalty and trust" (154). Thus we have moved from the plays as a record of public orthodoxy, through the plays as a palimpsest of varying orthodoxies, to the plays as celebrations of private values. Two attempts to mediate these positions are Moody Prior's *The Drama of Power* (Evanston, Ill.: Northwestern Univ. Press, 1973) and Robert Weimann's *Structure and Society in Literary History* (Charlottesville: Univ. Press of Virginia, 1976). C. G. Thayer's *Shakespeare's Politics: Government and Misgovernment in the Great Histories* (Athens: Ohio Univ. Press, 1983), characterizes Shakespeare as a discreet dissenter from those orthodox Tudor doctrines "which would have to be described as objectionable by any standards held by reasonable people" (viii). For a mainstream account of current critical opinion on the histories, see O. B. Hardison's "Shakespeare's Political World," in *Politics, Power, and Shakespeare,* ed. Frances McNeely Leonard (Arlington: Texas Humanities Resource Center, Univ. of Texas at Arlington Library, 1981). My own reading of the play is an attempt to show that the two major themes of criticism—the question of rebellion and the question of Richard's subjectivity—are not two different "readings" of the play, but are historically shaped responses to its typical representation of royal power.

44. Weimann, *Structure and Society,* 53.

45. Karl Marx, *The Eighteenth Brumaire of Louis Bonaparte* (1869; New York: International, 1963), 122.

46. "An Homily against Disobedience and Willful Rebellion" in *Sermons or Homilies Appointed to be Read in Churches in the Time of Queen Elizabeth of Famous Memory,* 4th ed. (Oxford: Clarendon Press, 1816), 472; Stafford quoted in Michael Walzer, *The Revolution of the Saints: A Study in the Origins of Radical Politics* (New York: Atheneum, 1970), 86.

47. William Shakespeare, *The Tragedy of King Richard II,* ed. Herschel Baker, in *The Riverside Shakespeare* (Boston: Houghton Mifflin, 1974), 4.1. I have used the usual modern spelling, "Bolingbroke," for the Riverside's "Bullingbroke." Subsequent references are given parenthetically in the text.

48. E. M. W. Tillyard, "The Second Tetralogy," in his *Shakespeare's History Plays* (New York: Macmillan, 1946), 290; Cleanth Brooks and Robert B. Heilman, *Understanding Drama* (New York: Harcourt Brace, 1945).

49. Ronald Berman, "The Nature of Guilt in the Henry IV Plays," *Shakespeare Studies* 1 (1965), 18-28; Norman Holland, "Introduction to *Henry IV, Part Two,*" in *The Complete Signet Classic Shakespeare* (New York: Harcourt Brace Jovanovich, 1972), 678-85.

50. Gordon Ross Smith, "A Rabble of Princes: Considerations Touching Shakespeare's Political Orthodoxy in the Second Tetralogy," *Journal of the History of Ideas* 41, no. 1 (Jan.-March, 1980), 29-48.

51. Roman Ingarden, *The Literary Work of Art,* trans. George G. Grabowicz (Evanston, Ill.: Northwestern Univ. Press, 1973), 276 ff., and *The Cognition of the Literary Work of Art,* trans. Ruth Ann Crowley and Kenneth R. Olson (Evanston, Ill.: Northwestern Univ. Press, 1973), 12-14.

52. Ingarden, *Cognition,* 8.

53. Ibid., 54.

54. Wolfgang Iser, *The Act of Reading: A Theory of Aesthetic Response* (Baltimore: Johns Hopkins Univ. Press, 1978), 82.

55. Geoffrey Hartman, "Criticism, Indeterminacy, Irony," in his *Criticism in the Wilderness: The Study of Literature Today* (New Haven: Yale Univ. Press, 1980), pp. 265-84.

56. Jean Piaget, *Der Structuralismus*, trans. L. Haflinger (Olten, 1973), 134, quoted in Iser, *The Act of Reading*, 203-4.

57. Hegel, *Logic*, 227.

58. Walter Benjamin, *The Origin of German Tragic Drama*, trans. John Osborne (London: NLB, 1977), 31.

59. Hegel, *Logic*, 226; Theodor Adorno, *Negative Dialectics*, trans. E. B. Ashton (New York: Seabury, 1979), 153.

60. Adorno, *Negative Dialectics*, 150.

61. Bertolt Brecht, "Speech to Danish Working-Class Actors on the Art of Observation," in Brecht, *Poems, 1913-1956*, ed. John Willett and Ralph Manheim (London: Eyre, Methuen, 1976), 234.

62. See Herbert Marcuse, *Reason and Revolution: Hegel and the Rise of Social Theory* (Boston: Beacon, 1941).

63. It is here that my understanding of typicality and its role in representation departs most fundamentally from Lukács's, since Lukács considered typicality a means of developing the whole work as a concrete totality. This ill-considered importation of a feature of Hegel's universal notion, I would hold, provided the conceptual niche in Lukács's aesthetics that was all too easily filled by a reified Marxism. It also rationalized Lukács's rejection of those modernist works in which indeterminacy cannot be evaded. Paradoxically, the indeterminate aspects of the work cannot be denied without undermining the veracity of those typical images Lukács so valued.

64. Theodor Adorno, "Reconciliation under Duress," in *Aesthetics and Politics* (London: NLB, 1977), 162.

65. William Shakespeare, *A Midsummer Night's Dream*, ed. Anne Barton, in *The Riverside Shakespeare* (Boston: Houghton Mifflin, 1974), 1.1.16-19. Subsequent references are given parenthetically in the text. A similar reading can be found in David Marshall, "Exchanging Visions: Reading *A Midsummer Night's Dream*," *ELH* 49 (1982), 543-75.

66. See Marshall, "Exchanging Visions"; Lynda Boose, "The Father and the Bride in Shakespeare," *PMLA* 97, 3 (May 1982), 325-47; and Germaine Greer, "Love and Law," in Leonard, ed., *Politics, Power, and Shakespeare*, 28-45.

67. See the works of K. M. Briggs, especially *The Anatomy of Puck: An Examination of Fairy Beliefs among Shakespeare's Contemporaries and Successors* (London: Routledge and Kegan Paul, 1959). Also useful are Ernest Schanzer, "The Moon and the Fairies in *Midsummer Night's Dream*," *University of Toronto Quarterly* 24 (1955), 234-46, and scattered comments on the native tradition in Weimann's *Structure and Society in Literary History*. An essay by Paul Olson, "*A Midsummer Night's Dream* and the Meaning of Court Marriage" (*ELH* 24 [1957], 95-119), although marred by misogyny, has useful information on the "high literary" sources of the fairies.

68. Robert Kirk, in *Secret Commonwealth of Elves, Fauns, and Fairies*, quoted in Briggs, *Anatomy*, chapter 3.

69. David Young, *Something of Great Constancy: The Art of "A Midsummer Night's Dream"* (New Haven: Yale Univ. Press, 1966), and Bruce Erlich, "Queenly Shadows: On Mediation in Two Comedies," *Shakespeare Survey* 35 (1982), 66-67.

70. Paul Siegel, "*A Midsummer Night's Dream* and the Wedding Guests,"

Shakespeare Quarterly 4, no. 2 (1953) 139-45, and Olson, "*A Midsummer Night's Dream* and the Meaning of Court Marriage."

71. Robert Watkins, "Shakespeare in Performance: *A Midsummer Night's Dream,*" lecture at Univ. of Texas, Austin, Feb. 9, 1978.

CHAPTER 2: DOMINANCE OF THE TYPICAL, DOMINANCE OF THE INDETERMINATE

1. Karl Marx, *Grundrisse,* trans. Martin Nicolaus (New York: Random House, 1973), 100-101.

2. John Webster, *The Duchess of Malfi* (Cambridge, Mass.: Harvard Univ. Press, 1964), 34. Subsequent references are given parenthetically in the text. A full review of the literature on *The Duchess of Malfi* can be found in Joyce E. Peterson's *Curs'd Example: "The Duchess of Malfi" and Commonweal Tragedy* (Columbia: Univ. of Missouri Press, 1978), 1-13. To the works cited by Peterson should be added William Empson's essay "Mine Eyes Dazzle," *Essays in Criticism* 14 (1964), 80-86, and several recent works: R. B. Graves, "*The Duchess of Malfi* at the Globe and Blackfriars," *Renaissance Drama* 9 (1978), 193-209; Leslie Duer, "The Landscape of Imagination in *The Duchess of Malfi,*" *Modern Language Studies* 10, no. 1 (1979-80), 3-9; M. C. Bradbrook, *John Webster* (New York: Columbia Univ. Press, 1980); Jacqueline Pearson, *Tragedy and Tragicomedy in the Plays of John Webster* (New York: Barnes and Noble, 1980); and Lee Bliss, *The World's Perspective* (New Brunswick, N.J.: Rutgers Univ. Press, 1983).

3. Frankfurt Institute for Social Research, *Aspects of Sociology,* trans. John Viertel (Boston: Beacon, 1972), 135. See also Lawrence Stone, *The Family, Sex, and Marriage in England: 1500-1800* (New York: Harper, 1977). Stone holds that family relations in the sixteenth and early seventeenth centuries were so impoverished that many people "found it difficult to establish close emotional ties with any other person" (99).

4. New historical research seems to indicate that English families during the period of the play were relatively small, averaging about four persons per household, and usually consisted of a married couple, children, servants, and perhaps an additional inmate or two. These barren empirical statements could be made with equal accuracy about English families at any point from the early Renaissance through the nineteenth century, but they do not exclude the possibility of an ideological redefinition of the family that was not reflected in demographics. For research on the family, see Phillipe Ariès, *Centuries of Childhood: A Social History of Family Life,* trans. Robert Balick (New York: Random House, 1962); Peter Laslett, "Mean Household Size in England since the Sixteenth Century," in *Household and Family in Past Time,* ed. Peter Laslett and Richard Wall (Cambridge: Univ. Press, 1972), 125-29; and Stone, *The Family, Sex, and Marriage.*

5. I cite again the work by Michael Walzer, *The Revolution of the Saints: A Study in the Origins of Radical Politics* (New York: Atheneum, 1970), as well as an earlier essay by Christopher Hill, "The Spiritualization of the Household," in his *Society and Puritanism in Pre-Revolutionary England* (New York: Schocken, 1964), 443-82. The work by Hill analyzes the theme of the family as a "little church" (455).

6. See also Marie Axton, *The Queen's Two Bodies: Drama and the Eliza-*

bethan Succession, Royal Historical Society Studies in History (London: Royal Historical Society, 1977).

7. Jürgen Habermas, "Critical Hermeneutics," in *Contemporary Hermeneutics: Hermeneutics as Method, Philosophy, and Critique*, by Josef Bleicher (London: Routledge and Kegan Paul, 1980), 196.

8. Freud's essay "The 'Uncanny'" can be found in vol. 4 of his *Collected Papers*, ed. Ernest Jones (London: Hogarth Press, 1925), 368-407.

9. Ibid., 369-70. I am using Freud in the spirit suggested by Fredric Jameson's observation in *The Political Unconscious* (Ithaca, N.Y.: Cornell Univ. Press, 1981): "So great has been the suggestiveness of the Freudian model that terms and secondary mechanisms drawn from it are to be found strewn at a great distance from their original source, pressed into the service of quite unrelated systems" (61-62).

10. See Inga-Stina Ekeblad, "Webster's Realism or 'A Cunning Piece Wrought Perspective,'" in *John Webster*, ed. Brian Morris, Papers of the Second York Symposium on the Plays of John Webster, 1969 (London: Ernest Benn, 1970).

11. Jorge Luis Borges, "Tlön, Uqbar, Orbis Tertius," in *Labyrinths*, trans. James Irby (New York: New Directions, 1962), 3-19. See J. Hillis Miller's "The Figure in the Carpet," *Poetics Today* 1, no. 3 (Spring 1980), 107-18, for an analogous distinction; Miller's essay is also very useful on doubling and substitution in James.

12. Henry James, *The Turn of the Screw*, ed. Robert Kimbrough (New York: Norton, 1966). Subsequent references are given parenthetically in the text.

13. J. M. Cranfill and R. L. Clark, *An Anatomy of "The Turn of the Screw"* (Austin: Univ. of Texas Press, 1965), 30.

14. J. M. Lightwood, *Encyclopedia of the Laws of England* (1898), 10: 237, as quoted in the *Oxford English Dictionary* entry on "possession."

15. Leon Edel, *Henry James: The Treacherous Years, 1895-1901* (Philadelphia: Lippincott, 1969), 193.

16. Georg Lukács, *The Historical Novel*, trans. H. and S. Mitchell (London: Merlin Press, 1962), 19-89. For the contradictory status of the governess, see M. Jeanne Peterson, "The Victorian Governess: Status Incongruence in Family and Society," in *Suffer and Be Still: Women in the Victorian Age*, ed. Martha Vicinus (Bloomington: Indiana Univ. Press, 1974), 3-20; Heath Moon, "More Royalist than the King: the Governess, the Telegraphist, and Mrs. Gracedew," *Criticism* 25, no. 1 (Winter 1982), 16-36; and Elliot M. Schrero, "Exposure in *The Turn of the Screw*," *Modern Philology* 78, no. 3 (Feb. 1981), 261-74.

17. John Crowley, "Antiquities" in *Whispers: An Anthology of Fantasy and Horror*, ed. Stuart D. Schiff (Garden City, N.Y.: Doubleday, 1977), 114.

18. Edmund Wilson's opening shot was fired in "The Ambiguity of Henry James," *Hound and Horn* (7) (1934), 385-406. He was answered by R. B. Heilman in *"The Turn of the Screw* as Poem," *University of Kansas City Review* 14 (1948), 175-87, a militantly New Critical reading of the work, in which the children's corruption is seen as emblematic of the fall of man. Wilson was also answered by—among many others—Oliver Evans in "James' Air of Evil: *The Turn of the Screw*," *Partisan Review* 16 (1949), 175-87. Evans argues that James's letters, notebooks, and prefaces all show an intention to write a ghostly tale. A useful, but eccentric, summary of the first stages of this controversy appears in G. Willen's *A Casebook on Henry James' "Turn of the Screw"* (New

York: Crowell, 1960). Willen also reprints Wilson's essay and his two subsequent statements and includes the otherwise inaccessible radio symposium (1942) on the novella by Katherine Anne Porter, Allen Tate, and Mark Van Doren. A slightly more scholarly and less controversial selection of essays can be found in Robert Kimbrough's edition of *The Turn of the Screw*. Kimbrough includes contemporary reviews of the work, relevant selections from James's notebooks and letters, and full textual apparatus. Among works of criticism too recent for mention in either Willen or Kimbrough, I should note Cranfill and Clark's uncompromising antiapparitionist *Anatomy of "The Turn of the Screw"* and the modified Freudian reading of the story in Leon Edel's *Henry James: The Treacherous Years*. Two related articles in *Etudes Anglaises* (22, no. 3 [1969], 250-69), R. Ballorain's "L'adulte et l'enfant ou les deux regards" and C. Tournade's "Propositions pour une psychologie sociale de *The Turn of the Screw*," are very useful investigations of the social and psychological structure of the novella. Tournade's analysis is especially provocative. Conservative ideological studies in the tradition of Heilman continue to be produced, most notably in E. Voegelin's article *"The Turn of the Screw,"* reproduced with considerable apparatus in the *Southern Review* 7 (1970), 3-48. In another vein, E. A. Sheppard provides very useful material on James's connection with the Society for Psychical Research in her *Henry James and "The Turn of the Screw"* (London: Oxford Univ. Press, 1974). More focused work on the SPR can be found in E. Tuveson's *"The Turn of the Screw:* A Palimpsest," *Nineteenth Century Fiction* 12 (1972), 783-801.

    19. Shoshana Felman, "Turning the Screw of Interpretation," *Yale French Studies* 55 / 56 (1977), 171. Felman's otherwise useful essay is badly represented by this quotation.

    20. Sheppard, *Henry James and The Turn of the Screw*, 61.

    21. G. W. F. Hegel, *The Phenomenology of Mind*, trans. J. B. Baille (New York: Harper, 1967), 93.

    22. Edel, *Henry James: The Treacherous Years, 1895-1901*, 210.

CHAPTER 3: TYPICALITY AND INDETERMINACY
IN JACOBEAN CITY COMEDY

    1. This genre has been treated by Alexander Leggatt in *Citizen Comedy in the Age of Shakespeare* (Toronto: Univ. of Toronto Press, 1973).

    2. Fredric Jameson, *The Political Unconscious* (Ithaca, N.Y.: Cornell University Press, 1981), 109.

    3. Brian Gibbons, *Jacobean City Comedy: A Study of Satiric Plays by Jonson, Marston, and Middleton* (Cambridge, Mass.: Harvard Univ. Press, 1968); L. C. Knights, *Drama and Society in the Age of Jonson* (London: Chatto and Windus, 1951).

    4. Margot Heinemann, *Puritanism and Theatre: Thomas Middleton and Opposition Drama of the Early Stuarts* (Cambridge: Cambridge Univ. Press, 1980), 66.

    5. Mikhail Bakhtin, *Rabelais and His World*, trans. Helen Iswolsky (Cambridge: Mass.: MIT, 1968), 155. Subsequent references are given parenthetically in the text.

    6. Martin Rivington Holmes, *Elizabethan London* (New York: Präger, 1969), 30-48. Gresham's Exchange was the most notable example of this process.

    7. Ths discussion draws upon the extremely useful treatment of pre-

Civil War politics in London in Valerie Pearl's *London and the Outbreak of the Puritan Revolution: City Government and National Politics, 1625–43* (London: Oxford Univ. Press, 1964).

8. Ibid., chapter 1.

9. Perez Zagorin, *The Court and the Country: The Beginning of the English Revolution* (New York: Atheneum, 1970), 135–40.

10. Robert Brenner, "The Civil War Politics of London's Merchant Community," *Past and Present* 58 (February 1973), 53–108. I am drawing on this very useful article throughout my discussion of the three competing mercantile groups. See also Anne Jennalie Cook, *The Privileged Playgoers of Shakespeare's London, 1576–1642* (Princeton: Princeton Univ. Press, 1981), 40, for a description of rural MP's in Commons entering the colonial trade.

11. Ben Jonson, *Bartholomew Fair*, ed. E. A. Horsman (London: Methuen, 1960), 1.6.55. Subsequent references are given parenthetically in the text.

12. Cook, *The Privileged Playgoers*, 104.

13. Ben Jonson, *The Alchemist*, ed. S. Musgrove (Berkeley and Los Angeles: Univ. of California Press, 1968), 1.1.127-29. Subsequent references are given parenthetically in the text.

14. The same sense of *free-woman* is used by Jonson: "*Whit:* I will make thee a free-woman and a lady" (*Bartholomew Fair* 4.5.30).

15. Thomas Middleton, *Michaelmas Term*, ed. Richard Levin (Lincoln: Univ. of Nebraska Press, 1966), 1.2.43-55. Subsequent references are given parenthetically in the text.

16. Harbage's initial formulations can be found in his *Shakespeare's Audience* (1941; reprint, New York: Columbia Univ. Press, 1964). Later revisions of this theory are available in Gibbons, *Jacobean City Comedy*, 32–50, and throughout Cook, *The Privileged Playgoers*. See also André Bry, "Middleton et le public des 'city comedies,'" in *Dramaturgie et société: Rapports entre l'oeuvre theatrale, son interpretation et son public aux XVIe et XVIIe siècles*, ed. Jean Jacquot, 2 vols. (Paris: Editions du Centre National de la Récherche Scientifique, 1968), 709-27.

17. Cook's recent claim that the "privileged"—that is, those living above subsistence level—dominated Elizabethan audiences, obviously affects our understanding of the Jacobean private theater audience. But Cook's argument is somewhat tautological; the category of "privilege" is defined so broadly that it includes all those Londoners, perhaps 15 percent of the population, who could easily afford to see a play, hardly a coterie audience. Cook also neglects evidence suggesting that the theater was not especially expensive compared to other amusements, and she fails to draw the obvious conclusion from her own study of the ample size of the theaters. With 10,000 seats available and a total privileged population of some 52,000, the theaters could not have been filled six days a week with members of the privileged strata.

18. John Stow, *Survey of London*, ed. Charles Kingsford (Oxford: Clarendon Press, 1908), 101. See especially the chapters: "Of orders and customs of citizens," "Sports and pastimes of old time used in this Citie," "Watches in London," and "Liveries worne by Citizens at triumphs."

19. Ibid., 93.

20. *The Works of Thomas Middleton*, ed. A. H. Bullen (New York: AMS Press, 1964), 7:253.

21. Philip J. Finkelpearl, *John Marston of the Middle Temple: An Elizabethan Dramatist in His Social Setting* (Cambridge, Mass.: Harvard Univ. Press,

1969); *The Selected Plays of Thomas Middleton,* ed. David Frost (Cambridge: Cambridge Univ. Press, 1978), ix–x; Ben Jonson, *Works,* ed. C. H. Herford and P. Simpson (Oxford: Clarendon Press, 1925), 1:31.

22. C. L. Barber, *Shakespeare's Festive Comedy: A Study of Dramatic Form and Its Relation to Social Custom* (Princeton: Princeton Univ. Press, 1959).

23. Finkelpearl, *John Marston,* 45–62.

24. Emmanuel Le Roy Ladurie, *Carnival in Romans,* trans. Mary Feeney (New York: George Braziller, 1980).

25. John Marston, *Poems,* ed. Arnold Davenport (Liverpool: Liverpool Univ. Press, 1961), *The Scourge of Villanie,* "To Detraction I Present My Poesie," ll. 15–16, and "Satyre II," ll. 70–71.

26. Joseph Malof, *A Manual of English Meters* (Bloomington: Indiana Univ. Press, 1970).

27. John Marston, *The Malcontent,* ed. M. L. Wine (Lincoln: Univ. of Nebraska Press, 1964), 1.3.158–64.

28. Francis Beaumont, *The Knight of the Burning Pestle,* ed. T. Doebler (Lincoln: Univ. of Nebraska Press, 1967), Induction, ll. 16–29.

29. Ben Jonson, *Works,* ed. Hereford and Simpson, 3:421.

30. John Marston, *The Dutch Courtesan* (3.2.41–45), in *Four Jacobean City Comedies,* ed. Gamini Salgado (Baltimore: Penguin, 1975). Subsequent references are given parenthetically in the text.

31. Richard Horwich, "Wives, Courtesans, and the Economics of Love in Jacobean City Comedy," *Comparative Drama* 7 (1973–74), 291–309.

CHAPTER 4: THE HERMENEUTICS OF THE BILDUNGSROMAN

1. François Jost, "La tradition du *Bildungsroman,*" *Comparative Literature* 12 (1969), 97–115.

2. See Roy Pascal, *The German Novel* (Toronto: Univ. of Toronto Press, 1956), and two more recent works, W. H. Bruford's *The German Tradition of Self-Cultivation: Bildung from Humboldt to Thomas Mann* (London: Cambridge Univ. Press, 1975) and Martin Swales's *The German Bildungsroman from Wieland to Hesse* (Princeton: Princeton Univ. Press, 1978).

3. Friedrich Schleiermacher, *Monologen,* second soliloquy, quoted in Bruford, *The German Tradition,* 74.

4. G. H. Lewes, *The Apprenticeship of Life,* in *The Leader* 1 (June 1, 1850), 236 (ellipsis in original).

5. Lewes, "Shirley: A Tale," *Edinburgh Review* 91 (Oct. 1849–April 1850), 158, quoted in Carl Dawson, *Victorian Noon: English Literature in 1850* (Baltimore: Johns Hopkins Univ. Press, 1979), 173.

6. Coleridge, *The Friend,* quoted ibid., 106.

7. *Literary Criticism of George Henry Lewes,* ed. Alice Kaminsky (Lincoln: Univ. of Nebraska Press, 1964), 96, 95.

8. Friedrich Schiller, *On the Aesthetic Education of Man: In a Series of Letters,* ed. and trans. E. M. Wilkinson and L. A. Willoughby (Oxford: Clarendon, 1967), 33.

9. Immanuel Kant, *Was ist Aufklarung? Aufsätze zur Geschichte und Philosophie,* ed. J. Zehbe (Gottingen, 1967), 53, quoted in Swales, *The German Bildungsroman,* 17.

10. Wilhelm Dilthey, *Leben Schleiermachers* (Berlin: Gruyter, 1922), 282.

11. William Makepeace Thackeray, *Pendennis* (London: J.M. Dent, 1910), 1:xviii. Subsequent references are given parenthetically in the text.

12. Lewes, *Literary Criticism*, 96.

13. Beerbohm, "Quia Imperfectum" (1919), quoted in Bruford, *The German Tradition*, 42.

14. J.W. von Goethe, *Wilhelm Meister*, trans. Thomas Carlyle, vol. 2 (London: Chapman and Hall, 1899).

15. Here, as elsewhere in this chapter, I am transposing categories developed in Georg Lukács's *Theory of the Novel*, trans. Anna Bostock (Cambridge, Mass.: MIT Press, 1971) into ordinary literary critical language, with some loss of dialectical fluidity.

16. This position was taken most radically by Herbert Marcuse, "The Affirmative Character of Culture," in his *Negations* (Boston: Beacon Press, 1969), 88-134.

17. Schiller, *Aesthetic Education*, 60.

18. These thematic clusters have normally been used to ground a definition of the bildungsroman, with all the strengths and weaknesses that normally attend empirical analyses. The first critical work identifying some major English bildungsromans was Susanne Howe's *Wilhelm Meister and His English Kinsmen* (New York: Columbia Univ. Press, 1930). It has been superseded, especially for modern works, by Jerome H. Buckley, *Season of Youth* (Cambridge, Mass.: Harvard Univ. Press, 1974). A recent article by Marianne Hirsch, "The Novel of Formation as Genre: Between Great Expectations and Lost Illusions," *Genre* 12 (Fall 1979), 293-311, combines thematic and formal approaches.

19. I am heavily indebted to Dawson, " 'The Lamp of Memory': Wordsworth and Dickens," chapter 6 in his *Victorian Noon*, for his treatment of memory, especially as it figures in *David Copperfield*.

20. Swales discusses this as a tension between the *Nebeneinander* ("one-alongside-another") of possible selves within the hero and the *Nacheinander* ("one-after-another") of narration in his *German Bildungsroman*, 29.

21. Stendhal, *La vie de Henry Brulard*, trans. J. Steward and B.C. Knight (London: Merlin Press, 1968).

22. Goethe, *Wilhelm Meister*, 1:327.

23. Alfred Lord Tennyson, *In Memorian A.H.H.*, CXXI, in *Poems*, ed. Christopher Ricks (London: Longmans, 1969), 988.

24. Charles Dickens, *David Copperfield*, ed. Nina Burgis (Oxford: Clarendon Press, 1981), 1. Subsequent references are given parenthetically in the text.

25. J. Hillis Miller, *The Form of Victorian Fiction: Thackeray, Dickens, Trollope, George Eliot, Meredith, and Hardy* (Notre Dame, Ind.: Univ. of Notre Dame Press, 1968).

26. Lukács, *Theory of the Novel*, 115.

27. Karl Marx, *Capital* (New York: International, 1967), 1:42-47.

28. Charles Dickens in *Mr. and Mrs. Charles Dickens: His Letters to Her*, ed. Walter Dexter (London: Constable, 1935), 227.

29. A.O.J. Cockshut, *The Imagination of Charles Dickens* (New York: New York Univ. Press, 1962), 114-27.

30. Walter Benjamin, "Theses on Philosophy of History," in *Illuminations*, trans. H. Zohn (New York: Schocken, 1969), 264.

31. Buckley, *Season of Youth*, 121.

32. Jost's article "La tradition du *Bildungsroman*" includes a useful survey of French criticism.

33. Stendhal, *La Chartreuse de Parme* (Paris: Garnier Flammarion, 1964). Subsequent references are given parenthetically in the text. Translations are mine, checked against Margaret B. Shaw's Penguin translation (Harmondsworth: Penguin, 1958).

34. Thomas Hardy, *Jude the Obscure* (New York: Harper and Row, 1966), 377.

35. Doris Lessing, *The Four-Gated City* (1969; reprint New York: Bantam, 1978). Subsequent references are given parenthetically in the text.

36. Doris Lessing, *A Ripple from the Storm* (New York: New American Library, 1958). Subsequent references are given parenthetically in the text.

CONCLUSION: THE PUBLIC, THE PRIVATE,
AND THE DIALECTICS OF REPRESENTATION

1. Richard Sennett, *The Fall of Public Man: On the Social Psychology of Capitalism* (New York: Vintage, 1977), 17.

2. William Shakespeare, *The Rape of Lucrece*, in *The Riverside Shakespeare*, ed. G. Blakemore Evans (Boston: Houghton Mifflin, 1974), ll. 1478-79; Robert Ornstein, *A Kingdom for a Stage* (Cambridge, Mass.: Harvard Univ. Press, 1972), 154; Karl Marx, *The Eighteenth Brumaire of Louis Bonaparte* (1869; New York: International, 1963), 107; William Wordsworth, *The Prelude* (1805-6), ed. J. C. Maxwell (Harmondsworth: Penguin, 1971), bk. 12, ll. 70-77.

3. Jürgen Habermas, "Technology and Science as 'Ideology,'" in his *Toward a Rational Society: Student Protest, Science, and Politics*, trans. Jeremy Shapiro (Boston: Beacon, 1970), 62-80.

4. Bertolt Brecht, "The Playwright's Song," in Brecht, *Poems, 1913-1956*, ed. John Willett and Ralph Manheim (London: Eyre Methuen, 1976), 260.

INDEX

Abstraction: abstract labor, 152; in Hegel, 22; and indeterminacy, 49–50; in Marx, 27, 152; in *A Midsummer Night's Dream*, 57, 59; and typicality, 49. *See also* Indeterminacy
Adorno, Theodor, 52, 54; and subjectivity, 14
Alchemist (Jonson), 120, 125
Allegory, 120, 122; in de Man, 2; in *Richard II*, 38; in *The Turn of the Screw*, 92
Althusser, Louis: critique of the subject, 13; in de Man, 3; in Jameson, 10

Bakhtin, Mikhail, 123; and billingsgate, 117; and the body, 122; and intersubjectivity, 5; and the marketplace, 106; and student festivals, 116
Balzac, Honoré de, 15, 21, 35, 82
Barber, C. L., 116
Bartholomew Fair (Jonson), 110, 111, 120, 126-28, 129
Beaumont, Francis, 112, 118-19
Beerbohm, Max, 137
Benjamin, Walter, 154
Beyle, Marie Henri [pseud. Stendhal], 133; *La Chartreuse de Parme*, 141, 154, 155-59; *La vie de Henry Brulard*, 140, 154
Bildungsroman, 133-64; and part-whole relations, 134. See also *Chartreuse de Parme, La; David Copperfield;* Lessing, Doris; Self-formation
Billingsgate, 125; in city comedy, 121
Body: in Bakhtin, 106; in city comedy, 122; in *The Duchess of Malfi*, 62, 65, 70-71; in Jonson, 126; in *Richard II*, 40

Brecht, Bertolt, 53, 169
Brontë, Charlotte, 141, 154
Butler, Samuel, 154

Chartreuse de Parme, La (Stendhal), 141, 154, 155-59
Chaste Maid in Cheapside, A (Middleton), 129-30, 171
Chernishevsky, N. G., 20
City comedy, 103-32
Coleridge, Samuel Taylor, 134
Communist Party of the USSR, and typicality, 32
Cook, Anne J., 187n.17
Critique, 131; in the bildungsroman, 141; in *David Copperfield*, 150; in Jacobean London, 118. *See also* Indeterminacy

David Copperfield (Dickens), 19, 141, 144-54, 155, 159
Dekker, Thomas, 103, 112
Deleuze, Giles, and Félix Guattari: critique of the subject, 12
De Man, Paul, 1; and indeterminacy, 3, 46; and rhetoric, 2, 5-6; *Allegories of Reading*, 2-8; *Blindness and Insight*, 2, 8
Derrida, Jacques, 1, 172
Dialectics, 165; and genre, 104; relation between typical and indeterminate registers, 50, 82, 136-37, 142; and reflexivity, 133
Dickens, Charles, 82, 152; *David Copperfield*, 19, 35, 141, 144-54, 155, 159
Dilthey, Wilhelm, 136; typicality in, 28-29

THE JOHNS HOPKINS UNIVERSITY PRESS

THE DIALECTICS OF REPRESENTATION

This book was composed in Baskerville text type by A. W. Bennett, Inc., and Cheltenham display type, from a design by Martha Farlow. It was printed on 50-lb. Glatfelter B-31 by Thomson-Shore, Inc., and bound in Kivar 5.